MW00818321

The Gospel in Latin America

The Gospel in Latin America

Historical Studies in Evangelicalism and the Global South

David W. Bebbington

Editor

BAYLOR UNIVERSITY PRESS

Cover and book design by Kasey McBeath
Cover art: Unsplash/Kseniya Lapteva

The Library of Congress has cataloged this book under ISBN 978-1-4813-1-7238.
Library of Congress Control Number: 2022938564

Paperback ISBN: 978-1-4813-1723-8
Printed Case ISBN: 978-1-4813-1722-1

CONTENTS

FOREWORD

David W. Bebbington

The World Missionary Conference held at Edinburgh in 1910 proposed to consider how far the gospel had progressed in the various lands across the globe. A preparatory commission took into account "the two Americas," North and South. The evangelical Christians planning the conference naturally hoped for the conversion of Latin America. Yet only the "Indians" and the "immigrant Orientals" of the Americas were covered in the report that was drawn up in advance of the conference.[1] The great bulk of the population of the Hispanic and Lusophone world between Mexico and Argentina was left out. The explanation of this striking omission is that Anglo-Catholics supporting the conference regarded this vast territory as already part of Christendom. It was a portion of the patrimony of the Roman Catholic Church and so should not be regarded as a section of the foreign mission field. On that understanding Latin America was off limits to Protestants.[2] By the date of the conference, in fact, there had been little progress in planting evangelical faith in the region. There were a number of missionaries working in most of the countries as well as a scattering of churches serving expatriates, but there had been no mass movement of the inhabitants into Protestant churches. Latin America was then a largely barren land from an evangelical point of view.

[1] W. H. T. Gairdner, *"Edinburgh 1910": An Account and Interpretation of the World Missionary Conference* (London: Oliphant, Anderson & Ferrier, 1910), 70–71.
[2] Brian Stanley, ed., *The World Missionary Conference, Edinburgh 1910* (Grand Rapids: Eerdmans, 2009), chap. 3.

A century later the religious situation had been transformed. The proportion of the population professing some form of Protestant faith had risen to 19 percent, and nearly all of them were evangelicals of some type or another.[3] In the early twenty-first century by far the largest section of the Latin American evangelical world consisted of Pentecostals or Neo-Pentecostals, but there had also been significant growth in other bodies including Methodists and Baptists. The region, having become the home of huge new denominations, was sending missionaries to some of the countries which in 1910 had been seen as the "home base" of missions. Thinkers from Latin America were setting the pace of theological change among evangelicals in other parts of the globe. Politicians from outside the movement competed to recruit *evangélicos* to their cause. Nobody could pretend that Latin American Protestantism was a force that could be ignored. An evangelical age had dawned.

Consequently, when the subject for the first conference of the Evangelical Studies Program at Baylor University in October 2020 was considered, the evangelical movement in Latin America was an obvious choice. The history of a major phenomenon of the modern world could be addressed in a number of presentations. Those papers, together with a couple of additional ones, form the contents of this volume. The conference was to have been an in-person gathering, but the spread of coronavirus dictated that it should be conducted online instead. A happy result was that it attracted far more attenders from Latin America itself than could have been possible if it had been held under traditional circumstances.

The editor is very grateful to Byron R. Johnson, the director of the Baylor Institute for Studies of Religion, and to Thomas S. Kidd, associate director, for their sponsorship of the conference. He also greatly appreciates the willingness of Ronald J. Morgan to take on the task of composing the introduction and afterword when the original author was unavoidably prevented from participation in the project. It is appropriate that Baylor University Press should publish a volume deriving from a conference at the university and thanks are due to its staff for producing it. The result is a book of essays that help to place the evangelicals of Latin America in their historical setting without losing sight of the core priorities of a movement identified with the spread of the gospel.

David Bebbington
Stirling, October 2021

---

[3] *Religion in Latin America: Widespread Change in a Historically Catholic Region* (Washington, D.C.: Pew Research Center, 2014), 4, https://www.pewforum.org/2014/11/13/religion-in-latin-america/.

CONTRIBUTORS

Editor

David Bebbington is emeritus professor of history at the University of Stirling in Scotland. An undergraduate at Jesus College, Cambridge (1968–1971), he began his doctoral studies there (1971–1973) before becoming a research fellow of Fitzwilliam College, Cambridge (1973–1976). From 1976 he taught at the University of Stirling, where from 1999 to 2019 he was professor of history, and he has acted on many occasions as Visiting Distinguished Professor of History at Baylor University, Texas. He has served as president of the Ecclesiastical History Society (2006–2007) and as president of the Scottish Church History Society (2016–2020). In 2016 he was elected a Fellow of the Royal Society of Edinburgh. His publications include *Evangelicalism in Modern Britain: A History from the 1730s to the 1980s* (Unwin Hyman, 1989), *Patterns in History*, 4th ed. (Baylor University Press, 2018), *Baptists through the Centuries: A History of a Global People*, 2nd ed. (Baylor University Press, 2018), and *The Evangelical Quadrilateral*, 2 vols. (Baylor University Press, 2021).

Writer of Introduction and Afterword

Ronald J. Morgan (PhD in Latin American history, University of California, Santa Barbara) is professor of history at Abilene Christian University (ACU) and former director of ACU's undergraduate study program in

Oxford, England. He and his wife worked in church planting and leadership training in Brazil for six years. His publications, which focus primarily on Roman Catholicism in early modern Spanish America, include a monograph entitled *Spanish American Saints and the Rhetoric of Identity, 1600–1810* (University of Arizona Press, 2002) and various articles on Jesuit spirituality and the global imaginary. In tandem with scholars from several public universities in Mexico, he co-organized a conference in Mexico City with the theme "Protestantism, Identity, and History in Latin America" (2011). More recently, Morgan published *Brazilian Evangelicalism in the Twenty-First Century: An Inside and Outside Look* (coedited with Eric Miller, Palgrave Macmillan, 2019).

Chapter Authors

Pedro Feitoza is a postdoctoral fellow at the Brazilian Center of Analysis and Planning, São Paulo. He completed his PhD in history at the University of Cambridge in 2019 with a thesis titled "Protestants and the Public Sphere in Brazil, c. 1870–c. 1930." In 2018 he won the inaugural World Christianities Essay Prize from the *Journal of Ecclesiastical History* with an article on the history of Brazil's first Protestant periodical. His current research project on the social and intellectual history of Brazilian evangelicalism, 1860–1950, is funded by the São Paulo Research Foundation.

Joseph Florez is assistant professor of religious studies at California State University, Bakersfield. He received his PhD from the University of Cambridge and completed a postdoctoral fellowship at Union College. He has published on topics related to Pentecostalism and the Chilean dictatorship in *Pneuma* and the *Journal of Religion and Society*. He is also the author of *Giving Life to the Faith: Pentecostalism, Everyday Experience, and Social Activism in Authoritarian Chile* (Brill, 2021).

Virginia Garrard is professor of history and religious studies at the University of Texas at Austin. Her most recent work is *New Faces of God in Latin America: Emerging Forms of Vernacular Christianity* (Oxford University Press, 2020). She is coauthor, with Peter Henderson and Bryan McCann, of *Latin America and the Modern World* (Oxford University Press, 2018); with David Orique and Susan Fitzpatrick-Behrens she coedited *The Oxford Handbook of Latin American Christianity* (Oxford University Press, 2020); and with Stephen Dove and Paul Freston, *The Cambridge History of Religions in Latin America* (Cambridge University Press, 2016).

Her research interests include historic memory and human rights during the Cold War in Latin America, contemporary Central American history, and religious movements and ethnic identity in Latin America.

Philip Jenkins received his doctorate from the University of Cambridge (1978). He is presently distinguished professor of history at Baylor University, where his main appointment is in the Institute for Studies of Religion. He has published thirty books, including *The Next Christendom: The Coming of Global Christianity* (Oxford University Press, 2002); *Fertility and Faith: The Demographic Revolution and the Transformation of World Religions* (Baylor University Press, 2020); and *Climate, Catastrophe, and Faith: How Changes in Climate Drive Religious Upheaval* (Oxford University Press, 2021).

David C. Kirkpatrick is an assistant professor in the Department of Philosophy and Religion and teaching faculty in Latin American, Latinx, and Caribbean Studies at James Madison University. Previously he was the Timothy Gannon Postdoctoral Associate in American Religious History at Florida State University. He is the author of *A Gospel for the Poor: Global Social Christianity and the Latin American Evangelical Left* (University of Pennsylvania, 2019) and coeditor of *Global Visions of Violence: Persecution, Media, and Martyrdom in World Christianity* with Jason Bruner (Rutgers University Press, 2022). His most recent research appears in the *Journal of the American Academy of Religion*, *Oxford Encyclopedia of American Religion*, and the *Journal of Ecclesiastical History*, as well as public-facing outlets such as the *Washington Post* and the *Los Angeles Review of Books*. He is currently writing his third book with Oxford University Press under the title *Blood and Borders: Violence and the Origins of the "Global War on Christians."*

Véronique Lecaros is a full-time professor in the Department of Theology at Pontificia Universidad Católica del Perú (PUCP). She holds a doctorate in theology from the University of Strasbourg. She was a Tinker Visiting Professor at Stanford in 2019. Her field of expertise is religious phenomena in Peru, with a special focus on Pentecostalism, religious conversion, Catholic institutions, and secularization. She is the author of several articles, book chapters, and books, among them, *La conversión al evangelismo* (PUCP, 2016).

John Maiden is Senior Lecturer and Head of the Department for Religious Studies at The Open University (UK). He researches the history of global evangelical, pentecostal, and charismatic cultures and networks. He is author of the forthcoming *Age of the Spirit: Charismatic Renewal, the Anglo-World and Global Christianity, c. 1945–1980* (Oxford: Oxford University Press, 2022) and co-editor of *Transatlantic Charismatic Renewal, c. 1950–2000* (Leiden: Brill, 2021).

Matt Marostica has a PhD in political science and a juris doctorate from the University of California, Berkeley. Currently, Matt is associate university librarian for collection development in the Stanford University Libraries. He was previously a civil litigator at the Dentons law firm and an assistant professor of political science at Brigham Young University. He is the author of "La nueva política evangélica: el movimiento evangélico y el complot Católico en la Argentina" (The New Evangelical Politics: The Evangelical Movement and Catholic Conspiracy in Argentina), *Religión y Sociedad*, Porto Alegre, 2:2 (2000); and "Religion and Global Affairs: Religious Activation and Democracy in Latin America," *SAIS Review of International Affairs*, 18:21 (1998).

Matheus Reis, from Manaus, Brazil, is an adjunct professor in the School of Ministry at Palm Beach Atlantic University. He received his PhD in World Christianity from the University of Edinburgh with a thesis entitled "Brazilian *Evangélicos* in Diaspora in South Florida: Identity, Ecclesiology, and Mission." He also received a B.A. in Christian Ministry and a Master of Divinity from Palm Beach Atlantic University. He has contributed to the website of the Centre for the Study of World Christianity at Edinburgh.

J. Daniel Salinas, from Bogotá, Colombia, received a PhD in historical theology from Trinity International University. He is professor of theology and church history with the Biblical Seminary in Medellín, Colombia; and Asian Theological Seminary in Manila, Philippines. He is the author of several books and articles in both Spanish and English, including *Latin American Evangelical Theology in the 1970s: The Golden Decade* (Brill, 2009); *Taking Up the Mantle: Latin American Theology in the 20th Century* (Langham, 2017); and *Teología con alma Latina* (Puma, 2018). He serves as associate director of the Theological Education Initiative, a program of the United World Mission.

INTRODUCTION

Ronald J. Morgan

The shift of the center of gravity in world Christianity from Global North (Europe and North America) to Global South (Africa, South and East Asia, and Latin America) was one of the most notable developments in the faith during the twentieth century. As social scientists David Martin and David Stoll demonstrate in their influential 1990 studies, one of the most salient dimensions within that worldwide evolution was the emergence of evangelical Protestantism in Latin America, a process that has only intensified since their publications.[1] The continent which was excluded from the agenda of the 1910 Protestant-organized World Missionary Conference in Edinburgh on the grounds that it was Roman Catholic territory has become, around a century later, the home of flourishing evangelical communities.

The purpose of this volume is to extend the historical scholarship on this dynamic phenomenon. Most of the chapters here were originally presented as papers at a conference hosted by Baylor University in October 2020. The online event was the first venture of the Evangelical Studies Program (ESP) sponsored by Baylor's Institute for Studies of Religion, building on the legacy of the Institute for the Study of American Evangelicals (ISAE) at Wheaton College, Illinois. From 1982 to 2014, the

---

[1] David Martin, *Tongues of Fire: The Explosion of Protestantism in Latin America* (Oxford: Blackwell, 1990); David Stoll, *Is Latin America Turning Protestant? The Politics of Evangelical Growth* (Berkeley: University of California Press, 1990).

ISAE promoted historical research on the evangelical movement within the United States, transforming that field into a thriving subdiscipline of North American historiography. Under the leadership of its director David Bebbington, Baylor's Evangelical Studies Program now aspires to do something similar, while taking the whole world as its province. To mark that ambition, it chose Latin America as the focus for its first conference and publication.

The fact that the Evangelical Studies Program and this particular book are heirs of the earlier ISAE work, with its focus on North American evangelical Christianity, deserves some comment from the outset. In the first place the Evangelical Studies Program's scholarly focus on evangelical faith worldwide will do more than identify discrete examples of evangelical Protestant Christianity in each unique cultural context; rather, careful attention to each part should bring the whole into greater focus. In that regard, for example, these chapters on Latin America should elucidate contemporary debates about the nature of British or North American evangelicalism, a point emphasized by historians Mark Noll, Jay Case, Kelly Cross Elliott, and others.[2] In this regard, Mark Noll borrows an analogy from sports, proposing that in order to understand evangelicalism today, one should approach it as the World Cup (global) rather than the World Series (U.S.-centered).[3]

Secondly, while so much of the historical scholarship focused on North American evangelicals has privileged questions of terminology and categorization—for example, what defines an evangelical, the viability (or not) of the inclusive noun "evangelicalism," and, more recently, laments about how political pollsters have undermined religious and theological definitions by including among "evangelicals" the religious

---

[2]   See Mark A. Noll, David W. Bebbington, and George M. Marsden, eds., *Evangelicals: Who They Have Been, Are Now, and Could Be* (Grand Rapids: Eerdmans, 2019). Noll, who has been at the forefront of the historiography of U.S. evangelicalism, observed that when one gives attention to "evangelical-like movements around the world . . . any coherent understanding of evangelicalism" should focus more on "mind-boggling diversity" than on "[U.S.-centric] political or theological standoffs" (11). See also Jay Case, *Unpredictable Gospel: American Evangelicalism and World Christianity, 1812–1910* (New York: Oxford University Press, 2012); and Kelly Cross Elliott, "The Bebbington Quadrilateral Travels into the Empire," in Noll, Bebbington, and Marsden, eds., *Evangelicals*, 126–36.

[3]   Noll, Bebbington, and Marsden, eds., *Evangelicals*, 300–316.

right and the so-called Trump evangelicals[4]—the chapters in this study largely ignore that debate. Readers will not find here any systematic attempt to characterize "Latin American evangelicalism" as some coherent whole. Instead, the chapters in this volume validate Mark Noll's observation that although many expressions of evangelical-like Christianity worldwide have roots in the missionary efforts of Western evangelicals, "their shape, their chief concerns, their preoccupations, and their goals often lie very far from the politics and preoccupations of the contemporary American media."[5] This is not to suggest that there is no overlap between the foregoing debates and the sorts of questions being pursued by scholars of Latin American evangelicalism. For example, as we shall see in the chapters of this volume by Virginia Garrard and Véronique Lecaros, there has been a significant political turn among conservative evangelicals across the region that shows parallels with developments in the United States. Similarly, while it is true that no contributor to this volume takes on the complex task of delineating the nomenclature and categories, the constantly shifting socio-religious landscape has made such labeling a contested arena of discourse.

Before proceeding, then, a word or two about terminology. There has been the tendency in Latin America to employ the labels "Protestant" and "evangelical" as alternative expressions describing the same concept,[6] although the shifting religious landscape since the 1980s has generated debate about such categories.[7] For example, evangelical social scientist Orivaldo Pimentel Lopes Jr. has recognized the challenges inherent in any attempt to articulate an "evangelical" identity within the Brazilian church. In Brazil, he notes, some who formerly wore the label *evangélico* are now ambivalent, resenting having been robbed of their identity by

---

[4] For a recent scholarly update of these debates, see Noll, Bebbington, and Marsden, eds., *Evangelicals*.

[5] Mark A. Noll, "Introduction: One Word but Three Crises," in Noll, Bebbington, and Marsden, eds., *Evangelicals*, 11.

[6] For a nuanced discussion of factors that make religious census-taking a challenge for Latin America, see Paul Freston, "Contours of Latin American Pentecostalism," in Donald M. Lewis, ed., *Christianity Reborn: The Global Expansion of Evangelicalism in the Twentieth Century* (Grand Rapids: Eerdmans, 1995), 221–70.

[7] See Ronald J. Morgan and Henrique Alonso Pereira, "Which *evangélicos*? An Analysis of the Broad Diversities within Latin American Protestantism," in Eric Miller and Ronald J. Morgan, eds., *Brazilian Evangelicalism in the Twenty-First Century: An Inside and Outside Look* (Cham, Switzerland: Palgrave Macmillan, 2019), 65–81.

"unscrupulous religious groups" who have appropriated the name.[8] Moreover, census takers face similar dilemmas. On the one hand, they distinguish between "historical" and "Pentecostal" as distinct categories. But that latter subset is no cut-and-dried umbrella term; while most observers differentiate between "Pentecostal" and "Neo-Pentecostal" denominations, such distinctions are not always precise. With such complexity in mind, I follow the Pew Research Center survey of 2014, employing the broad term "Protestant" as a catchall. I employ the words "evangelical" and "evangelical Protestant" when speaking of groups that display the characteristics normal among evangelical Christians throughout the world. To differentiate between diverse classifications or groupings, I will use more specific nomenclature.

The remainder of this introduction consists of two complementary parts. First, I offer a historical overview of Protestantism in Latin America from 1492 to the twenty-first century, with a constant eye on the relationship of Protestant groups to national societies characterized by Roman Catholic monopoly or hegemony. Thereafter follows a review of recent Anglophone and Latin American historiography of the evangelical Protestant phenomenon. At the end of the book, in the afterword, I highlight prevalent historiographical themes, noting how the chapters from this current collection develop and extend the scholarly discourse.

Protestantism in Latin America since 1492

The Protestant Reformation that spread across Europe and into North America from the sixteenth to the eighteenth centuries did not take root in Spain or her New World colonies. That is not to say there was no interest in the calls for ecclesial and theological reform that slipped across the Pyrenees from regions farther north, nor that the possibility of reading the Bible in the vernacular held no appeal for Spanish Catholics.[9] But the Spanish monarchs Charles V and Philip II, armed by instruments of suppression like the Holy Office of the Inquisition, nipped any serious

---

[8]   Orivaldo Pimentel Lopes Jr., "A espiritualidade e a identidade evangélica nacional," in Nelson Bomilcar, ed., *O melhor da espiritualidade Brasileira* [The Best of Brazilian Spirituality] (São Paulo: Mundo Cristão, 2005), 73–91, at 75.

[9]   In regard to sixteenth-century humanistic and proto-Protestant leanings in Spain, see Marcel Bataillon, *Erasmo y España: estudios sobre la historia espiritual del siglo XVI* (Mexico City: Fondo de Cultura Económica, 1950).

Protestant leanings in the bud.[10] Aware of the political implications of theological dissent, first in the Holy Roman Empire and subsequently in their provinces in the Low Countries, the Spanish Habsburgs were loath to allow the contagion of "Lutheranism"—a term which always implied something heterodox, rebellious, and foreign—to spread to the Spanish realm they had inherited through Charles' maternal line.[11]

Thus, the history of Protestantism during the three centuries of Spanish and Portuguese colonial rule in the Americas is a rather short read. True, French Huguenots established a brief foothold in the Baía de Guanabara (Rio de Janeiro) during the 1550s. And when the Dutch occupied northeastern Brazil in 1630, they brought their Calvinism with them, only to lose that region back to staunchly Catholic Portugal in 1654. As Pedro Feitoza demonstrates in chapter 6, nineteenth-century Protestant writers would reclaim this history as a way to demonstrate the rootedness of non-Catholic Christianity in Brazil.

For the Spanish and Portuguese authorities from colonial New Spain (Mexico) to Greater Peru to Brazil, such Protestants were the culturally alien "other," associated with imperial rivals, and a commercial threat to their regulated mercantilist systems. Spanish colonial records are replete with references to Protestant privateers and black-market traders detained not only for their commercial violations, but often for the more serious crime of heresy. English Protestants who were captured and handed over to the Mexican Inquisition in the 1570s suffered a violent fate. The much-venerated St. Rose of Lima famously protected the consecrated host from the sacrilegious intentions of Calvinist Dutch pirates who plundered Peru's viceregal capital in 1615.[12]

---

[10] Fermina Álvarez Alonso, "Herejes ante la Inquisición de Cartagena de Indias" [Heretics before the Cartagena Inquisition], *Revista de la Inquisición* 6 (1997): 239–69; Christine Wagner, "Los luteranos ante la Inquisición de Toledo en el siglo XVI" [Lutherans before the Toledo Inquisition in the Sixteenth Century], *Hispania Sacra* 46 (1994): 109–65; and Ander Berrojalbiz Echevarría, *Los herejes de Amboto: "Luteranos" en el año 1500* [Heretics of Amboto: "Lutherans" in the year 1500] (Arre, Spain: Pamiela argitaletxea, 2016).

[11] On the debate about whether early Spanish proto-Protestants were Lutherans or Erasmians, see José C. Nieto, "Luther's Ghost and Erasmus' Masks in Spain," *Bibliothèque d'Humanisme et Renaissance* 39:1 (1977): 33–49.

[12] Lourdes de Ita Rubio, "Extranjería, Protestantismismo e Inquisición: presencia inglesa y francesa durante el establecimiento formal de la Inquisición en Nueva España," *Signos Históricos* 19:38 (2017): 8–55; and *Viajeros isabelinos en la Nueva España* [Elizabethan Travelers in New Spain] (Morelia, Michoacán: Universidad

In the wake of Napoleon's invasion of the Iberian Peninsula in 1808, movements for independence from imperial rule spread at differing rates across Spain's New World territories. From those movements emerged new republics over the course of about fifteen years; all Spanish colonies except Cuba and Puerto Rico attained nationhood in the early decades of the nineteenth century. Though it gained autonomy from Portugal in the early 1820s, Brazil did so as an independent Brazilian Empire under the rule of Dom Pedro I, son of King João VI of Portugal.

The significance of these political breaks from direct Spanish or Portuguese control cannot be overstated for the future of Protestantism in Latin America. From the outset, national politics across the region divided around the question of what status the Roman Catholic Church should enjoy. From Mexico to the Rio de la Plata region, liberal ideology emphasized Progress (uppercase *P*) over tradition. Liberal parties (uppercase *L*) often expressed their modernizing outlook not only through admiration for things British, French, or American, but also through repudiation of many Iberian and Roman Catholic cultural holdovers. The pursuit of Progress was multidimensional, touching on social structures, international relations, economy, education, and more. For proponents of these liberal ideals, the power of the Roman Catholic Church posed a barrier to societal renewal. As a result, Latin American Liberals made common cause with the Protestant merchants and diplomats who began to enter the region, while the foreign Protestants were happy to reciprocate the favor.[13]

Historians point to Scotsman James "Diego" Thomson as "the forerunner of Protestant mission in Latin America."[14] An advocate for biblical literacy and mass education, Thomson arrived in the River Plate region in 1818, soon moving on to Chile, from there up the spine of the Andes to Gran Colombia, and eventually to Mexico and the Caribbean. Thomson found a warm reception not only among the national liberators like Bernardo O'Higgins and José de San Martín, but also among some Catholic priests and religious who were open to the new ideas of education and

---

Michoacana de San Nicolás de Hidalgo, 2001). On Rosa de Lima, see Ronald J. Morgan, *Spanish American Saints and the Rhetoric of Identity, 1600–1810* (Tucson: University of Arizona Press, 2002), 67–97, at 90–91.

[13] Ondina E. González and Justo L. González, *Christianity in Latin America: A History* (Cambridge: Cambridge University Press, 2008), 184–205.

[14] González and González, *Christianity in Latin America*, 209.

biblical literacy. In the process, he laid early foundations for the establishment of Protestant worship in the years to follow.[15]

To explain the gradual emergence of the Protestant presence in nineteenth-century Latin America, scholars distinguish between "immigrant churches" and "missionary churches." In the former case, young Latin American governments keen to attract trade partners and labor made treaty agreements with European governments, allowing Protestant immigrants to worship discreetly and in their own language, albeit without proselytizing. Indeed, Diego Thomson was among a small group of Scots who, in 1820, held what is believed to be the first Protestant service in Buenos Aires. From the middle decades of the nineteenth century, the Brazilian empire and republics in the southern cone were the biggest recruiters of European labor, and thus hosts to Lutheran, Anglican, and Waldensian immigrant communities, among others.[16]

The second half of the century witnessed the arrival across Latin America, through fits and starts, of the "mission Protestants." From 1855, the government of Brazilian Emperor Dom Pedro II allowed Protestant missions to settle and work in various regions, from Bahia in the northeast to the far southern province of Rio Grande do Sul.[17] In Guatemala, Liberal President Justo Rufino Barrios made overtures to the U.S.-based Presbyterian Board of Missions as part of his anticlerical conflict with the Roman Catholic hierarchy, enlisting the Protestants' aid in establishing schools in his nation. By 1884, the first Presbyterian church was established on a site in the center of Guatemala City where it still worships in 2021. A similar scenario played out in Colombia during three decades of Liberal rule from 1849 to 1880, as Protestant-founded *colegios americanos* ("American schools") came to play a key role in the emergence of the national middle class.[18]

Several dynamics characterized the next generations of these immigrant and mission churches, also known in the scholarship as mainline or "historical" denominations. The 1916 Congress on Christian Work in Latin America (or Panama Conference), the significance of which David

---

[15]   On the influence of James Thomson, Bible Societies, and the Lancasterian method of education, see González and González, *Christianity in Latin America*, 209–16.

[16]   González and González, *Christianity in Latin America*, 184–239, at 209.

[17]   "Introdução," in Elizete da Silva, Lyndon Araújo dos Santos, and Vasni de Almeida, eds., *Fiel é a Palavra: leituras históricas dos evangélicos protestantes no Brasil* [Faithful Is the Word: Historical Readings of Evangelical Protestants in Brazil] (Feira de Santana, Bahia: UEFS Editora, 2011), 13–19.

[18]   González and González, *Christianity in Latin America*, 220–23.

Kirkpatrick and Pedro Feitoza examine in this collection, increased tensions over national versus foreign leadership of the Protestant churches and stimulated processes of interdenominational cooperation for the sake of mission. From the late nineteenth century to the late twentieth, Protestants across Latin America sought to articulate and practice an evangelical faith that was not a foreign import, but authentically rooted in the local context. As late as 1980, notes Brian Stanley, non-Pentecostal Protestants accounted for around one-half of Latin America's evangelicals. Baptist denominations alone had increased from around 250,000 region-wide in 1965 to 1.4 million by the mid-1990s.[19]

As these historical denominations continued to forge their identities within the Latin American religious economy, a new evangelical Protestant phenomenon appeared on the scene just after the turn of the twentieth century. According to the established historiography, Pentecostalism gained its first permanent footholds in Chile and in two very different regions of Brazil in the first decade of the twentieth century. In the two Brazilian cases, Europeans who had encountered Pentecostal doctrine in the United States arrived in Brazil to evangelize and plant churches. By contrast, an American mainline Methodist missionary couple working in Chile came into contact with Pentecostal teaching through a transnational network of influences. As Joseph Florez explains in chapter 7, when they and some of their Methodist congregants began to practice the gifts of the Spirit, a rift occurred within the national Methodist fellowship, resulting in the formation of the *Iglesia Metodista Pentecostal* (Pentecostal Methodist Church).[20] From such beginnings in three distant corners of the South American continent, Pentecostalism has spread and undergone significant transformations over the past century and more, though at varying paces and in diverse ways.[21]

Through a variety of demographic studies over the past few decades, academics and public entities have charted the growth of Pentecostal and

[19]   Brian Stanley, *Christianity in the Twentieth Century: A World History* (Princeton, N.J.: Princeton University Press, 2018), 304–10. Statistics for Brazil, at least, show that the numerical growth of historical Protestants had flattened between the census reports of 2000 and 2010. See Morgan and Pereira, "Which *evangélicos*?" 65–71.

[20]   In a chapter entitled "Pentecostalism and Autochthonous Movements," Ondina and Justo González caution that, until further research is completed, "it is . . . impossible at this time to present an orderly and critical review of the origins and growth of the movement." Even so, they begin their narrative with Chile, "the first country in which Pentecostalism made a significant impact." *Christianity in Latin America*, 270–96, at 271.

[21]   Freston, "Contours," 224–27.

Neo-Pentecostal groups. Well into the middle twentieth century, Chile and Brazil contained the highest national percentages of Protestants and Pentecostals. Even as late as 1985, Chile (21.6 percent), Guatemala (19 percent), and Brazil (16 percent) had the highest proportions of Protestants across Latin America. Even so, national growth rates during the quarter century between 1960 and 1985 favored Central American and Andean nations, while earlier leaders Chile and Brazil were experiencing flattening growth rates.[22]

In 1995, Paul Freston estimated the general Protestant population continent-wide at forty-five to fifty million, roughly 10 percent of the regional population, with Pentecostals comprising around 60 percent of those Protestant totals (approximately thirty million). Such general statistics might be misleading, since the degree of "Pentecostalization" of general Protestant populations varied widely by nation, from approximately 30 percent in some Andean countries to as high as 80 percent in Chile. Acknowledging the dynamic situation, Freston added that both in terms of Protestants as a percentage of national population and the Pentecostal ratio to historical Protestants, most Central American nations had already surpassed early front runners Brazil and Chile.[23] As Matt Marostica demonstrates in his contribution to this collection, these shifts over time are more than numerical—they also represent, as in his case study of Argentina, ever-changing ways of being Pentecostal and conceiving of evangelical identity within a national context.

A 2014 survey by the Pew Research Center verifies trends highlighted in the 1990s by Stoll and Freston. First, across Latin America as a whole, 19 percent self-identified as Protestant, up from Freston's estimated 10 percent about two decades earlier. Region-wide, 65 percent of those evangelical Protestants claimed a Pentecostal identity and/or institutional affiliation. One valuable feature of the Pew survey was its attention to religious change within a single generation. Thus, while 84 percent of respondents

---

[22] Stoll, citing *Operation World*, provides the following rates of evangelical growth: Guatemala (from 2.81 to 18.92 percent); Honduras (1.51 to 8.75 percent); El Salvador (2.45 to 12.78 percent); Colombia (0.39 to 2.43 percent); Ecuador (0.48 to 2.75 percent); Bolivia (1.27 to 6.51 percent); Peru (0.63 to 2.98 percent). See appendices 2 and 3 in Stoll, *Is Latin America Turning Protestant?* 335–38.

[23] Freston, "Contours," 228–29. One remarkable statistic for Central America stands out. In that region, the "Pentecostalization" of the general Protestant population multiplied over a half century from 2.3 percent in 1936 to 37 percent in 1965, surging to above 50 percent by the 1980s.

reported that they had been raised Roman Catholic, only 69 percent continued to identify as such. Conversely, while only 9 percent of respondents reported being raised as evangelical Protestants, 19 percent were claiming an evangelical identity in 2014. Moreover, in this survey and others, the increase in religiously "unaffiliated" persons is confirmed by Philip Jenkins' forecast in chapter 4 of a likely decline in religious practice over the years to come. And those reporting unaffiliated status had reached 8 percent, up from 4 percent who claimed to have been raised with no affiliation.[24]

The Recent Historiography of Evangelical Protestantism in Latin America

Any consideration of recent historical scholarship on the evangelical phenomenon in Latin America must give ample tribute to David Martin's *Tongues of Fire* and David Stoll's *Is Latin America Turning Protestant?* In his 1991 review of these two groundbreaking monographs, Paul Freston called their appearance "a somewhat belated recognition by academics of a major cultural shift."[25] But if the arrival of such scholarly attention was tardy, it certainly ignited its own scholarly conflagration, one that stimulated further academic study of the religious transformations of the region by the continued proliferation and growth of Pentecostal and Neo-Pentecostal denominations.

In *Tongues of Fire*, British sociologist Martin examines Pentecostalism within a broader historical framework of earlier evangelical Protestant revolutions: Puritanism and Methodism. To a large degree, Martin explains the *why* of conversion in relation to social migration, "the mass movement of people from countryside or hacienda to the mega-city."[26] And like several contributors to this volume, he is concerned with the question of cultural authenticity, "the extent of . . . the Latin Americanization of Protestantism." Acknowledging that "[w]hat historic

---

[24] *Religion in Latin America: Widespread Change in a Historically Catholic Region* (Washington, DC: Pew Research Center, 2014), 4–5, 8, https://www.pewforum.org/2014/11/13/religion-in-latin-america/.

[25] Paul Freston, "Tongues and Politics: The Protestantization of Latin America; A Review Essay," *Crux* 27:3 (1991): 38–41, at 38.

[26] Martin, *Tongues of Fire*, 284. Such emphasis on the socioeconomic implications of conversion also characterizes Sheldon Annis' monograph entitled *God and Production in a Guatemalan Town* (Austin: University of Texas Press, 1987). Annis applied Weberian analysis to a highland indigenous town during the 1970s and 1980s, documenting how conversion to Pentecostalism resulted in greater economic prosperity for many.

Protestantism has lacked and still lacks is precisely the capacity to 'go native,'" he suggests that Pentecostalism is more adept, pointing to the Methodist Pentecostal Church of Chile as "the first important case of 'inculturation.'" Recognizing that features of such inculturation often draw criticism, he offers a sort of silver lining: "[T]hat Pentecostalism reproduces some of the characteristics of *caudillismo* (authoritarian leadership) and of 'patriarchal relations' on the hacienda is to say that it lies close to the social roots."[27]

For his part, U.S. anthropologist David Stoll scrutinizes the evangelical moment in Latin America in terms of the politics of religion, arguing "that polemics against the 'invasion of the sects' have tended to obscure a fact of great significance, the emergence of debates *among evangelicals* over how to respond to the social and economic crises swelling their congregations."[28] In what has become a central theme in the recent analysis of evangelical growth, Stoll juxtaposes such expansion with Roman Catholic numerical decline, placing much of the blame on "the Catholic Church's inability to decentralize its system of authority."[29] At the same time, distinguishing between diverse strands of evangelical Protestantism across the region,[30] Stoll highlights the work of the Latin American Theological Fellowship (FTL), a globally influential movement whose significance Daniel Salinas narrates in chapter 2 of this volume.[31] Responding to the frequent criticism of recent evangelical politics—tendencies examined below by Garrard and Lecaros—Stoll expresses a hope that the "third way" inspired by the generation of Samuel Escobar, José Míguez Bonino, and René Padilla—"theologically but not politically conservative"— might offer a social vision with the potential to alter Latin America's cultural, moral, and political landscape.[32] Short of such an outcome, he expresses a concern that many evangelicals in Latin America will follow the U.S. religious right in exchanging the former apoliticism for

---

[27] Martin, *Tongues of Fire*, 282.

[28] Stoll, *Is Latin America Turning Protestant?* xvi (emphasis added).

[29] Stoll, *Is Latin America Turning Protestant?* xvi–xvii.

[30] In the aforementioned review article, Paul Freston observes the following: "Stoll is strong on the increasing differentiation of the Protestant world, unlike other authors who do not go beyond a simplistic dichotomy of 'ecumenicals' and 'fundamentalists'" ("Tongues and Politics," 39).

[31] See also Daniel Salinas, *Latin American Evangelical Theology in the 1970s: The Golden Decade* (Leiden and Boston: Brill, 2009).

[32] Stoll, *Is Latin America Turning Protestant?* 10.

a theocratic vision, the goal of which is to "take dominion" over the earth, a theme that Garrard nuances in this volume.[33]

Nearly a quarter century after Martin and Stoll called attention to the changing shape of evangelicalism across Latin America, historian Todd Hartch weighed in with *The Rebirth of Latin American Christianity*, part of the Oxford Studies in World Christianity series. A key to the author's approach is to be found in the title term "rebirth." Unlike other regions of the Global South like Africa and Asia, regions that have witnessed "the sudden and massive growth of a new faith," he characterizes the transformations taking place in Latin America as "a simultaneous fragmentation and revitalization that threatened, awakened, and ultimately brought to greater maturity a dormant and at times parochial religion."[34] Eschewing the sort of zero-sum game analysis which equates evangelical numerical growth with Roman Catholic decline, Hartch's central theme is the "surprisingly fruitful" relationship between Pentecostalism and the Catholic Charismatic Renewal, a point developed by John Maiden's chapter in this volume. Calling Pentecostalism "the true magical realism" that "brought the supernatural back into urban, industrial Latin America," Hartch notes that scholars who are content to analyze religion on moral, ethical, ritual and liturgical bases have not known what to do with "a movement utterly out of step with the spirit of the age."[35]

Despite various signs of revitalization of Latin American Christianity, however, Hartch identifies major challenges that Christians of all stripes must confront if their witness and influence are to remain relevant to their societies. Central to his concern is the danger that "the newly revitalized mestizo Protestantism and Catholicism" might become culturally captive. He points to the tendency for the "mestizo" church—by which he means that of national majorities—to confuse the gospel with their own cultural values and forms, thus endangering the authentic Christianization of indigenous peoples in the region.[36] In addition, he laments the inability of Latin America's Christians to provide their region with a new "master key for perceiving reality," a phrase he borrows from Peruvian novelist Mario Vargas Llosa. Instead, much like the secular culture of the early twenty-first century, whose products "are ephemeral and commercial,"

---

[33]   Stoll, *Is Latin America Turning Protestant?* xvii.

[34]   Todd Hartch, *The Rebirth of Latin American Christianity* (New York: Oxford University Press, 2014), 2.

[35]   Hartch, *Rebirth of Latin American Christianity*, 207.

[36]   Hartch, *Rebirth of Latin American Christianity*, 223–26.

Latin American Christians have become consumers of their own cultural products, following market-driven trends with short-term aims instead of "communicating Christianity as a total way of life, or . . . as something to which elites should give serious attention."[37]

Of course, Spanish- and Portuguese-language scholars across Latin America have shown interest in the Protestant phenomenon for decades, led by the pioneering work of several European-born scholars, including Reformation historian Émile Léonard (d. 1961), social scientists Emilio Willems (d. 1997) and Pierre Lalive D'Epinay (d. 2014), and historian Jean-Pierre Bastian.[38] The work of these scholars lent credibility in the early days to critical, scientific approaches to the study of Latin American religion, particularly Protestantism, as did the subsequent formation of professional academic organizations like the Commission for Historical Studies of the Church in Latin America (CEHILA, 1973) and the Brazilian Association for the History of Religions (ABRA, 1999). Comprised of Protestant scholars exploring their own traditions and their nonreligious colleagues, these organizations and more informal networks have been largely responsible for the growth and increasing sophistication of the historiography of evangelicalism in Latin America.[39]

---

[37]   Hartch, *Rebirth of Latin American Christianity*, 211–16.

[38]   Émile Léonard, *O Protestantismo Brasileiro: estudo de eclesiologia e história social*, trans. Linneu de Camargo Schützer (São Paulo: JUERP and ASTE, 1963). Léonard delivered these lectures while at the University of São Paulo between 1948 and 1950, publishing them at that time in article form. See also Emilio Willems, *Followers of the New Faith: Culture, Change and the Rise of Protestantism in Brazil and Chile* (Nashville: Vanderbilt University Press, 1967); Christian Lalive D'Epinay, *Haven to the Masses: A Study of the Pentecostal Movement in Chile* (London: Lutterworth, 1969); and Jean-Pierre Bastian, *Historia del Protestantismo en América Latina* (Mexico City: Ediciones CUPSA, 1990).

[39]   Consider two academic conferences of 2010 and 2011. In June 2010, several Latin American evangelical historians gathered in Lima, Peru, to commemorate two hundred years of Latin American independence. Their essays were subsequently published in English translation in Lindy Scott, ed., "Special Issue on Nineteenth-Century Latin American Protestantism," *Journal of Latin American Theology* 6:2 (2011). A second conference in Mexico City in October 2011, entitled "History, Protestantism and Identity in the Americas," drew academic participants and observers from public universities, religious seminaries, parachurches, and denominations across Latin America. Cosponsored by the Universidad Nacional Autónoma de México (UNAM), the Conference on Faith and History, and the Nagel Institute, this groundbreaking academic conference represented for several of the Mexican hosts a milestone in the legitimization of the academic study of Protestantism within Latin American public institutions of higher learning.

The scholarship of historian Jean-Pierre Bastian in particular has been a major factor in the transition from hagiographic Protestant narratives, often produced under the auspices of denominations, to more critical approaches that privileged the relationship between the religious sphere and dynamics in wider society. In a 1990 monograph, Bastian offers a broad analysis of the Protestant phenomenon in the region, emphasizing its status as a minority subculture in societies that were overwhelmingly Roman Catholic in composition. He notes the "organic ties" between Protestants and Latin American Liberals, characterizing Protestant "societies" (churches or denominations) as spaces in which modern values such as democratic practice and egalitarian ethics could begin to weaken the authoritarian culture that the Roman Catholic monopoly had reinforced. In this regard, he links nineteenth- and early twentieth-century Protestantism to Latin American reform movements of various stripes, with particular attention to Mexico. Moreover, Bastian gives attention to matters of transmission, integration, and Latin Americanization of the phenomenon, themes elaborated in this volume by Maiden, Salinas, Kirkpatrick, Feitoza, and Florez.[40] In so doing, he challenges the assumption that Protestantism in the region has served as a mere arm of U.S. interests or a quiescent rubber stamp of the sociopolitical status quo.[41]

Inspired by Bastian, the intersecting themes of Protestantism, religious plurality, and democratic culture have inspired multidisciplinary studies on minorities in Latin America. For example, Mexican scholar Carlos Mondragón González, psychologist and historian at the Universidad Nacional Autónoma de México, has headed the wide-ranging project entitled *Minorías, sociedad y subjetividad: Desde los márgenes de la historia* ("Minorities, Society and Subjectivity: From the Margins of History"), resulting in extensive scholarly production. One such edited collection, entitled *Minorías religiosas: el Protestantismo en América Latina* (Religious Minorities: Protestantism in Latin America), reveals

---

[40] Bastian, *Historia del Protestantismo.*

[41] Jean-Pierre Bastian, *Protestantismos y modernidad latinoamericana: historia de unas minorías religiosas activas en América Latina* (Mexico City: Fondo de Cultura Económica, 1994); and Jean-Pierre Bastian, *Los disidentes: Sociedades protestantes y revolución en México, 1872–1911* (Mexico City: Fondo de Cultura Económica and El Colégio de México, 1989). In a similar vein, see Norman Rubén Amestoy, "Protestantismo, nación y modernidad en la Argentina, Siglo XIX," in Carlos Mondragón González and Carlos Olivier Toledo, eds., *Minorías religiosas: el Protestantismo en América Latina* (Mexico City: Universidad Nacional Autónoma de México, 2013), 97–125.

concerns on the part of many Latin American scholars that evangelical Protestants may be drifting from their historical commitment to religious pluralism and the lay state, concerns that Garrard and Lecaros raise below.[42]

In one chapter of *Minorías religiosas*, coeditor Carlos Mondragón follows Serge Moscovici in arguing that social minorities, with their heterodox practice and discourse, bring dynamism to societies. He praises the role played by "the more radical sectors" of nineteenth-century Latin American Liberalism, who "stimulated the growth of tolerance and religious liberty, freedom of conscience, the rise of the state and of lay education, etc."[43] On the one hand, Mondragón laments how whole sectors of evangelical Protestants in the mid-twentieth century bought into an anti-Marxist, antisocialist rhetoric, and thus supported or acquiesced in repressive governments across the region. Others, he notes, declared a sort of "social strike" (*huelga social*), backing away from the social commitments of early Protestant generations. Turning to the more recent political engagement of some evangelical groups, he expresses concern that generations conditioned to be apolitical were now ill-prepared to put their beliefs into practice "in the social realm." His concluding question is crucial: "How do the churches aid in the formation of engaged citizens who are conscious of their civil obligations and rights?"[44]

In the concluding essay of the same volume, Leopoldo Cervantes-Ortiz addresses the historical and present relationship between Mexican Protestants and national culture. Referring to a past in which to be a Protestant made one a "bad Mexican" and a threat to national wellbeing, he concludes by providing a list of Mexican "Protestants or sympathizers of certain renown"—protagonists in the 1910 Revolution and public officials, educators, and popular cultural figures. The purpose of offering this panoply, he notes, is to help readers understand "the sociocultural repercussions of the Protestant presence in Mexico."[45]

---

[42] Mondragón González and Olivier Toledo, eds., *Minorías religiosas*.

[43] ". . . impulsaron la tolerancia y la libertad religiosa, la libertad de conciencia y el surgimiento del Estado y la educación laica, etc." In Carlos Mondragón González, "Minorías religiosas y contexto social en la América Latina, Siglo XX," in Mondragón González and Olivier Toledo, eds., *Minorías religiosas*, 37–52, at 37.

[44] Mondragón González, "Minorías religiosas y contexto social," in Mondragón González and Olivier Toledo, eds., *Minorías religiosas*, 37–52, at 50 (translation mine).

[45] Leopoldo Cervantes-Ortiz, "Los Hijos de Lutero en México," in Mondragón González and Olivier Toledo, eds., *Minorías religiosas*, 246–52 (translation mine).

Minorías religiosas: el Protestantismo en América Latina is simply one example of a very extensive scholarship among Latin American historians on the historical link between evangelical Protestants and the creation of the secular or "lay" state across the region.[46] These historians, many of them either active evangelicals or products of evangelical Protestant formation, have also produced important historical scholarship on Protestantism, education, and modernization in nineteenth- and early twentieth-century Latin America.[47]

To some degree, the history of Pentecostalism in Latin America remains to be written. In a 1995 essay entitled "Contours of Latin American Pentecostalism," Paul Freston describes "a mass phenomenon [that] is now attracting increasing academic scrutiny," though he credits social scientists, more than historians, for making Latin American Pentecostalism a growing field of study.[48] Positing that the lack of historical scholarship leaves those same social scientists with little "information on the large churches as *dynamically evolving institutions*," Freston himself takes up the slack in his 1995 study of the Brazilian context. Spotlighting six denominations (two per period) to illustrate "three waves of institutional creation," Freston highlights the flexible relationship between Brazilian culture and various Pentecostalisms, as well as the historical restraints that limited the ability of each wave to adapt to changing times. In regard to the first wave, to which we alluded above, he examines how the Swedish and Italian American ori-

---

[46]   For an analysis of Protestant support for President Benito Juarez' Liberal *Reforma* of the 1850s, see Ariel Corpus, "Secularism and Freedom of Conscience: The Historical Tie to Mexican Presbyterianism," in Lindy Scott, ed., "Special Issue on Nineteenth-Century Latin American Protestantism," *Journal of Latin American Theology* 6:2 (2011): 89–106. On how Protestantism shaped the nineteenth-century legislative battles that accompanied the formation of the secular state in Argentina, see Eunice N. Rebolledo Fica and Norman Rubén Amestoy, "El Protestantismo y el proceso de laicización en Argentina: las luchas legislativas del siglo XIX," *Revista Teología y Cultura* 23:1 (2021): 34–55.

[47]   Rubén Ruiz Guerra, *Hombres Nuevos: Metodismo y Modernización, 1873–1930* [New Men: Methodism and Modernization in Mexico, 1873–1930] (Mexico City: CUPSA, 1992); and Juan Fonseca Ariza, *Misioneros y civilizadores: Protestantismo y modernización en el Perú, 1915–1930* [Missionaries and civilizers: Protestantism and modernization in Peru, 1915–1930] (Lima: PUCP, 2002). In English, see various articles in Lindy Scott, ed., "Special Issue on Nineteenth-Century Latin American Protestantism."

[48]   Freston, "Contours," 220–24, at 221. Pedro Feitoza addresses such scholarly imbalance in "Experiments in Missionary Writing: Protestant Missions and the *Imprensa Evangelica* in Brazil, 1864–1892," *Journal of Ecclesiastical History* 69 (2018): 585–605, at 586–87.

gins of the Assembleia de Deus and the Congregação Cristã, respectively, shaped their planting and development in Brazil's far north and in São Paulo state.[49] A key feature of the mid-twentieth-century second wave was a move from church buildings to the streets, as first the U.S.-import Foursquare denomination and then the native-born Brazil for Christ (Brasil para Cristo) employed new methods and infused their preaching with "the felt needs of physical and psychological healing."[50] Finally, the third wave, notes Freston, "fits into urban culture influenced by television and the yuppie ethic."[51] These Neo-Pentecostals, best exemplified by the Universal Church of the Kingdom of God (IURD) (f. 1977) and International Church of the Grace of God (f. 1980), began to be characterized by more emphasis on prosperity and less on moral austerity (e.g., women's dress style), while they built media empires (e.g., TV Record), engaged more directly in electoral politics, stressed healing and exorcism, and began to treat Afro-Brazilian groups, more than Roman Catholicism, as their primary spiritual antagonists. In relation to this latter feature, Brian Stanley has observed how "the panoply of spirits associated with the . . . [Afro-Brazilian] context have been interpreted [by Pentecostals] as emissaries of Satan."[52] This points to a growing preoccupation in the social scientific and historical literature on Neo-Pentecostalism, namely, its intolerance for the sort of religious freedom that earlier generations of evangelical Protestants argued for and defended.

It should be noted here that Freston's focus on three distinctive waves, with its clear emphasis on Brazilianization over time, omits any attention to charismatic renewal within the historical denominations. While there are many studies on charismatic renewal within Roman Catholicism, including that by Todd Hartch (see above), very little scholarly attention has been given to the same phenomenon among Presbyterians, Baptists, and Methodists in the mid- to late twentieth century, though John Maiden addresses these developments in his chapter of this volume.[53] U.S.-based anthropologist Andrew Chesnut has authored insightful assessments of

---

[49] Paul Freston, "Pentecostalism in Brazil: A Brief History," *Religion* 25:2 (1995): 119–33, at 120–25.

[50] Freston, "Pentecostalism in Brazil," 126–29, at 126.

[51] Freston, "Pentecostalism in Brazil," 129–32, at 129.

[52] Stanley, *Christianity in the Twentieth Century*, 308.

[53] For one dissertation on the origins and growth of charismatic renewal among mainline Baptists in Brazil, see Thiago Moreira, "Da tradição à renovação na Igreja Batista da Lagoinha: um olhar sobre o Protestantismo renovado" [From Tradition to Renewal in the Baptist Church of Lagoinha: A Look at Renewed Protestantism] (PhD diss., Universidade Federal de Juiz de Fora, 2016).

the current success of charismatic Christianity in the Latin American religious marketplace.[54] And in his influential monograph entitled *Born Again in Brazil*, Chesnut achieves three things in one book: a historical overview of Brazilian Pentecostalism and Neo-Pentecostalism; a participant-observer analysis of how poor northerners surrounded by "pathogens of poverty" find their way to Pentecostal churches; and a history of early Pentecostal forays into legislative politics in the northern state of Pará.[55]

Garrard's chapter in this collection builds upon her influential studies of civil war and ethnic cleansing during a period of rapid Pentecostal and Neo-Pentecostal growth. In *Protestantism in Guatemala: Living in the New Jerusalem*, she explores the development of Protestantism in the central American nation up through the presidency of José Efraín Ríos Montt in the early 1980s.[56] Garrard's *Terror in the Land of the Holy Spirit* is an attempt to account for the convergence of evangelical numerical growth and rising violence, especially under the presidency of former military general Ríos Montt.[57] Of course, the theme of religious competition and violence is not confined to recent decades, nor to the growth of Pentecostalisms, as Erika Helgen has recently demonstrated in her monograph on the transition in Brazil from a hegemonically Catholic society to one increasingly characterized by religious pluralism.[58]

When Paul Freston complained of the lack of historical scholarship on Latin American Pentecostalism, he found a partial explanation in features within Pentecostalism, which "has a tense relationship with history." Not only do Pentecostal denominations lack written sources with which scholars might work, he notes, but they have also tended to value origin

---

[54] Andrew Chesnut, "Latin American Charisma: The Pentecostalization of Christianity in the Region," in Martin Lindhardt, ed., *New Ways of Being Pentecostal in Latin America* (Lanham, Md.: Lexington Books, 2016), 1–14; and *Competitive Spirits: Latin America's New Religious Economy* (Oxford: Oxford University Press, 2007).

[55] Andrew Chesnut, *Born Again in Brazil: The Pentecostal Boom and the Pathogens of Poverty* (Rutgers, N.J.: Rutgers University Press, 1997).

[56] Virginia Garrard-Burnett, *Protestantism in Guatemala: Living in the New Jerusalem* (Austin: University of Texas Press, 1998).

[57] Virginia Garrard-Burnett, *Terror in the Land of the Holy Spirit: Guatemala under General Efraín Ríos Montt* (Oxford: Oxford University Press, 2010).

[58] Erika Helgen, *Religious Conflict in Brazil: Protestants, Catholics, and the Rise of Religious Pluralism in the Early Twentieth Century* (New Haven, Conn.: Yale University Press, 2020).

events, relegating change over time to the footnotes.[59] That being said, Latin American Pentecostal historians like Norberto Saracco (Argentina) and Juan Sepúlveda (Chile)[60] were making valuable scholarly contributions even before the influential publications by David Martin, David Stoll, Andrew Chesnut, and Virginia Garrard. In this vein, in 1998 Pentecostal scholars formed the Latin American Network of Pentecostal Studies (RELEP) to promote such scholarship. Led by David Mesquiati, Néstor Medina, Sammy Alfaro, and others, these scholars are producing interdisciplinary work in the growing field of Pentecostal studies.[61]

Recently, scholars have begun to highlight the diversity within Pentecostalism across Latin America. Danish scholar Martin Lindhardt led a multi-scholar study of the recent and ongoing reinvention of Pentecostal theologies, practices, and identities in Latin America. Acknowledging the validity of earlier scholarly interpretations, Lindhardt argues that "certain developments and transformations of Latin American Pentecostalism within recent decades call for a broadening and partial renewal of scholarly focus." Among the said transformations were the emergence of "an individually confessed and a *sui generis* Christian identity"; new types of intra-Pentecostal competition; new generations raised in Pentecostal traditions; and new positions on politics, citizenship, and "the world."[62]

Naturally, the increased interest in transnational approaches to the study of global Christianity has weakened the rather arbitrary boundary between Latin American and U.S. Latino studies. Gaston Espinosa, a prolific researcher on U.S. Latino religiosity, has described the Pentecostalization of evangelical Christianity both north and south of the U.S.-Mexican border, as well as the impact of Latino Pentecostals on U.S. politics. As noted earlier, to be Protestant in much of Latin America has historically

[59] Freston, "Contours," 223.

[60] Norberto Saracco, "Argentine Pentecostalism: Its History and Theology" (PhD diss., University of Birmingham, 1989); "Charismatic Renewal and Social Change: A Historical Analysis from a Third World Perspective," *Transformation* 5:4 (1988): 14–18; and Juan Sepúlveda, "Pentecostalismo y democracia: una interpretación de sus relaciones," in Arturo Chacon, ed., *Democracia y evangelio* (Santiago: Rehue, 1998), 229–50.

[61] See David Mesquiati de Oliveira, "The FTL, Pentecostal Theology, and the Academy in Brazil," *Journal of Latin American Theology* 11:2 (2016): 103–20; and Mesquiati de Oliveira and Gedeon Freire de Alencar, "Research note: The Contribution of the Rede Latino-americana de Estudos Pentecostais," *International Journal of Latin American Religion* 1:1 (2017): 156–65.

[62] Lindhardt, ed., *New Ways of Being Pentecostal in Latin America*, vii–ix.

presented challenges of identity and citizenship. For the U.S. context, Arlene Sánchez-Walsh has examined ways in which Latino Pentecostals have differentiated themselves from the larger Latino Catholic culture. Daniel Ramírez has placed transnational migratory routes at the center of his analysis of how the U.S.-Mexican borderlands shaped the origins and ongoing development of Pentecostalism both north and south, arguing that the region was fertile ground for religious innovation on the part of large populations whose world was in motion. Such historical analysis of Latino religious identities in flux has not been limited to Pentecostalism, as Felipe Hinojosa's fine study of how Mexican and Puerto Rican American Mennonites negotiated and blended their religious and ethnic identities in several far-flung corners of the United States and Puerto Rico.[63] In the final chapter of this volume, Matheus Reis contributes to the expanding transnational scholarship on evolving ethnic and religious identities among Latin American migrant communities in the United States.

In the chapters that follow, ten authors from Latin America, Britain, France, and the United States build on the foregoing scholarship. The papers for the conference on which the collection is based were invited with a view to assembling a broad range of studies in the history of Latin American evangelicalism. Of necessity the treatment of the many lands could not be comprehensive, but the contributors were selected as experts on various dimensions of the subject, national and denominational. Thus, while five chapters address issues affecting the whole of Latin America, a further five concentrate on specific national case studies. Pentecostalism is included, but does not dominate the collection, allowing the full range of religious groups to find a place. Politics is certainly not omitted, but the main concern is with the core religious priorities of the movement associated with the spread of the gospel. The various contributions go a long way toward enriching our understanding of the very complex tapestry that is evangelicalism in Latin America.

---

[63] Gaston Espinosa, "The Pentecostalization of Latin America and U.S. Latino Christianity," *PNEUMA: The Journal of the Society for Pentecostal Studies* 26:2 (Fall 2004): 262–92; *Latino Pentecostals in America: Faith and Politics in Action* (Cambridge, Mass.: Harvard University Press, 2014); Arlene M. Sánchez-Walsh, *Latino Pentecostal Identity: Evangelical Faith, Self, and Society* (New York: Columbia University Press, 2003); Daniel Ramírez, *Migrating Faith: Pentecostalism in the United States and Mexico in the Twentieth Century* (Chapel Hill: University of North Carolina Press, 2015); and Felipe Hinojosa, *Latino Mennonites: Civil Rights, Faith, and Evangelical Culture* (Baltimore: Johns Hopkins University Press, 2014).

I
General Studies

1

Looking South

Latin America and Charismatic Renewal in the United States and United Kingdom, 1945–1980

John Maiden

"In these last days the Holy Spirit is doing a new thing in Argentina and in all of Latin America and in many other parts of the world. The Holy Spirit is starting to regroup us into only two groups: those who love one another and those who *do not* love one another."[1] Of the Latin American contributions to the 1974 Lausanne Congress, a crucial international evangelical gathering, the presentation by Juan Carlos Ortiz is usually overlooked. While Samuel Escobar and René Padilla challenged Western Christians to consider the social dimensions of the gospel, Ortiz brought to those gathered in Switzerland a distinctively charismatic challenge, born out of his ministry in Buenos Aires: the renewal of the churches, Protestant and Catholic, in the unifying power of the Spirit. Ortiz' message was apparently well received at the congress. A review in *Church Growth Bulletin* suggested, "When you think of what Juan Carlos Ortiz has been saying to us all it is remarkable . . . here he is, guiding Western churchmen desperately looking for some way to put fire into their churches."[2] Switzerland was only one stop in a busy

[1]   Juan Carlos Ortiz, "The Work of the Holy Spirit in Evangelization, Individually and through the Church," *Lausanne 1974 Documents*, accessed December 21, 2020, https://www.lausanne.org/content/lausanne-1974-documents.

[2]   Herbert Works, "Lausanne—A Catalyst for World Evangelization," *Church Growth Bulletin*, September 1974, 1.

global schedule for Ortiz, with the United States, Australia, New Zealand, and the United Kingdom each on his itinerary in the mid-1970s. Most of the gatherings at which he spoke were associated with the charismatic renewal. For the purposes of what follows, this is defined as a loose and trans-local imagined community of the Spirit, involving mainline, independent, and Pentecostal Christians, which was established through the course of the long 1960s. It was constructed, as with the global evangelical imagined community of the nineteenth century, very largely through media. Texts (books, pamphlets, and magazines) and audio (reel-to-reel and cassette tapes) circulated Spirit baptism testimonies and teachings, with video and television offering a further audiovisual medium to be exploited from the late 1960s. In the West, Ortiz was something of a teaching celebrity within the charismatic subculture, yet he is rarely mentioned in the scholarly literature on the movement. In this chapter, we will see that this is in fact symptomatic of a wider historiographical problem.

As is very evident in the work of historians such as David Swartz, Melani McAlister, Mark Noll, Brian Stanley, and others, scholarship on the history of conservative and progressive evangelicalism is increasingly taking into account the "global reflex." By this we mean the ways in which the Global South, either through the mobilities of its own religious actors and media or through the return of long- and short-term missionaries, has influenced the Global North.[3] This shift of emphasis in the scholarship has been rather less evident in the historiography of charismatic Christianity. However, as historians such as Mark Hutchinson and Paul Freston have asserted, the dominance of American-centric narratives of charismatic renewal is particularly problematic.[4] The established narrative of charismatic renewal, recited regularly by both participants and academic scholars, tends to emphasize two trajectories. One is Protestant and begins with High Church Episcopalians in the Los Angeles suburbs in 1959/60,

[3]   David R. Swartz, *Facing West: American Evangelicals in an Age of World Christianity* (New York: Oxford University Press, 2020); Melani McAlister, *The Kingdom of God Has No Borders: A Global History of American Evangelicalism* (New York: Oxford University Press, 2018); Mark A. Noll, *The New Shape of World Christianity: How American Experience Reflects Global Faith* (Downers Grove, Ill.: InterVarsity Press, 2009); and Brian Stanley, *The Global Diffusion of Evangelicalism: The Age of Billy Graham and John Stott* (Downers Grove, Ill.: InterVarsity Press, 2009).

[4]   Paul Freston, "Charismatic Evangelicals in Latin America: Mission and Politics on the Frontiers of Protestant Growth," in Stephen Hunt, Malcolm Hamilton, and Tony Walter, eds., *Charismatic Christianity: Sociological Perspectives* (London: Palgrave, 1997), 184–204.

and particularly the high-profile controversy (reported in both *Time* and *Newsweek*) regarding news of Dennis Bennett's baptism in the Spirit with tongues. The second, the Catholic trajectory, begins with faculty and students at Duquesne University in 1966 and 1967, among whom there was an inbreaking of "Pentecost," in part through the impact of reading David Wilkerson's account of ministry in the power of the Holy Spirit among New York City's gangs in *The Cross and the Switchblade*. From these starting points, the history of charismatic renewal inevitably becomes one of expansion and export *from* these places. While, clearly, transnational religion is not a level playing field, and the United States has indeed been the major exporter worldwide of Pentecostal and charismatic religious personnel and media, these narratives of the origins and development of the charismatic movement need to be complicated.

There is some existing literature specifically on interactions between charismatics in the United States and Latin America, with the focus generally on the late 1970s onward and on the politics of the "religious right." Sara Diamond's *Spiritual Warfare: the Politics of the Christian Right* (1989) is a helpful contribution, but tends to present a rather one-way pattern of export "south."[5] More recently, Lauren Turek's important work on California evangelical charismatic support for the Rios Montt regime in Guatemala argues "the web of influence that U.S. Christians wove—or found themselves woven into—in Guatemala in the early 1980s exemplified the transnational connectivity, shared evangelistic goals, and extensive reach of the global evangelical community."[6] This chapter seeks to adopt the kind of sensitivity to transnational connections and exchanges evident in Turek's work, but with a focus on religious identities and practices rather than politics. In what follows, furthermore, there is emphasis on the reception and representation of Latin America in Anglo-world contexts. Through a series of brief case studies, it explores multidirectional dynamics of encounter and exchange between the West and the "third world" in the emergence of charismatic renewal. Specifically, it will look at the relationship between Latin America (and also communities of Latin American heritage, the Mexican Americans) and the Anglo world, specifically the United States and the British Isles. The four studies concern

---

[5] Sara Diamond, *Spiritual Warfare: The Politics of the Christian Right* (Cambridge, Mass.: South End Press, 1989).

[6] L. F. Turek, "To Support a 'Brother in Christ:' Evangelical Groups and U.S.-Guatemalan Relations during the Ríos Montt Regime," *Diplomatic History* 39:4 (2015): 689–719.

the mainline *Renovação Espiritual* in Brazil, and American evangelical "higher-life" perceptions of the global work of the Spirit; the movement of the piety and communitarianism of the Catholic lay apostolate *Cursillos de Cristiandad* from Spain, through Mexican American communities, to the white middle-class Catholic environs such as the University of Notre Dame and Catholic-ecumenical prayer groups, from where they also influenced Protestants; the impact of the ecclesiology of Juan Carlos Ortiz on transatlantic restorationism; and the influence of charismatic renewal in Chile on Anglican and Episcopalian theories of church growth.

Brazilian Baptists, *Renovação Espiritual,* and the Evangelical Pursuit of Reanimated Piety

Hope for revival was in the air among evangelicals in the transatlantic world during the postwar years. The year 1949 had seen two contrasting revivalistic developments in very different contexts: in Los Angeles, Billy Graham arrived with his already well-oiled evangelistic machine; while on the Isle of Lewis, in the remote Outer Hebrides of Scotland, there were reports of spontaneous and emotional public expressions of repentance from sin. These events and others contributed to the heightened expectation of revival evident in evangelical publications such as *Christian Life*. The magazine was published in Chicago (as *Christian Life and Times*) beginning in 1946, before its purchase two years later by Robert A. Walker. The magazine sat in the broad tradition known variously as "deeper-," "higher-," or "victorious-" life evangelicalism, each a description of the spiritually empowered life. While most of the content was by American authors—including favorites such as A. W. Tozer—it also drew on material from the British evangelical scene. The magazine displayed the global imagination and ambition of evangelicalism, particularly where revival awakening was concerned. "Praise God for a world-sweeping revival now in progress," wrote Robert Walker in September 1949.[7] The desire for worldwide awakening was cultivated by the existential uncertainties which had come with the Soviet acquisition of the atomic bomb. It was "4 minutes to midnight," asserted one writer in 1950, a reference to the *Bulletin of the Atomic Scientists*.[8] Throughout the decade and into the next, *Christian Life* regularly published intelligence of global revival. A 1956 report in the magazine asked: "[C]an revival scenes from the 19th

---

[7]   Editorial, "Formula for Revival," *Christian Life*, September 1949, 6.

[8]   William W. Gothard, "4 Minutes to 12," *Christian Life*, January 1950, 11–13, 35.

century be duplicated in our modern, atomic-age world?" In answer, it mapped awakenings on every continent, including in Brazil, East Africa, the Belgian Congo, Korea, and Japan. One correspondent, Don Hoke, argued, "The prophecy of Joel was not exhausted but rather only initiated by Pentecost. I believe that we can expect from God in the last days a gracious outpouring of His Holy Spirit in revival."[9] Here was a restatement of the eschatology of the "latter rain" (the end-time outpouring of the Spirit, distinct from the "former rain" of Pentecost) which had been evident in some historical strains of radical evangelicalism—for example, the teachings of William Boardman, A. T. Pierson, and A. B. Simpson—before it became, in the early twentieth century, a key motif of Pentecostalism.[10]

A historian of American evangelicalism, Amber Thomas Reynolds, has discussed how the revivalism of *Christian Life* was accompanied by a desire to see empowerment and manifestation of the Holy Spirit. Indeed she presents *Christian Life* as a "missing link" in the origins of charismatic renewal in the United States.[11] Her observations about the magazine fit a wider pattern of dissatisfaction among higher-life evangelicals. In *Full Surrender* (1951), the Belfast-born revivalist and scholar of revivalism, J. Edwin Orr, had gone as far as to describe the period from 1908 to 1948 as a "forty years of the wilderness experience" because of the dearth of teaching on the filling of the Spirit.[12] Throughout the 1950s, *Christian Life* published articles criticizing the cerebral tendencies of evangelicalism, urging the recovery of a second-stage crisis experience of the Spirit distinct from conversion. This experience, it asserted in 1956, was the "need of the hour." It explained: "Terminology doesn't matter. You may call it victorious life of Keswick Conference fame, fullness of the Spirit, sanctification, deeper life experience, baptism in the Spirit, the life that wins of Charles G. Trumbull or the exchanged life of Hudson Taylor. Essentially they all mean the same thing."[13] Other articles discussed exorcism and supernatural healing, in a kind of evangelical backlash against interwar claims that

---

[9] "Revival Today," *Christian Life*, February 1968, 18–20, 45, at 45.

[10] See, for example, Edith Blumhofer, *Restoring the Faith: The Assemblies of God, Pentecostalism, and American Culture* (Chicago: University of Illinois Press, 1993), 95–96.

[11] Amber Thomas Reynolds, "Robert Walker's *Christian Life* Magazine: A Missing Link between Mainstream American Evangelicalism and Charismatic Renewal," in Andrew Atherstone, Mark P. Hutchinson, and John Maiden, eds., *Transnational Charismatic Renewal, c. 1950–2000* (Leiden: Brill, 2021), 37–60.

[12] J. Edwin Orr, *Full Surrender* (London: Marshall, Morgan and Scott, 1951), 72.

[13] "Need of the Hour," *Christian Life*, December 1956, 18–20, at 19.

the extraordinary gifts of the Spirit had ceased.[14] As *Christian Life* scanned world horizons for signs of revival, so it also looked to the third world for evidence of pneumatic empowerment and manifestations. A 1958 article on spiritual warfare, for example, referred to the experience of demons in the mission field in Acua territory in Ecuador. "In this enlightened, scientific age, is it possible to believe in demons?" it asked. "Are demons present on Main Street and Times Square, USA?"[15]

Brazil was one country in which the magazine began to take a particular interest. The country had been part of a wider resurgence, evident also in Central and East Africa and India, of a dynamic variety of higher life encounter with the Spirit which involved brokenness before God and confession of sin. "Evidence that the Spirit of God works in revival power" had come from "Catholic-dominated South America," a report asserted in 1950. The article mentions the work of the Worldwide Evangelization Crusade (WEC) in the Congo, and a Child Evangelism Fellowship conference at the Pedra Bible Institute near Rio de Janeiro, where representatives of eight denominations—pastors, students, and missionaries—had wept and confessed sins for four hours.[16] In 1952, a visit by J. Edwin Orr to Brazil brought further reports of united prayer and spontaneous revival. "When Spirit filled men and women unite in Spirit-directed prayers for revival, their persevering, persistent prayers will result in a mighty outpouring of God's Spirit such as the world has yet to see," argued Orr in *Christian Life*.[17] In the imaginary of these deeper-higher-life evangelicals, Brazil was becoming a place of pneumatic potential.

This was the background for a series of articles published in 1961 on the experience of "baptism in the Spirit" among Brazilian Baptists, along with some Methodists and Presbyterians. The background of these developments on the ground in Brazil has been discussed by the historian João B. Chaves. A key figure was Rosalee Appleby, a Southern Baptist missionary and church planter who served in Brazil from 1924 onward. Appleby taught an "advanced" version of Keswick doctrine—a second experience of the Spirit which endued the believer with power. Her teachings of *Renovação Espiritual* were to be criticized by the

---

[14] William H. Good, "I Saw a Miracle," *Christian Life*, July 1951, 21, 68–70; W. Douglas Roe, "I Clashed with the Spirit World," *Christian Life*, January 1952, 21, 64, 66; and Samuel Shoemaker, "Healing Prayer," *Christian Life*, August 1959, 16–17.

[15] "Demon Power Today," *Christian Life*, June 1958, 15.

[16] "In Brazil and the Congo," *Christian Life*, October 1950, 33.

[17] J. Edwin Orr, "Power in United Prayer," *Christian Life*, July 1958, 15–17.

Southern Baptists' Foreign Mission Board not only for being "Pentecostal" in tendency but also because they were said to be the product of psychological instability. The latter was a charge which carried sexist undertones when applied to a female missionary, but it was also a common evangelical anti-Pentecostal trope directed toward men. A Baptist minister who later became one of Appleby's mentees, José Rego do Nascimento of Sixth Baptist Church of Belo Horizonte, was baptized in the Spirit in 1954 following a period of personal spiritual searching and dissatisfaction with ministry. Along with another Appleby mentee, Enéas Tognini, the three worked to foster interest in the baptism in the Spirit among Baptists during the late 1950s.[18]

In 1961, *Christian Life* reported on the outbreak of empowered evangelicalism in Brazil and the role of Appleby, Nascimento, and Tognini. Robert Walker visited the country personally to observe the movement. He interviewed the Baptist Antonio Martins Vilas Boas, a chief justice of the Supreme Court, whom he quoted: "We have ignored the Person and work of the Holy Spirit. As a result we have failed to benefit from the power which God has intended Christians to enjoy . . . The baptism of the Holy Spirit, and the enduement of power which results, is being re-examined and rediscovered in some of the evangelical denominations today."[19] Walker's representation of these empowered Baptists in *Christian Life* was particularly significant. He informed his readers that the Brazilian mainliners saw the "current move of the Holy Spirit" as "something akin to, but totally different from, the pentecostal doctrine." Chaves' study of the public doctrinal debates within the denomination in Brazil confirm that Nascimento and Tognini, like Appleby, were eager to situate the experience within the historic Baptist tradition. Here, then, was a charismatic awakening that was recognizably evangelical; one that would have been more immediately recognizable and acceptable to the readers of *Christian Life* than the combination of High Church Episcopalianism and Pentecostalism that characterized the movement of the Spirit in Southern California heralded by Dennis Bennett. Indeed, it is significant that the developments in Brazil were reported in *Christian Life* three months before the magazine made any substantial mention of Bennett and the happenings

[18] João B. Chaves, "Exporting Holy Fire: Southern Baptist Missions, Pentecostalism, and Baptist Identity in Latin America," *Perspectives in Religious Studies* 2:1 (2020): 203–14.

[19] "Letter from the Editor," *Christian Life*, May 1961, 5–7. See also Robert Walker, "Spiritual Awakening in Brazil," *Christian Life*, August 1961, 24–27.

at St. Mark's, Van Nuys.[20] Brazil provided an example of mainline renewal in the Spirit for higher-life evangelicals before the Californian version of "charismatic renewal" was popularized in the United States.

Mexican *Cursillistas* and Catholic Charismatic Renewal

Cursillos de Cristiandad (Short Courses of Christianity) was a Catholic apostolate which involved small group meetings. These aimed at the intensification of lay—and initially male—piety. It was founded on the Spanish island of Mallorca in 1944 and just over a decade later, was brought to the United States by Spanish Air Force cadets. Cursillo, of course, was not evangelical. However, it played a critical, preparatory role in the origins of charismatic Catholic-ecumenical prayer groups, which displayed some markedly "evangelical" characteristics. Upon its arrival in the United States, in Texas, the course initially appealed to a first generation of Mexican Americans who had experienced significant marginalization. Kristy Nabhan-Warren argues that it initially "offered family, a new community to call home, and emotional release from the every-day oppression Mexicanos experienced in mainstream America."[21] The first Spanish-speaking group was held in Waco, Texas, in 1957, initially just for men, but women's courses were established shortly after. By 1962 English-speaking groups were established, which tended to attract a white, middle-class, urban and suburban demographic of baby boomers.[22]

The key components of the Mallorcan Cursillo spirituality were Marian devotion, mystical relationship with Christ, and the experience of the fire of the Spirit.[23] The groups' activities involved reading the Bible, discussion, and spontaneous elements of worship and prayer. These characteristics endured after they were transferred to the American context, but here, too, synergies were developed with what Joseph Chinnici describes as a "pedagogy of participation," which the Catholic hierarchy had encouraged

[20]   Jean Stone, "What is Happening Today in the Episcopal Church," *Christian Life*, November 1961, 38–42.

[21]   Kristy Nabhan-Warren, "'Blooming Where We're Planted': Mexican-Descent Catholics Living Out *Cursillo de Cristiandad*," *U.S. Catholic Historian* 28:4 (2010): 99–125, at 102.

[22]   Kristy Nabhan-Warren, "'We are the Church': The Cursillo Movement and the Reinvention of Catholic Identities in Postwar America and Beyond," *U.S. Catholic Historian* 33:1 (2015): 81–98.

[23]   Kristy Nabhan-Warren, *The Cursillo Movement in America: Catholics, Protestants and Fourth Day Spirituality* (Chapel Hill: University of North Carolina Press, 2013), 3, 38, 47.

in recent decades.[24] Two upper-Midwest dioceses where English-language Cursillo established strong roots were Fort Wayne-South Bend and Lansing. These were the homes of the University of Notre Dame, Michigan State, and the University of Michigan, all of them locations where from 1967, the charismatic experience of baptism in the Spirit spread rapidly through the existing nexus of Cursillo networks.[25] There was something about their involvement in Cursillo which predisposed Catholics such as Steve Clark and Ralph Martin toward charismatic piety and which shaped their pioneering (while members of the National Cursillo Secretariat between 1965 and 1970) of the inchoate The Word of God Catholic-ecumenical community in Ann Arbor. Involvement in Cursillo, Clark argued, meant that *cursillistas* (participants in Cursillo groups) were likely "to find all the good that was in the 'new thing'" where Pentecostal practices were concerned.[26] It was the "seed-bed out of which the Charismatic Renewal blossomed," Martin argued.[27]

The role of Mexican Americans in mediating the spirituality of Cursillo to the white, upper-Midwest pioneers of "Catholic Pentecostalism" is yet to be properly explored. The emotional, experiential side of Mexican American Cursillo groups had initially been critiqued by some white American Catholics as excessive; however, for Catholic baby boomer seekers looking for a "conventional" but authentic expression of faith, this dimension made it appealing.[28] Clark had become aware of Cursillo through an American priest who had described the movement in Mexico City in "Pentecostal terms" as men "filled with the Holy Spirit," empowered to become effective apostles. Later Clark met Mexican *cursillistas* who struck him as "stronger Christians than the Americans." He came to think that the courses might effectively disciple white American Catholics also.[29] As

---

[24] Joseph P. Chinnici, "The Catholic Community at Prayer, 1926–1976," in James M. O'Toole, *Habits of Devotion: Catholic Religious Practice in Twentieth-Century America* (Ithaca, N.Y.: Cornell University Press, 2004), 48–49.

[25] Jim Manney, "Before Duquesne: Sources of Renewal," *New Covenant*, February 1973, 12–17.

[26] Virginia Beach, Regent University Special Collection and Archives, Dennis Bennett Papers, Box 4: Steve Clark, "Renewal in the Catholic Church," *Pastoral Newsletter*, June 1970.

[27] Quoted in Patti Gallagher Mansfield, *As by a New Pentecost: The Dramatic Beginning of the Catholic Charismatic Renewal* (Steubenville, Ohio: Franciscan University of Steubenville, 1992).

[28] Nabhan-Warren, "Blooming Where We're Planted," 107.

[29] Clark quoted in Manney, "Before Duquesne," at 15.

Cursillo groups were established at the University of Notre Dame, they cultivated an appetite for New Testament Christianity; during a meeting in 1965, there was even a case of tongues.[30] Ralph Martin was in fact converted through Cursillo and later recalled an experience of being filled with "power from on high." Months after this, without pursuing a Pentecostal experience, he manifested tongues, but without understanding what was happening at the time.[31]

Cursillo influenced the social dynamics of the Catholic-ecumenical prayer groups and later a number of covenant communities. For Clark, one aspect of these collective expressions of charismatic renewal that Cursillo had introduced consisted of practices of embodied affection. His time doing apostolic work in Mexico and his involvement in Cursillo, Clark asserted, had shown him how to be more freely affectionate. In 1975, looking back at these earlier experiences, he argued the following:

> We need to avoid attitudes like, "I'm an American and American men don't hug one another; that's just for those Latins." We discovered that affection among men was liberating for us. In fact, if we had not learned to express love to one another in a much freer way than most Americans do, Christian community would have been a lot harder.[32]

These encounters with Mexican American and Mexican *cursillistas* shaped Catholic charismatic renewal from its inception. A strong sense of affinity remained—for example, at the International Conference on the Charismatic Renewal in the Catholic Church in 1978, Eduardo Bonnín, founder of the Cursillo, was an invited speaker.[33] Cursillo's experiential piety and communitarian form was a Hispanic contributor to charismatic origins. Catholic-ecumenical charismatic communities such as Clark and Martin's The Word of God in Ann Arbor were to wield a significant influence on Protestant charismatic conceptions of community, for example, through their links with the nondenominational Christian Growth Ministries (mentioned below). This meant that aspects of Cursillo's approach to authentic and spontaneous interpersonal relationships permeated beyond Catholicism, into evangelicalism.

---

30 Manney, "Before Duquesne," 17.
31 Mansfield, *As by a New Pentecost.*
32 Steve Clark, "Learning from other Cultures," *New Covenant* 4:11 (1975): 13–15.
33 Louise Bourassa, "You Shall Be My Witnesses," *New Covenant* 8:3 (1978): 4–8.

Renovación, City-Wide Churches, and Authority in Buenos Aires

In the mid-1970s, some charismatic leaders, particularly those associated with Christian Growth Ministries (CGM), Fort Lauderdale, Florida, began to put their weight behind the idea of the "city-wide church." CGM was established at the end of the previous decade as the Holy Spirit Teaching Mission. It had drawn together diverse elements of the charismatic ecosystem in the United States, although it increasingly represented the "restorationist" stream of the movement. According to the model of local church they began to disseminate, pastors of different churches should submit to each other, regarding themselves collectively as co-elders of the ecumenical body of Christ in that geographical area. The restoration of the putatively New Testament "one church, one city," or "city government," was supported in the magazine *New Wine* and particularly in the ministry of CGM's Derek Prince. "It doesn't make any difference," Prince asserted, "if your bone comes from a Baptist graveyard, a Catholic graveyard or a Pentecostal graveyard. When the bones are joined together, it will not be on the basis of which graveyard they come from; it will be on the nature of their function in the Body."[34] This primitivist concept had various lineages. It was one example of continuity between charismatic renewal and the Latter Rain movement of 1948. It was also advocated in the writings of the Chinese leader of the Little Flock movement, Ni Doushen, or Watchman Nee. His *Concerning Our Missions* (1939) urged this approach to the local church in order to "return to the beginning." In 1962 the book was republished in Los Angeles as *The Normal Christian Church*. However, if these were ideological sources of inspiration for this ecclesiology, the exemplar of the citywide church in action was Buenos Aires, Argentina, and the ministry of Juan Carlos Ortiz and others.[35]

The *renovación* in Buenos Aires began around 1969 among the open Brethren in the city, and soon drew in Mennonites, Baptists, and Catholics. One of those impacted was the Assemblies of God pastor Ortiz. His church, *Tabernáculo de la Fe* (Tabernacle of Faith), had been planted by American missionaries following the Tommy Hicks crusade the previous decade. Ortiz' church was revitalized and grew significantly in the context of this wider renewal, later moving into a large theater in the

[34] Derek Prince, "Can These Bones Live?" *New Wine*, January 1973, 5–10, at 10.
[35] Jim Hamann, "One City One Church," *New Wine*, February 1974, 25–27; Frank S. Longino, "City Government—Can it Work?" *New Wine*, June 1974, 15–18.

city. Ortiz developed strong links with other church leaders in Buenos Aires, and through his friendship with a priest, Julio Elizaga, had ecumenical connections with Roman Catholics, including the archbishop. Catholics even preached at the *Tabernáculo*, a move which produced significant consternation in the American Assemblies of God.[36] Alongside other pastors in the city, Ortiz also became an advocate for "one city, one church"—or, as he would explain it in his preaching, including at Lausanne in 1974, "many potatoes but one *mashed* potato." He later described his experience of this ecclesiology as follows: "Little did I know how much I had to learn until I came together with other pastors—Baptists, Presbyterians, Plymouth Brethren, and Catholics. As a proud Pentecostal I had to become a humble elder in the church."[37] Ortiz and others from the city traveled widely throughout Latin America, where their ministry was particularly significant because of its breaking barriers between Catholic and Protestant. Buenos Aires became a hub for the renewal on the continent. Its reputation was consolidated in 1972, when the First Latin American Renewal Congress was held in the city, at a Catholic retreat center. By the time of the 1974 Lausanne conference, Ortiz' church was regarded as the "fastest growing charismatic congregation in Argentina."[38]

The Buenos Aires experiment had an impact on charismatic ecclesiology in the English-speaking world. Ortiz, Orville Swindoll, Ivan Martin Baker, and others from the city appeared in CGM's *New Wine* magazine. In 1975, Logos International Fellowship, the publishing house for luminaries of the charismatic renewal, published Ortiz' *Call to Discipleship*. The reputation of the wider church in Buenos Aires was highlighted in the introduction to the book, which was authored by the leading American independent charismatic, Jamie Buckingham. "'The church of Buenos Aires' has come very close to being a prototype of the New Testament church in the twentieth century," he claimed.[39] Ortiz was one of the few Global South charismatics to become an established participant in the international conference circuit of the charismatic renewal in the

[36] Juan Carlos Ortiz and Martha Palau, *From the Jungles to the Cathedrals: The Captivating Story of Juan Carlos Ortiz* (Miami: Editorial Vida, 2011), 325–50.

[37] Juan Carlos Ortiz, *Call to Discipleship* (Plainfield, N.J.: Logos International Fellowship, 1975).

[38] Herbert Works, "The International Congress on World Evangelization," *Church Growth Bulletin*, July 1974, 2.

[39] Ortiz, *Call to Discipleship*, xii.

mid-1970s, visiting the United States in 1973, Australia and New Zealand in 1974, and the United Kingdom in 1976.

The influence of Ortiz' ecclesiology went beyond the "one city, one church" model. *Call to Discipleship* described discipleship as a spiritual "law." "There will be no formation in life without submission," Ortiz asserted.[40] Significantly, in 1973 Ortiz had been invited to speak in Fort Lauderdale by Don Basham, Bob Mumford, and Derek Prince—the CGM men who became key proponents of the so-called discipleship or shepherding movement. Later, Bob Mumford recognized the extent of Ortiz' influence on his own teaching on submission.[41] The back cover of *Call to Discipleship* claimed that "some see him as a man like Watchman Nee"—and indeed Nee's writings, including his views on the local church, were influential on Ortiz' ecclesiology and authority.[42] Buenos Aires was a Latin American laboratory for Nee's approach. In the few years after 1974, "shepherding" nearly broke what unity existed in the charismatic movement in the United States, Australia, and New Zealand, and to a lesser extent, the United Kingdom. Where Ortiz' own teaching on submission was concerned, it was not so much the substance of his teaching that some charismatics opposed as the clearly abusive ways in which it could be (and was) put into practice locally. Michael Harper, the English charismatic leader, said of Ortiz' teaching on the matter before his invited visit by the British Evangelical Alliance in 1976: "I was as impressed with the book [*Call to Discipleship*] as I have been disturbed by some of its attempted expressions in this country. If the word 'nurturing' had been used it might have helped."[43] In advocating a radical submission to authority as part of discipleship, Ortiz and others from Buenos Aires contributed indirectly to the most significant controversy to face the charismatic renewal in the West during the 1970s.

Latin America and Anglican "Power Evangelism"

The Anglican Church in Latin America—that is, Province IX of the American Episcopal Church, the Missionary District of Mexico, the Province of Brazil, and the English-influenced Province of the Southern Cone—was

---

[40] Ortiz, *Call to Discipleship*, 73.

[41] S. David Moore, *The Shepherding Movement: Controversy and Charismatic Ecclesiology* (London: T & T Clark, 2003), 58. Moore notes that another leading CGM figure, Charles Simpson, was not influenced by Ortiz.

[42] Ortiz and Palau, *Jungles to Cathedrals*, 363–64, 381.

[43] Michael Harper, "Hot Issue," *Renewal* 60 (1975/1976): 8.

a tiny denomination in Latin American terms. However, from the early 1970s, news of Anglican renewal in Chile was reaching the networks of Anglican and Episcopal renewalists in the United States and England. In April 1971, the Rev. Dennis Bennett in Seattle received a letter from the Assemblies of God missionary Arthur Lindvall, describing how he had been invited to visit the Valparaíso home office of the English churchman David Pytches, the assistant bishop for the region. Upon entering the room, he was told, "Start talking about the Holy Spirit. We want to know about Him." The previous month, the bishop's wife, Mary Pytches, had experienced Spirit baptism while traveling back from furlough in England. Lindvall was invited to join Kathleen Clark, a Spirit-baptized South American Missionary Society worker in the south of Chile, in bringing teaching to the bishop and his Valparaíso pastors and in ministering in the supernatural gifts. The Anglican work in Chile, Lindvall argued, was on the brink of renewal.[44]

Pytches' memoirs describe Clark's visit as the "beginnings of a glorious visitation of the Holy Spirit."[45] The ministry in the charismatic gifts was new to Pytches, a South American Society missionary who had been wary of Pentecostalism and described himself as a "Bible loving, card carrying evangelical."[46] In Valparaíso and elsewhere in Chile, Pytches—who became bishop of Chile, Bolivia, and Peru in 1973—witnessed scenes of Anglican growth. He described the church in the 1970s as being "in the throes of spiritual revival" and as having a significant charismatic element.[47] One such example was the church in Gomez Carreño, led by Omar Ortiz, where meetings were held every night and reportedly on one occasion at least one hundred were baptized in the nearby river.[48] Pytches became increasingly aware of the power of the Spirit to heal. After the organist of St. Paul's, Valparaíso, claimed to have had a painful tooth healed by the visiting healing evangelist Gigi Avila, Pytches took

[44] Arthur Lindvall to Dennis Bennett, South America, April 14, 1971, in Regent University Special Collections and Archive.

[45] David Pytches, *Living at the Edge: The Autobiography of David Pytches* (Bath: Arcadia, 2002), 145.

[46] Pytches, *Living at the Edge*, 139.

[47] Pytches, *Living at the Edge*, 180. Figures are difficult to obtain, but available figures show that average growth rate increased from 4.3 percent prior to 1970 to 7.5 percent between 1970 and 1995. See Henri Gooren, "The Growth and Development of Non-Catholic Churches in Chile," *Review of Religious Research* 57:2 (2015): 191–218.

[48] Pytches, *Living at the Edge*, 186–87.

his whole family to see this Puerto Rican at the football stadium. "I had never seen anything like it," he later recalled.[49]

Pytches was one of many Western missionaries who had their first and most profound experiences of the work of the Spirit and of the supernatural world in Latin America or other parts of the Global South. It is notable that apart from some available literature by American authors such as Kathryn Kuhlman and Francis MacNutt, Pytches had no links with charismatic renewal. In fact, he admitted to not really understanding the work of the Spirit at this stage. On one occasion he was asked by a woman in Achupallas, a poor area by Viña del Mar, north of Valparaíso, to pray for a sick baby (who apparently the local hospital had said was beyond help). Pytches prayed for healing somewhat reluctantly and with little expectation ("there was no way out. I'd just have to give it a go!"). He was surprised to be told by the woman a few days later that the baby was healed. Even after this, Pytches seems to have been unsure in the operation of the gifts. "I didn't realise it at the time," he said, that this experience "opened the door to a whole new range of possibilities for me."[50] As Pytches observed the revival, he had no real "model" for integrating signs and wonders into local church life. Nevertheless, Pytches' own experience of Christianity, and of the relationship between evangelism and the supernatural, was transformed during his time in Chile.

Pytches brought news of Anglican growth in his Latin American diocese to England and the United States. In 1975 he was invited to speak to those Pittsburgh Episcopalians who would soon take an important role in the coordination of evangelical charismatic resurgences in their denomination.[51] Then, after returning to England, in 1977 he took over the congregation of St Andrew's, Chorleywood, to the northwest of London. Here, Pytches was finally able to experiment with how to incorporate the charismatic gifts into the life of a parish. Another former South American Missionary Society worker, Eddie Gibbs, had also settled in Chorleywood. Gibbs recommended the ministry of John Wimber, the American church planter. Wimber's every-member lay "power" ministry might be interpreted as a Californian attempt to indigenize the Latin American church growth and power movement, which C. Peter Wagner had described in his *Look Out: The Pentecostals Are Coming!* (1973).

---

[49] Pytches, *Living at the Edge*, 195.

[50] Pytches, *Living at the Edge*, 189.

[51] Jeremy Bonner, *Called out of Darkness into Marvelous Light: A History of the Episcopal Diocese of Pittsburgh, 1750–2006* (Eugene, Ore.: Wipf and Stock, 2009), 265.

While spending some time teaching on church growth at Fuller Seminary, Pasadena, Wimber had encounters with students from the third world, as well as with former missionaries on faculty, such as Chuck Kraft, which led him to question the rationalistic assumptions of the Western Christian mindset. Pytches invited him to England in 1981, and St Andrew's was impacted profoundly.

Pytches had returned from Chile at a time when English renewalists were looking for a "new thing" that might provide a second wind for the movement. St Andrew's became a charismatic flagship, growing significantly and sending out lay teams to other congregations throughout the country to model their "every-member-ministry" in the power of the Spirit. It played a key role in laying the groundwork for what later became the New Wine network of churches. Pytches' *Come Holy Spirit* (1985) became a charismatic best seller in the United Kingdom, arguing that confirmation of the gospel through signs and wonders was "more relevant than ever in the 1980s." It related, too, some of the experiences from Chile. It mentioned the impact of Gigi Avila (although Pytches, like Wimber, wanted to emphasize that the miraculous gifts were not only for the big names, but for every member to practice).[52] It described also how in Petraco, south Chile, following an exorcism, Pytches had seen people "flock to the church" and new congregations planted.[53] In 1987 and 1988, Episcopal Renewal Ministries invited Pytches to teach on power evangelism and power ministry.[54] By a circuitous route, denominational connections meant that Pytches had an important role in mediating Wimber's approach to Americans.

Conclusion: Latin America and the Global Charismatic Reflex

During the 1960s, amidst concerns about secular trends in their own societies, various Christian leaders in the West looked elsewhere for signs of life and strategies for mission. In 1967, for example, Donald Coggan, then the Anglican Archbishop of York, reminded a congregation that in Latin America "four out of five non-Roman Christians are Pentecostals." He went further to ask if the church might require less organization and more of the Spirit. "Is it possible that they have the gifts of the Spirit which

[52] David Pytches, *Come Holy Spirit* (London: Hodder and Stoughton, 1985), 1.
[53] Pytches, *Come Holy Spirit*, 15.
[54] "What Do You Mean by 'Signs and Wonders'?" *Acts 29*, February 1987, 8; "Pytches's 'Power Ministry,'" *Acts 29*, July 1987, 1–2, at 1.

we have not?" he asked.[55] In 1963, a piece by Daniel J. O'Hanlon in the Jesuit magazine *America* spoke of the potential lessons to be drawn from the Pentecostals of Latin America, including their connection with the poor and the power of emotion in worship and devotion.[56] Charismatics, then, were not the only Christians in the West to wonder if some kind of re-enchanted faith might be found in the "third world." Between the 1950s and the 1970s, the impetus for charismatic renewal in the West was very often a sense of disillusionment with the situation facing Christianity. Michael Harper believed that the rapid, empowered expansion of Christianity described in the Acts of the Apostles made "embarrassing reading" for churches in Britain, particularly with all their "up-to-date techniques and novel methods of mass communication." "Only in the third world," he asserted, "is anything comparable taking place, and it is not without significance that it is being done largely through Pentecostals."[57] The interest of Western charismatics and proto-charismatics in the work of the Spirit in Latin America should be seen in this wider context. In the four case studies discussed in this chapter, we have demonstrated the significance of Latin America in charismatic renewal in the West. Transnational exchanges contributed to the very idea of a mainline awakening of the Spirit at the beginning of the 1960s; to the Catholic search for empowerment and then approaches of Catholics to community life in the Spirit in the mid- and late 1960s, which in turn would permeate into evangelical Protestantism; to the restorationist ecclesiology of some charismatics in the 1970s; and to Anglican and Episcopal approaches to church growth, through signs and wonders, in the late 1970s and 1980s. Across these four decades, then, Latin America played a vital role in the imagination, identity, and practice of charismatics in the Global North.

---

[55]   "Wind and Fire," *Logos* (New Zealand) 1:3 (1967): 11.

[56]   Daniel J. O'Hanlon, "The Pentecostals and Pope John's 'New Pentecost,'" *America* 108:18 (1963): 634–36.

[57]   Michael Harper, *Walk in the Spirit* (London: Hodder and Stoughton, 1968), 9–10.

2

The Theological Revolution in Latin American Evangelicalism of the 1970s

J. Daniel Salinas

Recent scholarship has made it clear that liberation theology is not the only Latin American theology.[1] In the 1970s, simultaneously with liberation theologies, an evangelical Latin American theology was developing. To have a more complete picture of Christian doctrine in Latin America, it is necessary to be acquainted with this theology. The Latin American Theological Fraternity (*Fraternidad Teológica Latinoamericana* [FTL]) was not the first theological forum in the region, nor the only one; however, its half a century of existence has galvanized and consolidated the growth and development of Latin American evangelical theological thought. This article tells the story of the formation of the FTL in 1970 and its relevance and influence for further theological developments in Latin America and other parts of the world.

[1] Sharon E. Heaney, *Contextual Theology for Latin America: Liberation Themes in Evangelical Perspective* (Eugene, Ore.: Wipf and Stock, 2008); David C. Kirkpatrick, *A Gospel for the Poor: Global Social Christianity and the Latin American Evangelical Left* (Philadelphia: University of Pennsylvania Press, 2019); Daniel Salinas, *Latin American Evangelical Theology in the 1970s: The Golden Decade* (Leiden: Brill, 2009); J. Daniel Salinas, "The Evangelical Theological Production in Hispanic Latin America between 1969 and 1979 (A Reception History)" (PhD diss., Trinity International University, 2004); and Daniel Salinas, *Taking up the Mantle: Latin American Theology in the 20th Century* (Carlisle, UK: Langham, 2017).

Rationale for an Evangelical Latin American Theology

Argentinean Methodist theologian and pastor José Míguez expressed in 1970 his concern about the lack of a proper Latin American evangelical theology.

> The Christian Church has a longstanding debt to Latin America: four and a half centuries of Roman Catholicism and one of Protestantism have not produced the minimum of creative thought . . . The scarce literature that has been produced until recent years has done no more than translate, reproduce, or imitate materials from other latitudes . . . The lack of theology in a continent where the Church has such a wide human base is symptomatic . . . Let us propose a hypothesis: neither Roman Catholicism nor Protestantism have had (as churches) deep enough roots in Latin American reality to give light to creative thought. In other words, both churches have remained marginal to the history of our people.[2]

A couple of years later, Ecuadorian New Testament scholar René Padilla pointed in the same direction as Míguez:

> The Latin American church is a church without its own theological reflection . . . our Christian literature is translated from English . . . our preaching is reduced to a mere repetition of badly assimilated doctrinal formulas, without any insertion in our historical reality. The analysis of all these aspects of our ecclesiastical reality shows that our "theological dependency" is . . . real and urgent . . . the total picture the church in Latin America presents [is] a church without a theology, without conscientious reflection that serves the Word of God.[3]

Míguez and Padilla described the state of theological reflection in Latin America and expressed a concern for an authentic growth of the church.

However, something was brewing in the 1970s. Peruvian missiologist Samuel Escobar explained in 1978:

> At the bosom of the Latin American evangelical churches, a theological reflection has been gestating for the last few years wishing to be faithful to its evangelical past and at the same time paying attention to the Latin American reality. This is not an academic theology taking the latest findings of some German or English thinkers to a laboratory and

---

[2]   Preface to Rubem Alves, *Religión: ¿Opio o instrumento de liberación?* (Montevideo: Tierra Nueva, 1970), I–II.

[3]   C. René Padilla, "La Teología en Latinoamérica," *Pensamiento Cristiano* 19:75 (1972): 205–13, at 206.

after a few modifications has added a "Made in Latin America" label. It is a reflection born in the midst of evangelical communities characteristic of a more dynamic sector of Latin American Protestantism.[4]

A few years later Salvadoran theology professor Emilio Núñez explained:

> What we are lacking is an *evangelical* theology which is systematized and authentically *Latin American*. But there is a group of evangelical thinkers in pursuit of that theology. With great effort they have begun to make progress in the theological field and are on the way to some reflections, with the intense desire to hear the Word of God and pronounce that Word for the people of Latin America.[5]

The dire social, economic, and political situation of most Latin American countries begged for biblical and theological answers that imported theologies could not provide. Puerto Rican seminary professor, pastor, and missiologist Orlando Costas summarized Latin America in the early 1970s as dominated by "oppression and repression, imperialism and colonialism, starvation and poverty, power and powerlessness, frustration and despair."[6] No wonder Latin American theologians were feeling the theological vacuum and the need for an autochthonous theology.

The "Rocky" Beginnings of the FTL

In November 1969 in Bogotá, Colombia, nine hundred participants from all over the continent were invited to the First Latin American Congress of Evangelism (CLADE I) organized and sponsored by the Billy Graham Evangelistic Association (BGEA). This congress was part of the plan by the BGEA to hold congresses in the Global South as a follow-up to the Berlin Congress of 1966.[7] At CLADE I there were some people from all over the continent who had been working independently on a theology by Latin Americans for Latin America. Bogotá provided the *kairos* for them to meet,

---

4   Samuel Escobar, "La Teología Evangélica Hoy," *Pensamiento Cristiano* 24:4 (1978): 232–37, at 232.

5   Emilio Antonio Núñez C., "Towards an Evangelical Latin American Theology," *Evangelical Review of Theology* 7 (1983): 123–31, at 123–24 (emphasis in original).

6   Orlando Costas, "Evangelism and the Gospel of Salvation," *International Review of Mission* 63:249 (1974): 24–37, at 25.

7   For the Berlin Congress, see Carl F. H. Henry and W. Stanley Mooneyham, eds., *One Race, One Gospel, One Task. World Congress on Evangelism, Berlin, 1966. Official Reference Volumes: Papers and Reports*, 2 vols. (Minneapolis: World Wide Publications, 1967), I.

interchange ideas, talk about their interests, compare notes, and become friends. They realized that, for the most part, their goals intersected, that they had similar feelings about the predominant theological dependency, that their questions in spite of their isolation and distance were alike, and that they longed for a strong theological fellowship. They decided it was time to join forces, to stop being solitary voices in the wilderness.

In Bogotá they made a commitment to keep in touch, to share their writings, and to form a theological group that would serve as the main forum for their theological enterprise. Peruvian Baptist Samuel Escobar expressed the general feeling by saying that they were "tired of the evangelical centers of power in North America telling us how to think, who to read, and what it meant to be evangelical," and therefore "we decided it was time to start reflecting the faith as grownups and on our own."[8]

During CLADE I, quite unintentionally, C. Peter Wagner's book on Latin American theology, distributed at no cost to all the delegates in Bogotá, started a flash flood.[9] Wagner, who had lived in Bolivia as a missionary for over a decade, was one of the leading exponents of the church growth movement in the United States, which concentrated on single-minded efforts to bring larger numbers of converts into the church.[10] Wagner described three groups of Christians in Latin America: "the conservative evangelical Protestants, the conservative Catholics of the establishment, and the radical left-wing group made of both Protestants and Catholics." The main argument of the book was that the last group, characterized by "secular theology and revolutionary politics," was outnumbering the evangelicals in theological publishing and scholarship.[11]

---

[8]   Samuel Escobar, "Heredero de la Reforma radical," in C. René Padilla, ed., *Hacia una teología evangélica Latinoamericana: Ensayos en honor a Pedro Savage* (San José, Costa Rica: Editorial Caribe, 1984), 51–71, at 64.

[9]   C. Peter Wagner, *Teología Latinoamericana ¿Izquierdista o evangélica?* (Miami: Editorial Vida, 1969); C. Peter Wagner, *Latin American Theology: Radical or Evangelical? The Struggle for the Faith in a Young Church* (Grand Rapids: Eerdmans, 1970), 118.

[10]   For a sample of articles on the Church Growth movement, see Orlando Costas, "Church Growth as a Multidimensional Phenomenon: Some Lessons from Chile," *International Bulletin of Missionary Research* 5:1 (1981): 2–8; Samuel Escobar, "El crecimiento de la iglesia en América Latina y la teoría del 'Iglecrecimiento,'" *Misión* 8:1 (1989): 15–19; Emilio Antonio Núñez C., "Crecimiento numérico versus crecimiento integral," *Misión* 8:1 (1989): 20–25; and C. René Padilla, "La unidad de la iglesia y el principio de las unidades homogéneas," *Misión* 2:3 (1983), 2–3.

[11]   Wagner, *Latin American Theology*, 9.

Reactions to Wagner's book came loud and strong. Samuel Escobar was indignant.[12] Orlando Costas felt offended by the purpose, the content, and the methodology of the book.[13] For René Padilla the book was unfair, "since some of the authors he mentioned—Justo Gonzalez, José Míguez Bonino, Emilio Castro—were the people trying to find some answers to our problems from a Latin American perspective. There were no others."[14] Mortimer Arias, a Methodist pastor from Bolivia, considered Wagner as dualistic on two counts: first, a dualism between the people of God and the world, and second, a dualism between preaching the gospel (*kerygma*) and social action (*diakonia*).[15] This is just a small sample of the predominant tone of the reception of the book.

There was no doubt that the challenges Wagner posed demanded a clear answer. Talks and plans brewed during CLADE I. This was the first embryonic stage for what was to become the *Fraternidad Teológica Latinoamericana*. One year later twenty-five arrived in Cochabamba, Bolivia, for the initial meeting, December 12–18.[16] A dream came true. There were twelve nationalities and nine denominations represented. Samuel Escobar remembered that

> from the Wesleyan background were the Mexican Hector Espinoza (Methodist) and the Argentinean Ismael Amaya (Nazarene.) Andrew Kirk, an evangelical in his Anglican tradition. Presbyterians were Pedro Arana and Pablo Perez . . . From the student movement [International Fellowship of Evangelical Students] came René Padilla, Samuel Escobar, and Robinson Cavalcanti . . . Virgilio F. Vangioni and Emilio Antonio Núñez were from a dispensationalist background; while Oscar Pereira and Ricardo Sturz were professors at Baptist seminaries. Gerardo Avila was from the Pentecostal perspective. Independent and interdenominational missions were represented through Peter Wagner, Asdrubal Rios, and David Jones.[17]

---

[12] Samuel Escobar, "Del CLADE I al CLADE II: Evangélicos en busca de una evangelización contextual," *Pastoralia* 2:3 (1979): 22–30, at 25.

[13] Orlando Costas, "Teólogo en la Encrucijada," in C. René Padilla, ed., *Hacia una teología evangélica Latinoamericana*, 13–35, at 26.

[14] C. René Padilla, interview by author, Wheaton, Ill., March 7–8, 2003.

[15] Mortimer Arias, "Polemics and Restatement," *Christian Century* 88:22 (1971): 698–700, at 699.

[16] For a complete list of names and biographical information on all the participants, see Peter Savage, *Fraternidad de teólogos Latinoamericanos* (Cochabamba, Bolivia: FTL, 1971).

[17] Escobar, "Del CLADE I al CLADE II," 28.

With such an assortment of ecclesiastical backgrounds and levels of experience, there were many possible points of contention. When this group met for the first time, there were many sharp edges. Most of them were not used to this kind of interaction. Most of them were "lone rangers" in their countries. And sure enough, discussions were "heated" at times.[18] Two examples suffice.

René Padilla's paper on the authority of the Bible produced quite a racket.[19] Padilla, among other things, discussed one of the most cherished doctrines of North American theology in regard to the Bible—inerrancy. Padilla did not deny the possibility that the original manuscripts were without error. What he said was that the Bible we have today is a Bible "of which the minimum we could say is that it has transmission errors," as well as translation errors. Padilla's conclusion was the apple of discord:

> Either we receive it [the Bible] from God *as it is* and accept it as authoritative in spite of those minor errors with faith that none of them affect the substance of the Gospel, or we insist on the indispensability of an absolutely inerrant Bible and we are left without an authoritative Bible. There is no other alternative![20]

Even though Padilla dedicated to inerrancy only one and a half pages out of twenty-nine, the discussion immediately became polarized.[21] Several argued that the word "inerrancy" was absolutely necessary in the final declaration. Others, more supportive of Padilla, recognized that "even though inerrancy was a theme which some sectors in the United States considered crucial, it was not so in Latin America."[22] However, the fact that the final declaration did not include the term "inerrancy" did not mean that the nascent FTL was abandoning the supreme authority of the Bible:

> We believe special revelation is the first and unavoidable condition to know God and to understand the meaning of life and human history. Even though God has made himself partially known by nature and by the law written in human hearts, He has revealed himself clearly and in

---

[18] Samuel Escobar, "La fundación de la Fraternidad Teológica Latinoamericana: Breve ensayo histórico," *Boletín teológico* 59:60 (1995): 7–25, at 19.

[19] C. René Padilla, "La autoridad de la Biblia en la teología Latinoamericana," in Peter Savage, ed., *El debate contemporáneo sobre la Biblia* (Barcelona: Ediciones Evangélicas Europeas, 1972), 121–53.

[20] Padilla, "La autoridad de la Biblia," 130.

[21] Escobar, "La fundación de la Fraternidad," 20.

[22] Escobar, "La fundación de la Fraternidad," 20.

a definite way through Jesus Christ, of whom the Bible testifies. It is on this fact that we base our theological reflection and we force ourselves to understand our mission as God's people in Latin America.

The Bible is inseparable from the history of salvation, in which it originated by the action of the Holy Spirit . . . The Bible is inseparable from Jesus Christ and from the internal witness of the Holy Spirit. God exercises his authority through the written Word and through the Spirit. And this authority is the norm for everything that relates to Christian faith and practice.[23]

The second example was related to adopting as the final declaration of the meeting a document produced in Europe. Padilla said the following:

A main problem came when Peter Wagner had a document already prepared with a declaration made in Frankfurt about missionary work and what the Third World had to do. He presented it translated and printed on paper with the name of the FTL, even before there was any FTL, as if it were the product of the FTL. He wanted to impose that document for us to sign. He wanted the FTL to adopt that declaration as its own. I said it was a bad start. I was opposed to that. I said absolutely no. What does a declaration made in Germany have to do with this meeting? Here we are going to write our own declaration.[24]

From its beginnings the FTL had to deal with the issue of what Latin American evangelical theology would look like. What were the questions the FTL should address? Whence should come the agenda for a Latin American theology? What to do with external pressures? How to engage in a relevant theological dialogue when the push was toward polarization? However, in spite of differences of opinion and the initial disputes, the participants decided nonetheless to go ahead and form a *Fraternidad de Teólogos Latinoamericanos*. For Escobar, "it was evident that there was a fundamental basis of common convictions, a deep desire for communion, stimulation, and fellowship, as well as a need for organized cooperation in order to promote theological reflection and its pastoral application."[25]

[23] Peter Savage, ed., *El debate contemporáneo sobre la Biblia* (Barcelona: Ediciones Evangélicas Europeas, 1972), 225–26.

[24] Padilla, interview by author. For the Frankfurt declaration, see Alfred C. Krass, *Evangelizing Neopagan North America: The Word That Frees* (Scottdale, Pa.: Herald Press, 1982).

[25] Escobar, "La fundación de la Fraternidad," 20.

The FTL had three objectives, as expressed in its first constitution:

1. To promote reflection on the gospel and its significance for Latin American people and society. This means stimulating the development of evangelical thought, which listens to the Word of God and takes seriously the questions it raises regarding life in Latin America; accepting the normative character of the Bible as the written Word of God and straining to hear, under the guidance of the Holy Spirit, the biblical message as it relates to the relativities of any concrete situation.
2. To be a platform for dialogue for thinkers who confess Jesus Christ as Lord and God, and who are willing to meditate upon the Bible in order to bridge the gospel with the Latin American culture.
3. To contribute to the life and mission of the church of Christ in Latin America, without pretending to speak on behalf of the church or assuming the position of theological voice of the evangelical people in the Latin American continent.[26]

In Cochabamba, Samuel Escobar proposed that a genuine Latin American evangelical theology starts when Latin Americans critically evaluate their Anglo-Saxon religious heritage in order to separate the permanent from the accessory. His challenge was to "leave the [Christian] ghetto and understand the current Latin American atmosphere with the questions it poses to our faith, its schools of thought, its challenges to the believer today."[27] Escobar proposed seven tasks as an agenda for an evangelical theology from Latin America: reevaluating any redeemable Hispanic elements in the culture, rediscovering the sixteenth-century Reformation, maintaining an atmosphere of maturity and freedom, opposing any blocks pushing for denominational or missionary interests, adding a pastoral dimension to the theological production, understanding the ongoing climate of revolution, and recovering the Christian hope.[28]

---

[26] Anonymous, "Estatutos de la Fraternidad Teológica Latinoamericana" (Cochabamba, Bolivia, 1970), 1–2.

[27] Samuel Escobar, "El contenido Bíblico y el ropaje Anglosajón en la teología Latinoamericana," in Savage, ed., *El debate contemporáneo sobre la Biblia*, 17–36, at 31; and Samuel Escobar, "Biblical Content and Anglo-Saxon Trappings in Latin American Theology," *Occasional Bulletin of the Latin American Theological Fraternity* 3 (1972): 1–32.

[28] Escobar, "El contenido Bíblico," 32–35.

However, reporting about Cochabamba, Peter Wagner's column for *Christianity Today* started a squall that almost blew the newborn FTL out of existence.[29] From all possible presentations and interesting participants, Wagner singled out Padilla's comments on inerrancy, giving his readers the impression that inerrancy was the only thing debated for the whole week, an impression far off the mark. Wagner should have been more careful with his choice of words. He should have been aware that "inerrancy" was a loaded word in the United States. It had a history of heated debates and theological warfare. Harold Lindsell voiced in his explanation how most of the people felt on this issue:

> I will contend that embracing a doctrine of an errant Scripture will lead to disaster down the road. It will result in the loss of missionary outreach; it will quench missionary passion; it will lull congregations to sleep and undermine their belief in the full-orbed truth of the Bible; it will produce spiritual sloth and decay; and it will finally lead to apostasy.[30]

In fact, the mention of inerrancy meant for North Americans a trip down memory lane of decades of theological conflict, *déjà vu*. By choosing that word, Wagner led them to a wrong conclusion. At Cochabamba there were no North American theologians with North American categories discussing the topic; they were Latin Americans with another linguistic, religious, and theological history. While in North America the issue of inerrancy had been at the core of evangelical identity, in Latin America it was unheard of, it never had been an issue; it was not even a question. Actually, "modernism never really arrived in Latin America;" the theological battles in Latin America did not have their "roots in the modernist-fundamentalist controversy of past decades in the United States. North Americans often do not understand this significant historical fact."[31]

Trying to unwind the debate, Wagner explained that for him, those like Padilla who held a different position "have chosen an option which does not necessarily remove them from the category of being called

---

[29] C. Peter Wagner, "High Theology in the Andes," *Christianity Today* 15:8 (1971): 28–29.

[30] Harold Lindsell, *The Battle for the Bible* (Grand Rapids: Zondervan, 1976), 25.

[31] John Howard Orme, "The Doctrine of Social Concern in Latin American Theology: A Critical Appraisal of the Evangelical Position" (ThD diss., Dallas Theological Seminary, 1975), 12.

evangelicals."[32] However, the damage was done. Wagner sent Padilla a letter expressing his wish to "do the whole thing over again."[33] After the article was printed, there was no way to stop the hurricane winds from all corners of the theological spectrum. For example, the president of a well-known Christian college in the United States wrote the following:

> The only thing high about "High Theology in the Andes" (January 15) is the location of the meeting. I believe you report some of the saddest news of 1970. When the reputed cream of evangelical theologians from a continent we have been led to believe is almost the private domain of conservative theology meets for the first time with its errant scripture ... it is indeed sad news.[34]

It is surprising that the FTL was able to launch. For Escobar what helped the FTL to survive its first major crisis was threefold: a firm definition of the common evangelical foundation, intentional search for pertinence, and resistance to any polarization by extra-theological factors.[35] The threat made the members join forces and put aside their differences, resulting in a stronger fellowship. Besides the factors Escobar listed, Padilla gives Peter Savage, the first general secretary of the FTL, the credit for continuing the efforts to keep the FTL on its tracks. Peter Savage was born in Peru of missionary parents and after studying in the United Kingdom, returned as a missionary to his country of birth. Padilla stated the following:

> Truly, had it not been for Peter Savage, I think the FTL would not have taken off ... At that time he used all his activism to lift the FTL up. He not only raised funds for the meetings, but also instigated those of us who had the task of producing something. He organized consultations, traveled, made other people interested in the FTL, found more members, even though there were no finances of any sort. He was the main promoter of the FTL. That is our great debt to him.[36]

---

[32] C. Peter Wagner to Clyde W. Taylor, January 22, 1971, in "Wagner, Charles Peter, 1930-," Collection 358, Box 8, Folder 1, Billy Graham Center Archives, Wheaton College, Ill.

[33] C. Peter Wagner to René Padilla, May 13, 1971, in "Wagner, Charles Peter, 1930-," Collection 358, Box 8, Folder 1, Billy Graham Center Archives, Wheaton College, Ill.

[34] J. Robertson Mcquilkin, "High Theology Low," *Christianity Today* 15:12 (1971): 20.

[35] Escobar, "La fundación de la Fraternidad," 21.

[36] Padilla, interview by author.

The FTL Goes "Glocal"

The FTL kept a heavy agenda during the following years. In 1971 there were three regional consultations on "the church" in Brazil, Mexico, and Peru. In April 1972, the FTL offered seminars for pastors with Dr. Saphir Athyal, from India, in Los Angeles, California, Mexico, Guatemala, Costa Rica, Bolivia, Argentina, and Brazil. Athyal was an orthodox theologian and a leading figure of World Vision in Asia. The same year the FTL also held a consultation on "social ethics"[37] and one on the "kingdom of God,"[38] both in Lima, Peru. In 1973 the FTL sponsored Dr. Carl Henry's visits to Mexico, Guatemala, Costa Rica, Peru, Chile, Argentina, Brazil, and Venezuela. His topic was "The Evangelical Responsibility in Today's Theology." Henry was the former editor in chief of *Christianity Today*. In January 1974, Dr. John Stott from England taught pastors in Argentina, Chile, Mexico, and Peru on the theme of "integral Christianity." Besides all of these regional activities, there were innumerable workshops in different countries and deliberative meetings of the different commissions. This heavy agenda shows not only local efforts to understand the pressing issues but also, by inviting international speakers, a continuous dialogue with the rest of the world. These double emphases—global and local—became ingrained in the FTL's DNA.

However, a bigger challenge for the FTL came at the International Congress of World Evangelization, in Lausanne, Switzerland, in July 1974.[39] This was part of a wider context at Lausanne that Mexican-American missiologist Charles Van Engen explains: "North American evangelicals were suddenly encountering hundreds of able evangelical leaders in the Third World churches."[40] Several Latin Americans were in the program at Lausanne: Manuel Bonilla (Mexico), Orlando Costas (Puerto Rico), Robinson Cavalcanti (Brazil), Juan Carlos Ortiz (Argentina), and Emilio Antonio

---

[37] C. René Padilla, ed., *Fe Cristiana y Latinoamérica hoy* (Buenos Aires: Ediciones Certeza, 1974).

[38] C. René Padilla, ed., *El reino de Dios y América Latina* (El Paso: Casa Bautista de Publicaciones, 1975).

[39] For the Lausanne congress, see J. D. Douglas, ed., *Let the Earth Hear His Voice: International Congress on World Evangelization Lausanne, Switzerland* (Minneapolis: World Wide Publications, 1975).

[40] Charles E. Van Engen, "A Broadening Vision: Forty Years of Evangelical Theology of Mission, 1946–1986," in Joel A. Carpenter and Wilbert R. Shenk, eds., *Earthen Vessels: American Evangelicals and Foreign Missions, 1880–1980* (Grand Rapids: Eerdmans, 1990), 203–32, at 217.

Núñez (Guatemala) among others. However, the contributions that "really set the Congress alight"[41] were those of René Padilla and Samuel Escobar, whose plenary papers[42] caused a "significant shift in Christian thinking,"[43] a "coming of age for evangelicals,"[44] and a "major breakthrough for evangelicals on questions of social ethics and openness in facing these issues."[45] Another participant commented that the results of Escobar's and Padilla's speeches "were much more deeply felt than many Western evangelical Christian leaders here could have expected."[46]

According to one observer, Padilla's presentation on "Evangelism and the World"[47] was considered by Billy Graham "one of the most brilliant contributions for the analysis of the evangelistic task today."[48] Escobar's presentation was "Evangelism and Man's Search for Freedom, Justice, and Fulfillment."[49] The contribution of Latin Americans in Lausanne was mostly evident in the writing of the final declaration—the Lausanne Covenant—which "had to be reviewed several times to incorporate the ideas introduced by Padilla and Escobar."[50] That was probably because Escobar was "the only representative of the majority world"[51] at the redaction subcommittee responsible for writing the covenant.

The inclusion of a complete section of the covenant on the topic of social responsibility indicated that the contribution by Padilla and Escobar was not easy to dismiss. Section 5 of the covenant includes mostly the ideas they presented and the conversations they provoked:

[41] Athol Gill, "Christian Social Responsibility," in C. René Padilla, ed., *The New Face of Evangelicalism: An International Symposium on the Lausanne Covenant* (Downers Grove, Ill.: InterVarsity Press, 1976), 87–102, at 91.

[42] Samuel Escobar, "Evangelism and Man's Search for Freedom, Justice, and Fulfillment," and C. René Padilla, "Evangelism and the World," in Douglas, ed., *Let the Earth Hear His Voice*, 303–18 and 116–33.

[43] John A. Coleman, "Aftermath of Lausanne! Evangelism in a Changing World," *New Life*, August 28, 1974.

[44] Gerald Davis, "A Coming of Age for Evangelicals," *Church Scene*, August 1, 1974.

[45] Bruce Kaye, "Lausanne: An Assessment," *CWN Series*, August 16, 1974.

[46] Alan Nichols, "Plain Speaking on Social Issues . . . ," *New Life*, August 8, 1974.

[47] Douglas, ed., *Let the Earth Hear His Voice*, 116–33.

[48] Armando Vargas, "La plenitud del discipulado evangélico hoy. Crónica del Congreso Internacional Sobre Evangelización Mundial," *Certeza* 56 (1974): 240–42, at 241.

[49] Douglas, ed., *Let the Earth Hear His Voice*, 303–18.

[50] Vargas, "La plenitud del discipulado evangélico hoy," 240.

[51] Brian Stanley, "'Lausanne 1974': The Challenge from the Majority World to Northern-Hemisphere Evangelicalism," *Journal of Ecclesiastical History* 64:3 (2013): 533–51, at 537.

We affirm that God is both the Creator and the Judge of all men. We therefore should share his concern for justice and reconciliation throughout human society and for the liberation of men from every kind of oppression. Because mankind is made in the image of God, every person, regardless of race, religion, color, culture, class, sex or age, has an intrinsic dignity because of which he should be respected and served, not exploited. Here too we express penitence both for our neglect and for having sometimes regarded evangelism and social concern as mutually exclusive. Although reconciliation with man is not reconciliation with God, nor is social action evangelism, nor is political liberation salvation, nevertheless we affirm that evangelism and socio-political involvement are both part of our Christian duty. For both are necessary expressions of our doctrines of God and man, our love for our neighbor and our obedience to Jesus Christ. The message of salvation implies also a message of judgment upon every form of alienation, oppression and discrimination, and we should not be afraid to denounce evil and injustice wherever they exist. When people receive Christ they are born again into his kingdom and must seek not only to exhibit but also to spread its righteousness in the midst of an unrighteous world. The salvation we claim should be transforming us in the totality of our personal and social responsibilities. Faith without works is dead.[52]

For James A. Scherer, a Lutheran observer, section 5 of the covenant was a turning point for the evangelical movement represented at Lausanne.[53] According to Padilla, section 5 of the covenant implied that social involvement had "finally been granted full citizenship in evangelical missiology."[54]

Thus, at Lausanne, Latin American evangelical theology was introduced to the world. Members of the FTL were active participants at many international forums and theological discussions that followed Lausanne.[55] John Stott invited René Padilla to the Colloquium on the Homogeneous Unit Principle, at Fuller Seminary in California, May 31 to June 2, 1977, with the idea that the most effective form of evangelism was for members of a congregation to reach people like themselves.[56] Latin

[52] Douglas, ed., *Let the Earth Hear His Voice*, 4–5.
[53] James A. Scherer, *Gospel, Church, and Kingdom: Comparative Studies in World Mission Theology* (Minneapolis: Augsburg Publishing House, 1987), 173.
[54] C. René Padilla, "Evangelism and Social Responsibility: From Wheaton '66 to Wheaton '83," *Transformation* 2:3 (1985): 27–33, at 29.
[55] See also Stanley, "'Lausanne 1974.'"
[56] For the "Pasadena Statement on the Homogeneous Unit Principle," see John Stott, ed., *Making Christ Known: Historic Mission Documents from the Lausanne Movement*,

Americans were also at the Consultation on the Gospel and Culture held January 7–12, 1978, in Willowbank, Somerset Bridge, Bermuda. Peter Savage acted as general coordinator; René Padilla presented a theological paper on hermeneutics and culture; and Orlando Costas contributed his personal testimony as a case study to understand Christian conversion as a complex experience.[57]

The Lausanne Theology and Education Group (LTEG) and the theological commission of the World Evangelical Fellowship (WEF) cosponsored a two-year study on the topic of "simple life-style."[58] This process culminated in another consultation, on March 17–21, 1980, in London with 85 evangelical leaders from 27 countries. René Padilla presented a paper at this consultation: "New Testament Perspectives on Simple Life-Style."[59]

The David C. Cook Foundation and Partnership in Mission, a service agency of the National Liberty Foundation, cosponsored the "Evangelical Literature in the Latin World Consultation," at Pinebrook Conference Center, Stroudsburg, Pennsylvania, June 23–27, 1975.[60] Peter Savage was the coordinator. Samuel Escobar acted as director and presented a paper on "Fostering Indigenous Authorship." Padilla presented the paper "Contextualization and the Gospel." The consultation discussed questions like, "Does evangelical literature produced in North America fail to show adequate appreciation for this cultural dynamic? To what extent has inappropriate literature been imposed on Latin America? Is the literature enterprise an authentic Christian vocation? Or is it a 'secular' pursuit?"[61] The consultation called publishers, mission executives, and distributors to intentionally promote Latin American authors and publishing.

1974–1989 (Grand Rapids: Eerdmans, 1996), 57–72. For Latin American reaction to the Homogeneous Unit Principle, see Escobar, "El crecimiento de la Iglesia en América Latina y la teoría del 'Iglecrecimiento,'" 15–19; Núñez C., "Crecimiento numérico versus crecimiento integral," 20–25; and Padilla, "La unidad de la Iglesia y el principio de las unidades homogéneas," 2–3.

[57] For the Willowbank Report on Gospel and Culture, see Stott, ed., *Making Christ Known*, 73–114.

[58] Stott, ed., *Making Christ Known*, 139–54.

[59] René Padilla, "New Testament Perspectives on Simple Life-Style," in Ronald J. Sider, ed., *Lifestyle in the Eighties: An Evangelical Commitment to Simple Lifestyle* (Philadelphia: Westminster, 1982).

[60] Anonymous, "Pinebrook Consultation on Latin America, June 1975," *RES News Exchange* 12:8 (1975): 1098–99.

[61] "Pinebrook Consultation on Latin America," 1098–99.

Latin Americans were also present at the consultation on "Church and Nationhood," cosponsored by the theological commission of WEF and the World Council of Churches (WCC), September 14–18, 1976, in St. Chrischona, near Basel, Switzerland.[62] Pablo Pérez, Peter Savage, Samuel Escobar, and Andrew Kirk represented the FTL. The consultation produced "The Basel Letter to the Churches." Pablo Pérez presented the paper, "The Third World of Emerging Nationalism–Latin America." A commentator said this was an opportunity for a "fertile dialogue, in the common framework of the evangelical theological heritage: respect for the Word of God, conviction about the need for a new birth, and a strong evangelistic and missionary vocation."[63]

Without any doubt the international exposure and dialogue in those years formed the launch pad for Latin American evangelicals to develop their theology and to learn from what others were doing in other parts of the world. However, the agenda at home was quite busy, too. There were consultations on "A Biblical Perspective on the Family" (Quito, 1974), "A Christian Perspective on Abortion" (Buenos Aires, 1975), "Our Mission in Latin America Today" (Buenos Aires, 1976), "Missions and Church" (Quito, 1976), "The People of God" (Itaici, Brazil, 1977), "Identity, Mission, and Future of Latin American Protestantism" (Mexico City, 1978), and "The Process of the Theological Task" (Buenos Aires, 1978).

The FTL continued inviting international speakers to the region. In 1976, Australian New Testament scholar Leon Morris spoke to pastors in Argentina, Brazil, Chile, Costa Rica, Ecuador, Guatemala, Peru, and Venezuela. Morris taught hermeneutics, "The Cross in the New Testament," and the Corinthian epistles. British theologian, Anglican pastor, and Christian apologist Michael Green presented the theme "Evangelization in the Early Church" to pastors in the Dominican Republic, Ecuador, Peru, and Puerto Rico in the summer of 1979.

Growth Pains

Nine years after it started, the FTL convened the Second Latin American Congress on Evangelism, CLADE II, in Lima, October 31 to November 8, 1979. CLADE II, in contrast to CLADE I, was completely planned,

---

[62] Lionel Holmes, ed., *Church and Nationhood: A Collection of Papers Originally Presented at a Consultation in Basel, September 1976* (New Delhi: Theological Commission, World Evangelical Fellowship, 1978).

[63] Anonymous, "Carta de Basilea sobre Iglesia y estado," *Certeza* 17:65 (1977): 26–28.

administered, and designed by Latin Americans. Reporter Arno W. Enns explained that "all papers were presented by Latin Americans except one presented by a professor of theology in Brazil who was born to missionary parents."[64] CLADE II was attended by 266 people from twenty-one countries and thirty-nine evangelical denominations. There were only twelve North Americans registered as participants, "plus a small number of observers and press representatives."[65]

A decade of international exposure and intense activity at home gave the FTL the experience needed for making CLADE II possible as the best platform to disseminate to a larger Latin American constituency the themes and conclusions that the FTL had developed so far. Also, they proved that Lindsell's misgivings about not professing inerrancy were invalid, as becomes clear in the final declaration, *Carta de CLADE II al pueblo evangélico de América Latina*:

> We have considered our mission submitting ourselves to the supreme authority of the Holy Scriptures, the sovereign guidance of the Holy Spirit and the lordship of Jesus Christ in an atmosphere of fraternal love . . . We resolve to dedicate ourselves with more intensity to study the Word in order to listen humbly and with an obedient spirit to what the Lord wants to tell us at this critical time of our history.[66]

The FTL became a leading fellowship for theological expression by Latin Americans, in Latin America, and for Latin America. Samuel Escobar explained in a nutshell the theological and programmatic agenda of the FTL in a comment on the decade of the 1970s extending into the 1980s:

> Evangelical theology . . . followed a two-way theological approach. On one side, a critical task including an on-going debate with two main interlocutors: Liberation Theologies on the left and the managerial missiology of "Church Growth" on the right. On the other side, a constructive task articulating a theology of mission that expresses the dynamic reality and the missionary impetus of Latin American evangelical churches. The intention was to provide a solid biblical foundation for new forms of evangelism and discipleship . . . This theology was devel-

---

[64] Arno W. Enns, *Report on CLADE II (Latin American Congress on Evangelism)* (Huampani, Peru, 1979).

[65] Partnership in Mission, *CLADE II Reports* (Abington, Pa.: Partnership in Mission, 1979).

[66] CLADE-II, *América Latina y la evangelización en los años 80. Un congreso auspiciado por la Fraternidad Teológica Latinoamericana* (Lima: FTL, 1979).

oped by thinkers who were actively involved in evangelism, teaching, and pastoral care in Latin America and the Hispanic community in the United States. As long as this evangelical theology remained linked to the life of these blooming churches, it took an integral impulse including themes like poverty and justice as well as those related to evangelistic activity.[67]

In the same way, another active person in the process, Emilio A. Núñez, expressed his involvement and defined his goals saying the following:

> One of my greater theological concerns in the last fourteen years relates to contextualization. I recognize that in order to be faithful to the Word of God I do not need to lose my Latin American identity nor to despise the rich doctrinal heritage I have received from my elders in the faith. At the same time, I understand that the Gospel has come to me with some cultural clothing from the Anglo-Saxon world and that I have learned and repeated a theology forged in a different social context than mine. It cannot be denied that within such a theology there are permanent values valid for all times and everywhere. But it is also true that it would be unjust to expect that theologians from other eras and latitudes could answer directly the problems Latin America has at the end of the twentieth century. It is our responsibility to answer with the Word and from our own social context the questions of the Latin American people.[68]

So, there were several factors that helped the development of an evangelical theology from Latin America in the 1970s. Peter Wagner's book and article became powerful incentives and catalysts for the decision to join forces. The book provoked a reaction to work together, while the article raised defense mechanisms adding cohesiveness and a sense of belonging, which were needed to continue the task. Also the Lausanne Congress of 1974, together with the other international forums where Latin Americans participated, served as springboards for Latin Americans to present their theology and to meet colleagues from other parts of the world, especially those also from the Global South. Other forums and theological meetings provided the incentive to keep writing and to participate in a global dialogue about different issues of their day.

---

[67] Samuel Escobar, "Mañana: discerniendo el Espíritu en América Latina," *Kairós* 20 (1997): 7–28, at 9.

[68] Emilio Antonio Núñez C., "Testigo de un nuevo amanecer," in Padilla, ed., *Hacia una teología evangélica Latinoamericana*, 101–11, at 109.

CLADE I stands as the initial venue where people met and started to change the theological dependency and theological vacuum among Latin American evangelicals. In Bogotá 1969, the first spark ignited that set the whole continent ablaze. Another important internal factor was people with doctoral degrees in theology and biblical studies with the acumen and the tools of their trade to move beyond the theoretical to reality. When they met in Cochabamba, a year after CLADE I, they became even more enthusiastic about the challenge of developing an evangelical theology that would deal with the region's crucial issues: poverty, violence, inequality, underdevelopment, political repression, and death, among others.

Undoubtedly, the formation of the FTL was the main factor that changed the situation of the evangelical theological vacuum that Míguez described in the 1970s. It was both the end of a process and the beginning of another one. Those who became members of the new fellowship were passionate about their call. They were active in their churches and ministries and wanted their theology to be relevant, a theology that spoke to the hearts of the people in their own language and gave the glory to God. Today the FTL has organized three more CLADEs, they have groups in many countries including Spain and the United States, and their members keep publishing relevant books and materials for believers. We can say that the founding of the FTL was an event that changed the state of Latin American evangelical theology for the better.

Wider Influence

After half a century, the legacy of the FTL is not limited to Latin America. Scholarship has noted that especially the concept of "integral mission" has been adopted by international Christian organizations and it has influenced important tendencies in evangelicalism worldwide.[69] For example, the Micah Network, a global Christian community of organizations and individuals founded in 1999, adopted Integral Mission as its theological

[69]   Robert Guerrero, "Networking for Integral Mission: El Camino Network, Latin America," in Tim Chester, ed., *Justice, Mercy and Humility: Integral Mission and the Poor* (Waynesboro, Ga.: Paternoster Press, 2002), 78–86; David C. Kirkpatrick, "C. René Padilla and the Origins of Integral Mission in Post-War Latin America," *Journal of Ecclesiastical History* 7:2 (2016), 351–71; and Kirkpatrick, *A Gospel for the Poor*. See also Daniel Salinas, "The Great Commission in Latin America," in Martin Klauber, Scott M. Manetsch, and Erwin Lutzer, eds., *The Great Commission: Evangelicals and the History of World Missions* (Nashville: B&H Publishing Group, 2008), 134–48; and Michael Clawson, "Misión Integral and Progressive Evangelicalism: The Latin American Influence on the North American Emerging Church," *Religions* 3 (2012): 790–807.

and programmatic agenda. Today, according to the information the Micah Network provides, it has over 750 members in at least ninety-five countries.[70]

> In 1999 a group of aid and mission organisations met in Kuala Lumpur to take time together and reflect on their response to God's Mission. They rejoiced in the successes of aid, the impact of mission and reflected on the evolving strengths, weaknesses, challenges and concerns that were arising within the sector and in the changing world contexts. Recognising that they were better together and that God was calling them to unite their effort and work towards a more holistic and integral approach, so as to contribute more comprehensively into God's transforming Mission, they established Micah Network to be a platform for Christian ministries involved in relief, development, creation care and justice responses to come together so as to strengthen their capacity and impact in making a biblically shaped response to the needs of poor and oppressed communities. Since its inception, Micah recognised the importance of building the capacity of members to embed integral mission approaches in and through all they do as well as to promote integral mission to Christian ministries around the world.[71]

And this is only one of the several global organizations and ministries that adopted the concept of "integral mission."[72]

Michael Clawson of Baylor University explains a link between the FTL and North American evangelicalism:

> Latin American theologian/practitioners like C. René Padilla and Samuel Escobar of the Latin American Theological Fellowship, promoted a holistic vision of the church's mission, what they called *misión*

---

[70] See https://www.micahnetwork.org/; and Steve Bradbury, "Introducing the Micah Network," in Chester, ed., *Justice, Mercy and Humility*, 13–16.

[71] https://live-micah-global.pantheonsite.io/historyofmicah/.

[72] Kirkpatrick says that "*misión integral*" has been adopted by about 600 organizations worldwide: Kirkpatrick, *A Gospel for the Poor*, 148. For a more detailed account, see C. René Padilla, "Wholistic Mission: Evangelical and Ecumenical," *Constructive Christian Theology in the Worldwide Church* (Grand Rapids: Eerdmans, 1997), 426–28; C. René Padilla, "Holistic Mission in Theological Perspective," in Tetsunao Yamamori et al., eds., *Serving with the Poor in Latin America* (Monrovia, Calif.: MARC Publications, 1997); C. René Padilla, "Integral Mission Today," in Chester, ed., *Justice, Mercy and Humility*, 59–64; and C. René Padilla and Chris Sugden, eds., *How Evangelicals Endorsed Social Responsibility* (Nottingham: Grove Books, 1985).

integral, seeking to integrate both evangelism and socio-political involvement on behalf of the poor and oppressed. These Latin American thinkers played a direct role in the rise of progressive evangelicalism in the United States in the 1970s. While overshadowed for a time by the Christian Right, the concept of *misión integral* and its Latin American exponents has continued to influence the resurgence of progressive social concerns among North American evangelicals in the first decade of the 21st century, and especially those associated with the emerging church movement.[73]

Robert Gallagher, a professor of intercultural studies at Wheaton College, concentrates on the contribution to spirituality and mission theory from the Latin American theologians we have mentioned here. Gallagher says the following:

> Protestant Latin American spirituality encouraged devotion to Christ, an incarnational lifestyle, and a faith that influenced society. With its distinctive features of prophetic daring, ecumenical sincerity, and pastoral dedication to bring about peace and social justice, Latino spirituality's greatest contribution comes from the integration of revelation and experience, in conjunction with contemplation and action.[74]

Justin Thacker, a British medical doctor turned theologian and former executive director of the World Evangelical Alliance Theological Commission, said that "frequently it is the case that Latin American theologians lead, and the rest of the evangelical world follows."[75] Thacker was speaking particularly about evangelicals in his country and indirectly in other countries where the WEA is involved. He added the following:

> Before Lausanne, before Padilla and Escobar, evangelicals in the United Kingdom had a tendency to ignore such concerns. No more—and I thank God for them. Lausanne put social concerns on the map. To be concerned for the gospel is to be concerned for the whole person.[76]

---

[73] Clawson, "Misión Integral and Progressive Evangelicalism," 790.

[74] Robert L. Gallagher, "Mission from the Inside Out: An Integrative Analysis of Selected Latin American Protestant 'Writings' in Spirituality and Mission," *Missiology* 40:1 (2012): 9–22, at 20. See also, from a Brazilian point of view, Valdir Steuernagel, "The Theology of Mission in Its Relation to Social Responsibility within the Lausanne Movement" (PhD diss., Lutheran School of Theology, 1988).

[75] Justin Thacker, "Opening Address at the World Evangelical Alliance, São Paulo, Brazil," *Journal of Latin American Theology* 5:2 (2010): 7–11, at 8.

[76] Thacker, "Opening Address," 9.

Conclusion

From a historiographical point of view, it could be argued that fifty years is not enough distance from the original events for a completely objective analysis. It is clear, however, that in comparison with the state of theological production in Latin America down to the 1960s, there had been a revolution. Instead of the continent being dependent on North American literature, with all its assumptions, the evangelical writers of the 1970s took into account the circumstances of Latin America. There was a sustained effort to apply biblical knowledge to the context of the Latin American experience. That change allowed social engagement to come to the fore as a component of evangelical missiology, alongside explicit evangelism and, indeed, established that the two should be combined as "*misión integral*," "Integral Christianity." Although many evangelicals in other parts of the world adhered to a traditional view of the exclusive priority of evangelism, a large proportion of evangelical missiologists elsewhere adopted the Latin American perceptions and applied them to their own situations. There was a revolution in global evangelical theology as a result of the Latin American initiatives in which the FTL was the chief agent. Latin America gave leadership to the world.

3

The Buried Giant

Dominion, Spiritual Warfare, and Political Power in Latin America

Virginia Garrard

On Easter Day 2018 Costa Ricans elected a new president, Carlos Alvarado, a member of the ruling Citizens' Action Party (PAC). Unlike most Costa Rican elections, which are usually democratic, fair, and predictable, the nation had collectively held its breath that year, due to predictions that a Pentecostal journalist named Fabricio Alvarado Muñoz (no relation to Carlos) might win the election instead. Fabricio was neither a seasoned politician nor a particularly well-known figure in Costa Rica prior to 2017, when he and his National Restoration Party (PNR) suddenly rose to the fore in the early stages of that nation's presidential campaign. Fabricio Alvarado's was a socially conservative message that pledged to "restore" Costa Rica to the pro-life, anti-LGBT, antigay marriage oasis where traditional family and Costa Rican values would be reclaimed. Despite the fact that Costa Rica is in many respects a progressive and forward-looking country, it is also, in the words of one pundit, "conservative from the waist down."[1] A ruling in 2017 that legalized gay marriage pushed many Costa Ricans into the Fabricio Alvarado camp

---

[1] Jim Wyss, "Are Evangelical Politics Reshaping Central America into the New Bible Belt?" *Miami Herald*, March 30, 2018, http://www.miamiherald.com/news/nation-world/world/americas/article207342744.html.

during the first round of presidential elections in February of the following year, although he ultimately lost by a slim margin. Since that time, however, Fabricio's notoriety has only increased, and his political future in Costa Rica seems assured.

The political rise of Fabricio Alvarado, however, is indicative of something more than a novelty in Costa Rican domestic politics. His Restoration party is part of a much larger movement across Latin America and, indeed, the world, that is hidden in plain sight to most observers, though it is clearly legible to the knowing, even boldly advertised in the party's name. This is a so-called Christian movement known as "Christian Restoration," associated with an international body of thought, "Dominion theology." In Latin America and elsewhere, the movement is closely linked to a broad network called the New Apostolic Reformation (NAR). These movements are not all precisely the same, but they are largely conterminous. While recognizing this imprecision, I will use the terms interchangeably with "Dominionism" in this chapter.

In actual terms, Dominion theology is not so much a "theology" per se so much as it is an ideology and practice for a specific type of conservative Christian political engagement. It is a theology derived from Christian Restorationism. Its goal is to adopt a mentality of cultural engagement to bring about political action resulting in modes of a specific variety of Christian political leadership across all nations; in the lexicon of the movements, advocates seek to "transform," "redeem," and "restore" culture, thus bringing "dominion" to the earth and restoring Christ's kingdom to precipitate his second coming. The movement is widespread, and its advocates are often politically influential, although it still remains a minority current within the stream of larger evangelical Christianity. Many outsiders including Christian fundamentalists, non-Dominionist Pentecostals, mainline Protestants, and Mormons view it with deep suspicion; these groups find its ideas unbiblical, threatening, and even abhorrent. Some even refer to it as "dark Christianity."

Even so, Dominionist thinking is widespread in Latin America; it has been a factor in an incipient form at least since the early 1980s, when in Guatemala, "church growth" specialists declared the appearance of the genocidal Rios Montt administration to be a "prophetic moment" when Christians would begin to take dominion over failed secular governments. But it is in the past ten years, not only in Latin America but in much of the world at large, that it has stepped out more boldly from the shadows.

The Roots of Christian Restorationism and Dominion Theology[2]

The roots of Dominion theology draw from Calvinism and an earlier fundamentalist mode known as "Christian Reconstructionism." Dominion theology demanded the politicization of the faith to reconstruct a godly society from the rubble of secular liberalism. Its early form, Christian Reconstructionism, called for an end to liberal democracy and for a new society to be built on Old Testament law, including Mosaic-era penalties such as execution by stoning for adultery and homosexuality, and the imposition of theonomy, a government based on divine law.[3] As early as 1973—not coincidentally, the same year that the United States Supreme Court legalized abortion—a University of California at Berkeley-trained Calvinist theologian and historian by the name of Rousas John (R. J.) Rushdoony published a treatise called *The Institutes of Biblical Law*. Rushdoony was a strict Calvinist and also sympathetic to the John Birch Society (JBS). The JBS was a fiercely conservative political movement that coalesced in the United States in the 1950s during, and partly in reaction to, the emergence of the Black civil rights movement. It thrived in opposition to the social turmoil of the 1960s, as the JBS cast itself as a champion of traditional values against the worst excesses of secular, libertine liberalism.

It was Rushdoony who most successfully fused this political tendency with an evangelical framework. His *Institutes of Biblical Law*, a highly parenetic work, readily revealed its deep Calvinist roots in its commitment to the ideas of "election" and "predestination," and would become the foundational book of Dominionism.[4] Although Rushdoony considered himself a Restorationist, not a Dominionist per se, he is nonetheless the genesis figure in the latter movement.

[2] Certain elements of this chapter also appear in "Hidden in Plain Sight: Dominion Theology, Spiritual Warfare, and Violence in Latin America," *Religions* 11:12 (2020): article 648, https://doi.org/10.3390/rel11120648.

[3] One of Rushdoony's most ardent apostles is Gary North, an economist and prolific writer who continues to produce extensively on Christian Restorationism. Perhaps his best-known work is the self-published *Dominion Covenant: Genesis* (Tyler, Tex.: Institute for Christian Economics, 1982), in which he argues in favor of economics based on biblical principles and that a libertarian political system corresponds with a return to biblical (Old Testament) law.

[4] Rousas John Rushdoony, *The Institutes of Biblical Law* (Dallas: Craig Publishers, 1973; reissued by the Chalcedon Foundation, 2013). The similarity in the name to John Calvin's seminal *The Institutes of Christian Religion* (Grand Rapids: Eerdmans, 1995 [1536]) is intentional.

Rushdoony's fundamental premise builds on four key principles: 1) Jesus calls on Christians to create a society that is founded and predicated on God's laws according to the Bible. 2) The United States is God's chosen and elect providential agent. 3) The United States cannot yet fulfill this destiny because of its sinful and fallen state, as evinced by key bellwether issues, particularly legal abortion, prohibition of public prayer in school, the teaching of evolution, approbation of same-sex marriage and other similar rights, compounded by the multiplicity of non-Christian voices and values corrupting American society. 4) The selection of "true" Christian leadership is essential to expunge and repent of these sins. Biblical law must replace secular legal codes, and Christian values should form the basis of the educational system. This leadership must restore a nostalgic "Christian" *imaginarie* where (white) men, acting with biblically sanctioned, benevolent, and godly *noblesse oblige*, dictate the lives of women, people of color, and all those outside the mainstream.[5]

Rushdoony's work directly or derivatively inspired three interrelated religio-political movements. The umbrella term *"Christian Restoration"* refers to the notion that the founding fathers of the United States never intended to create a truly secular nation, and demands that today's task is to restore the United States as a Christian nation defined by its adherence to precise biblical standards in all central aspects of public life: law, governance, gender and race interactions, reproductive health, and education.[6] The second is the closely related idea of *"Christian nationalism,"* which extrapolates these ideas into a direct-action political ideology, which in the United States has attached itself to the Republican Party. In the words of researcher Michelle Goldberg, "It is a conflation of scripture and politics that sees America's triumphs as part of a cosmic contest between God

<hr />

[5]   Chris Hedges, *American Fascists: The Christian Right and the War on America* (New York: Free Press, 2006), 11.

[6]   History shows clearly that several of the Founding Fathers, though raised as Christians, were Deists, in the fashion of the Enlightenment *philosophes*: this list is headed by no lesser figures than Benjamin Franklin and Thomas Jefferson, who penned the Declaration of Independence and served as the nation's third president. Jefferson's library, now housed at the Library of Congress, includes some two hundred different translations of the Bible and several Qurans, all of which he studied extensively as a scholarly exercise more than for spiritual edification. Among the most provocative is the Jefferson Bible, from which Jefferson had redacted and excised sections that he did not like. (See Denise Spellberg, *Thomas Jefferson's Qur'an: Islam and the Founders* [New York: Knopf, 2013].)

and the Devil."[7] The third current is Dominion theology, the specific topic of this chapter. This an international, perhaps more optimistic, derivation from Christian Restorationism that is less tied than the others to the specificity of the United States, but is still fiercely driven by a strident opposition to secular liberalism and demands society's "restoration" to godly rule as prescribed by Rushdoony a generation ago.

Because all of these propositions are so closely interwoven and because they bleed into one another, it is not always possible or even desirable to separate one from another. As Goldberg suggests, "It is a hydra-headed thing, sometimes contradictory but unified enough to be called by a single name."[8] As this chapter is concerned with Latin America, I will use the term "Dominionism" because of its more international, less U.S.-oriented implications, even as I acknowledge the imprecision of the nomenclature.

Rushdoony provides a series of propositions that translate readily into a methodology. The first and most important of these is the notion that because true Christian leadership is completely of God, all other political and societal figures are not merely in opposition, but literally Satanic, against God and his holy law. Because there can be no compromise with Satan, Dominionism eschews the traditional (but "secular") small-"l" liberal Western values that stem from the United States' Enlightenment-era founding documents: justice, equality, tolerance, reason, compassion, respect for dissent, and rationalism. In this theocratic thinking, there is no room for dissent or difference of opinion: it literally demonizes Others to the point of dehumanization. Such a framework offers fertile ground for the growth of conspiracy theories and absurd, even obscene, accusations against "enemies," because Satan, ever the trickster, is always prepared to colonize the human mind and soul.

One of the markers of Dominion theology is the reimagining of Jesus Christ as an aggressive, hypermasculine figure—a far cry from the iconic emaciated figure that traditionally appears on many crucifixes. Representations of Jesus that appear, for example, in social media often portray the Prince of Peace carrying a large sword or even an automatic weapon to lead the faithful into battle with the ungodly. This is a strident, martial image that calls for nothing short of the destruction of the liberal,

---

[7]   Michelle Goldberg, *Kingdom Coming: The Rise of Christian Nationalism* (New York: W.W. Norton, 2006), 6.

[8]   Goldberg, *Kingdom Coming*, 6.

enlightened secular state. It demands "spiritual warfare," and the restoration of "Christian values" by any means necessary. Although these references draw from the book of Revelation, it is only a short rhetorical leap from that world to the temporal one.

Its militant imagery and idiom notwithstanding, Dominion theology claims to be radically nonviolent in its methodology and ostensibly apolitical in its outlook to a degree not shared by other strands of Restorationism, particularly Christian nationalism. Dominionists believe that fervent and directed intercession, coupled with careful political slating, will bring about total "transformation"—a term of art—that will usher in a new age of peace, prosperity, and Christian benevolence to their troubled societies, the nations, and the global community at large. This process takes time and requires the patience that the Spanish axiom *Dios tarda pero nunca olvida* ("God may run late, but he never forgets") suggests. However, as we shall see below, when prayer, candidate slating, and voting fail to transform quickly enough, prayer warriors are increasingly willing to take matters into their own hands.

It is crucial to underscore that not all, nor even most, evangelicals are Dominionists, and many traditional conservative evangelical leaders, including evangelical icon Billy Graham, have publicly expressed severe discomfort with it.[9] (In Spanish and Portuguese, "*evangélico*" refers simply to a person who is a non-Catholic Christian. But by the same token, Latin America remains what might be considered an internal mission field, and the vast majority of *evangélicos* are, in fact, actually evangelicals. Of these in turn, the vast majority are Pentecostals and Neo-Pentecostals). Moreover, not all Dominionists are evangelicals; conservative, fiercely antiabortion Catholics also make up their numbers. As we shall see below in the case study of Bolivia, it was ultra-conservative Catholics, enjoying evangelical support, who headed the charge to expel "Satan" (President Evo Morales) from office in late 2019. Although Dominion theology has deep North American roots, preachers and politicians in Latin America have adopted it with enthusiasm, seeing in it a new opportunity to lay claim to another imported ideology (as they did in the late Cold War with anticommunism) and to adapt it to advance their own political and religious interests in their own countries.

---

[9]   See Katherine Stewart, *The Power Worshippers Inside the Dangerous Rise of Religious Nationalism* (London: Bloomsbury, 2020).

The New Apostolic Reformation

Many of the agents of Dominionism are part of an evangelical, mainly Pentecostal, current known as the New Apostolic Reformation (NAR). This network and movement of Dominion-minded "prophets and apostles" began in the 1970s and 1980s, also in the United States, when evangelicals began issuing cries to restore "traditional values" from a rapidly shifting and sometimes chaotic secular culture; this thinking coalesced in the 1990s.[10] The movement's most prominent advocate is C. Peter Wagner, a former missionary to Bolivia, prolific religious writer, and church growth professor at Fuller Theological Seminary in Pasadena, California. It was Wagner and his Fuller colleagues who fleshed out an idea that had rattled around for years in evangelical circles based on two verses in the book of Ephesians ("So Christ himself gave the apostles, the prophets, the pastors and teachers, to equip his people for works of service, so that the body of Christ may be built up"; Eph 4:11–12, NIV). These verses convinced Wagner that there was a need to restore "apostolic leadership" to church life. This leadership, in descending order, consists of a "five-fold ministry" of apostles, prophets, pastors, evangelists, and teachers.[11]

Thus was born the NAR, a movement that Wagner explores at length in his 1999 book *Church Quake! The Explosive Power of the New Apostolic Reformation*.[12] In this seminal work, Wagner highlights Latin America as one of the three areas of the world that God was "anointing with unusual blessing." Along with "Latin America's grassroots churches," he also underscores the emerging importance of African independent churches and China's house church movement as constituting a "pattern of divine blessing" that signaled the incipient emergence of the New Apostolic Reformation.[13]

---

[10] "American Dominionism and Europe's Evangelicals," The Pilgrim Path/Proto-Protestantism (blog), February 1, 2017, http://proto-protestantism.blogspot.com. The author of this blog credits—or blames—its emergence on Francis Schaeffer's address to the 1974 Lausanne Movement, in which he warned his hearers against embracing middle-class values and urged them to truth-test everything in biblical terms, including relations with evangelical and mainline Christian liberals.

[11] Sara Diamond, *Spiritual Warfare: The Politics of the Christian Right* (Cheektowaga, N.Y.: Black Rose Books, 1989), 112.

[12] C. Peter Wagner, *Church Quake! The Explosive Power of the New Apostolic Reformation* (Ventura, Calif.: Regal, 1999), 235.

[13] Wagner, *Church Quake*, 9–11.

The very name of NAR is simultaneously audacious and generic: in Wagner's words, "It's not a trademark."[14] The NAR movement itself is not dogmatic, nor is it highly centralized; instead it is dependent almost entirely on the revelations and whims of local "prophets and apostles," who are influenced by the movement but are also not directly accountable to it.[15] The NAR is not even really a coherent network per se, but its "apostles" are usually connected with one another either theologically or relationally, and it is they who set the NAR's vision and direction. This "vision" is often precisely that: the movement's "prophets" report direct revelations and interactions with God and angels (including visitations and out-of-body corporal migration); because of this direct access to the Divine, their teachings need not be burdened by conventional theology or close adherence to Scripture. In the words of Wagner, in the new world of the NAR "historians, Bible exegetes, and theologians in the church should be replaced by visionaries, cultural exegetes, and entrepreneurs"; this, Wagner assures us, promises "the most radical change in the way of doing church since the Protestant Reformation."[16]

The unbroken authority of NAR "apostles" extends to the political sphere, where they demand "apostolic governance," through the "restoration" of traditional values under the authority of a national leader who is elected with the prayerful influence of the NAR and guided entirely by its precepts. They see it as their duty both as Christians and as citizens to do as much as humanly possible to propel these divinely vested agents of transformation into high public office; this includes identifying and promoting suitable candidates, helping them to frame their message in alignment with NAR values, and, by the elevation of their apostles, saturating social media and church gatherings with the message that this is a direct advancement of God's will. (See chapter 9 by Véronique Lecaros in this volume.)

The NAR identifies apostles among individuals who evidence a strong ability to effect large-scale church growth. Evangelism, of course, has been a Christian mandate since Jesus himself issued the charge to "Go and make disciples of all nations" (Matt 28:19, NIV). But in the NAR, both "building the church" and "discipleship" are concepts coded with specific

---

[14] Wagner, *Church Quake*, 43, 33–49.

[15] Wagner, *Church Quake*, 55–80.

[16] Wagner, *Church Quake*, 36, 235; C. Peter Wagner, "The New Apostolic Reformation," *Renewal Journal*, April 12, 2012, 413; and John Weaver, *The New Apostolic Reformation: History of a Modern Charismatic Movement* (Jefferson, N.C.: McFarland, 2016).

meaning within the logic of a movement having to do with the trope of "church growth." Since the early 1970s evangelical missiologists—most notably the first dean of the School for World Mission at Fuller Theological Seminary, Donald A. McGavran—have placed great emphasis on church growth, as measured by careful record keeping, statistical analysis and case studies, and by incorporating the social sciences—anthropology in particular—much more fully into mission strategy. In his highly influential missiological study, *Understanding Church Growth* (1970), McGavran stressed that successful evangelism must produce not only numbers, but serious, committed members in local churches; he also pressed the then-radical notion (radical in Protestant circles, at least) that missionaries must learn the worldview of the recipients of the Christian message in order to convey the good news effectively.[17]

Much of McGavran's initial message was greatly transformed in the hands of Dominionists and the NAR (there is a dense Venn diagram that connects the two movements, and other sectors of evangelicalism over time have appropriated the heuristic of church growth, framing it less as a *method* of spreading the gospel, than as a *measure* of the gospel's, or at least a given pastor's or church's, success). McGavran's call for a fuller understanding of local culture and epistemologies has also transformed into something very different: a strongly held belief among many evangelicals, especially those associated with Dominionists, that native spiritual expressions are primitive, non-Christian, and literally demonic. They believe that a society's or a people's ills come from demonic forces that are present today either because of some sort of ancient Satanic pact, such as, in this case, devotion to indigenous religious practices and images, or because of an individual's or an identarian group's "flawed spiritual DNA." (This notion grew out of a trend in modern missionary strategy to try to evangelize "not one person at a time, but one people at a time.")[18] This is one of the distinguishing characteristics of Dominion theology both as a form of Christian Restorationism and as a theory of missions: that native, "folk," and hybrid religious expressions are not merely unbiblical, but the temporal work of the Evil One that must be expelled in the name of Jesus.

Given this Manichean divide, spiritual warfare and "deliverance ministry"—the casting out of demons—are key methods that help pave

[17] Donald A. McGavran, *Understanding Church Growth*, 3rd ed. (Grand Rapids: Eerdmans, 1990 [1970]).
[18] Weaver, *New Apostolic Reformation*, 57.

the way for the coming of Dominion. To be sure, deliverance and exorcism (both of which are based on biblical antecedents) and spiritual warfare (wherein Pentecostal "prayer warriors" organize to "map" locations plagued by demons and evil "principalities" and gather to expel them by prayer) are not unique to the NAR or Dominionism. In fact, they are spiritual exercises found widely throughout charismatic Christianity of many varieties. However, the NAR's contribution was to move deliverance ministry from the periphery and to codify it within a "standard" Pentecostal repertoire, and it has special resonance in colonialized localities where non-Christian religions retain a hold.

More importantly, the movement recentered deliverance ministry and spiritual warfare specifically from the mission field to one in which *local* spiritual leaders could take charge in naming and taming the "dark places" in which they and their own people lived and so extirpate the very beliefs and traditions to which they had subscribed and valued from time immemorial. It also strikes out hard against any effort to shift boundaries of understanding about gender or what they understand to be highly normative and "godly" family relations between men and women: any relationship or epistemology that bleeds beyond these fixed boundaries, they interpret to be transgressive, sinful, and deeply in need of moral restoration. There are obvious racial and ethnic implications in this equation, especially since non-Christian and above all ethnic—indigenous, Black—religious customs and images are typically identified as the historic hallmarks of "spiritual degeneracy." This is especially relevant to Latin America, where the legacies of indigenous and African-derived religious beliefs and practices are still quite pervasive.

When Wagner pronounced the beginning of "the second apostolic age" in 2001, there quickly emerged a cohort of autonomous rising stars in the movement in Latin America who enjoy a large popular following, either through their stature as the prominent pastors of megachurches, or as televangelists.[19] Early on, the Argentina preacher and televangelist, Carlos Annacondia, emerged as one of the most prominent evangelists of the movement worldwide.[20] (See chapter 8 by Matt Marostica in this volume.)

[19]   Frederick Osborn, *The New Reformation: An Assessment of the New Apostolic Reformation from Toronto to Redding* (San Bernardino, Calif.: self-published, 2015), 7.

[20]   See Matthew Marostica, "The Defeat of Denominational Culture in the Argentina Evangelical Movement," in Christian Smith and Joshua Prokopy, eds., *Latin American Religion in Motion* (London: Routledge, 1999), 150–54. For an example of Annacondia's work, see Carlos Annacondia, *¡Oígame bien, Satanás!* (Betania: Editorial Caribe,

By the first decades of the twenty-first century, NAR prophets and apostles were active across the entire region, adapting "Dominion" as a means to bring prosperity, good government, and modernity to their nations, by the grace of God and the advocacy by prayer, fasting, and direct political action of his people. This marked a dramatic departure for Latin America's Pentecostals, who traditionally maintained a fiercely *fugamundi* position that strictly separates "the church" from "the world."

Building Dominion in South America

Brazil

Political Neo-Pentecostals were closely involved in the constitutional *coup d'état* that removed Brazil's popularly elected leftist president, Dilma Rousseff, in 2016. The thirteen-member *bancada evangélica* (evangelical bloc) is arguably the most powerful lobby group in the Brazilian Congress. Alongside the well-known Pentecostal leader and speaker of the House of Deputies, Eduardo Cunha, these were active agents in the constitutional coup that ousted Rousseff.[21] Conservative *evangélico* support contributed to the rapid political rise and election of the far-right former military officer turned born-again "Christian" named Jair Messias Bolsonaro to the presidency of Brazil.[22] Bolsonaro, whom many aptly refer to as the "Brazilian Trump," is outspoken, bombastic, and authoritarian. His ferociously anti-immigrant views, his gloves-off law-and-order mentality, his outrageously misogynistic and homophobic statements, his disdain for Brazil's enormous non-white population, his enthusiasm for combating his political enemies through violence and even assassination, and his

---

1997), published in English as *Listen to Me Satan! Exercising Authority Over the Devil in Jesus' Name* (Mary Lake, Fla.: Creation House, 1998).

[21]   Omar G. Encarnación, "Amid Crisis in Brazil, the Evangelical Bloc Emerges as a Political Power," *The Nation*, August 16, 2017, https://www.thenation.com/article/amid-crisis-in-brazil-the-evangelical-bloc-emerges-as-a-political-power.

[22]   Bolsonaro's actual religious affiliation is hard to pin down. He is a baptized Catholic and claims to still be one, although he regularly attends a Neo-Pentecostal church. During the political campaign he took the precaution to be rebaptized in the Jordan River, a gesture clearly designed to attract evangelical voters. (Note: Pentecostal churches do not require a second water baptism for Catholic converts, but only baptism in the Spirit.) See Cheyenne Polimédio, "The Rise of Brazilian Evangelicals: Meet Jair Messias Bolsonaro, the Ultra-Conservative Military Officer-Turned-Politician Poised to Capitalize on the Fall of the Workers' Party," *The Atlantic*, January 24, 2018; and Kiko Nogueira, "Bolsonaro, os evangélicos e o que diz a Biblia sobre a burrice," September 1, 2018, https://www.diariodocentrodomundo.com.br.

flagrant disregard for democracy, do not on their face suggest much in the way of a Christian outlook.[23]

But all that aside, Bolsonaro's strong anticorruption stance, coupled with his profoundly unyielding views on gender and sexuality, make him a popular populist figure among conservative Brazilians well outside the *evangélico* community, but also deep within it.[24] To wit: On September 1, 2019, Edir Macedo, the founder and head of the Igreja Universal do Reino de Deus, one of Brazil's enormous and influential Neo-Pentecostal mega-churches with a worldwide presence, brought Bolsonaro into the sanctuary of the massive *Templo de Salomão* in São Paulo. As he blessed the president and anointed him with holy oil, Macedo—a devoted NAR prophet and Dominionist—declared Bolsonaro to be a *consegrado* (consecrated), *profético* (prophetic) leader, "filled with the Holy Spirit."[25] Charging the president to "lead the beloved country in the name of Jesus," Macedo declared that Bolsonaro will shepherd the Americas' largest nation to "apostolic governance," which will lead to the transformation of Brazil and far beyond.[26] In the following year, 2020, during which Brazil struggled under the multiple weights of the worldwide pandemic and threatened for some months to surpass the United States in mortality, vast wild-fires, grave economic stress, and public unrest, the problems were met with heavy repression. None of this boded well for Bolsonaro's prophetic authority, but pastors continued to remind their congregations, "God chooses flawed leaders for difficult times."

---

[23] David Biller and Bruce Douglas, "'The Donald Trump of Brazil' Soars in Polls," *Bloomberg Report*, October 13, 2017, https://www.bloomberg.com/news/articles/2017-10-13/ex-army-captain-rises-in-brazil-polls-as-threat-to-the-corrupt. See also "Jair Bolsonaro hopes to be Brazil's Donald Trump," *The Economist*, November 9, 2017, https://www.economist.com/the-americas/2017/11/09/jair-bolsonaro-hopes-to-be-brazils-donald-trump.

[24] It was Lula's departure from the political arena that significantly bolstered Bolsonaro's standing in national political polls. See Guilherme Venaglia, "Bolsonaro mantém liderança em cenário sem Lula, diz pesquisa CNT," *Veja*, May 14, 2018, https://veja.abril.com.br/autor/guilherme-venaglia/.

[25] Ricardo Chapola, Lilian Venturini e João Paulo Charleaux, "A parceria de Edir Macedo e Bolsonaro na eleição," *Nexo*, October 5, 2018, https://www.nexojornal.com.br/expresso/2018/10/06/A-parceria-de-Edir-Macedo-e-Bolsonaro-na-elei%C3%A7%C3%A3o.

[26] "Bispo Edir Macedo apresenta a vida de Jair Bolsonaro a Deus," Bispo Edir Macedo channel, posted September 1, 2019, https://www.youtube.com/watch?v=7LW5ehyaCnI.

Bolivia

It was only a matter of a few months later that "prophetic leadership" also came to Brazil's neighbor, Bolivia. Although the two countries border each other, they are different in every possible way. Bolivia is an Andean nation with a sizable indigenous population (Aymara and Quechua are the largest of the thirty-six indigenous groups) that makes up slightly more than 40 percent of the overall inhabitants. Its history is marked by overt racism, poverty, territorial loss, and political instability; for many years, Bolivia held the dubious distinction of having had more presidents serve in office than it had years of independence. It is a predominantly (65 percent) Catholic nation with a strong undertone of indigenous belief and practices, and like most other Latin American countries, it also has a rapidly growing *evangélico* population.[27]

Much of this changed in 2006 with the election of Evo Morales to the presidency. Morales was an Aymara coca grower who had cut his political teeth in fighting for the rights of native *cocaleros* (growers) to cultivate this ancient crop in the face of new restrictions due to coca's role in the production of cocaine. Morales, a socialist, would be Bolivia's first indigenous president and would also be one of its most enduring and successful leaders, serving from 2006 until the end of 2019. To the surprise of many pundits, Bolivia's economy throve under Morales, largely due to its extensive lithium resources, which moved into high demand for use in cellphone batteries, bringing an unaccustomed prosperity to the nation and an increase in basic services.

Morales made indigeneity the leitmotif of his administration, and he enjoyed immense popularity among the indigenous citizens, who benefited from vast improvements in literacy rates and reduced levels of poverty, alongside increased social access, justice, and respect during his thirteen years of rule.[28] Much less content, however, were white and other nonindigenous elites, who saw him as a dangerous upstart; Morales' insistence on voicing his full-throated support for leftist and anti-imperialist leaders elsewhere in Latin America, Venezuela's Hugo Chavez and Nicolás Maduro in particular, did him no favors among the traditional ruling class.

---

[27] "Afiliación religiosa en Bolivia a 2020, por tipo," *Statista*, https://www.statista.com/statistics/1066911/religious-affiliation-in-bolivia/.

[28] See Waskar Ari Chachaki, *Earth Politics: Religion, Decolonization, and Bolivia's Intellectuals* (Durham, N.C.: Duke University Press, 2014).

One of the domestic pressure points throughout the Morales administration was his position on religion; although Morales is a Catholic, he, like many other indigenous Bolivians, also observes certain native religious practices, and these he highlighted in his larger program to elevate indigenous rights and culture. For example, on January 21, 2006, prior to his national inauguration to the presidency, he participated in an indigenous power-conferring ceremony at *Tiwanuku*, a pre-Inca site near La Paz, where, after walking barefoot over coca leaves, he was blessed by Andean religious leaders and recognized as their Apumallku, or highest authority; he repeated this rite after each subsequent reelection.[29] The multicolored Andean indigenous *Wiphala* flag adorned the wall of his presidential office, and under his rule the government awarded it equal status with the Bolivian national flag.[30] Throughout his three terms, he took part in enculturated Catholic masses replete with Aymara elements, made libations to the Andean "earth mother," the *Pachamama*, and participated in rituals dedicated to the sun (the principal Incan deity) and to the ancestors.[31] In 2009 Morales promulgated a new law (Law 351) which declared Bolivia to be a "plurinational" nation *independent of religion*, rather than a Western-oriented Roman Catholic one. This was a move that alienated the Catholic Church in particular, which had long enjoyed a privileged status embodied

[29]   Nancy Postero, "The Emergence of Indigenous Nationalism in Bolivia: Social Movements and the MAS State," *The Indigenous State: Race, Politics, and Performance in Plurinational Bolivia* (Oakland: University of California Press, 2017), 37.

[30]   Sarah Hennessey, "A Tale of Two Flags: How Bolivia's Racial Divide Is Shaping Its Political Crisis," *The New Atlanticist*, December 11, 2019, https://www.atlanticcouncil.org/blogs/new-atlanticist/a-tale-of-two-flags-how-bolivias-racial-divide-is-shaping-its-political-crisis/.

[31]   The Pachamama was an important pre-Hispanic fertility goddess of the Incas who presided over planting and harvesting, and who they believed embodied the mountains and caused earthquakes. She is much revered today by many indigenous people in the Andes, who still evoke her as a mother of earth and time, as well as the holy being who has charge over the mountains, earthquakes, and harvests that are still very much a part of the region's current reality. While Catholics allow such beliefs to sit uneasily with Christianity, *evangélicos* consider the Pachamama to be Satanic. In October 2019 Pope Francis, a proponent of inculturation theology, permitted the celebration by some fellow South Americans of a Pachamama ritual in the Vatican Gardens, much to the outrage and consternation of anti-Francis conservative Catholics. See Francis X. Clooney, SJ, "The Pope, the Amazon, and Pachamama," *On the Inner Edge* (blog), Harvard University, February 20, 2020, https://projects.iq.harvard.edu/francisclooney/blog/pope-amazon-and-pachamama.

in prior constitutions.[32] Despite this statement of secularity, Morales required all members of the Constitutional Assembly to take a vow to "re-found Bolivia with the force of the Pachamama and by the grace of God."[33] This highly controversial move in a fiercely Catholic country to what a growing number of critics called the emerging "political religion of Evo Morales" marked a watershed in his administration's popularity and helped escalate opposition to his rule.[34] As one indigenous political scientist explained, Morales' administration introduced a fresh "political, cultural, and symbolic language from the native people (*los pueblos originarios*) of the Altiplano" that directly threatened the established power structure and traditional interests.[35] In this context, it would be religion that would serve as the unifying signifier of this discontent.

In 2016, to commemorate his first decade in power and third election to the presidency, Morales authorized the celebration of an enculturated *Te Deum*, presided over by both Catholic clergy and *yatiris*, indigenous religious specialists, who also performed a traditional cleansing ceremony on the president.[36] In his third term, he declared August the month of the Pachamama, a month of celebration that included the ritual slaughter of llamas on the shores of Lake Titicaca.[37] This is precisely the sort of activity that set Pentecostals' and conservative Catholics' teeth on edge.

All these elevations of Andean religion and cosmology helped gird the conservative political opposition already roused against Morales.[38] When Morales attempted to overthrow the law of term limitations that would

---

[32] Christine Delfour, "Etat et croyance(s) dans la Bolivie 'Plurinationale' d'Evo Morales," *Amni: Revue d'études des sociétés et cultures contemporaines Europe-Amérique* 11 (2012): https://journals.openedition.org/amnis/1755.

[33] Ministerio de la Presidencia, *Constitución política del estado plurinacional de Bolivia*, 2009, https://www.lexivox.org/norms/BO-CPE-20090207.html.

[34] Jorge Eduardo Velarde Rosso, "Iglesia-religión-Estado en el gobierno de Evo Morales," *Ciencia y cultura* 26 (2011): 129–44.

[35] Pablo Uc, *Tinku y Pachakuti: Geopolíticas indígenas originarias y estado plurinacional en Bolivia* (Buenos Aires: CLACSO, 2019), 63.

[36] Verushka Alvizuri, "Indianismo, política y religión en Bolivia (2006–2016)," *Caravelle: Croire aujourd'hui en Amérique latine* 108 (2017): 83–98, https://doi.org/10.4000/caravelle.2282.

[37] Matthew Peter Casey, "Old Religious Tensions Resurge in Bolivia after Ouster of Longtime Indigenous President," *US News and World Report*, November 20, 2019, https://www.usnews.com/news/best-countries/articles/2019-11-20/old-religious-tensions-resurge-in-bolivia-after-ouster-of-longtime-indigenous-president.

[38] See Rosso, "Iglesia-religión-Estado."

allow him to be elected president of Bolivia in 2019, it would be the religious charge that Morales had elevated "radical indigeneity" over Christianity that provided the ballast to bring down his government. As his third consecutive presidential term came to a close, Morales took the precarious step of bending Bolivia's constitution to allow himself to run for an unprecedented fourth term in office, an effort that even many of his supporters saw as a dangerous slide down the slippery slope of authoritarianism and *continuismo* that has plagued so much of Latin America's political history. Morales forged ahead with his project and won a fourth term in the October 2019 election itself, despite cries of fraud.[39] But he was shortly forced to relinquish office anyway.[40]

Evo Morales' overthrow in the bloodless coup on November 10, 2019, has many complex causes and actors, but for our purposes the salient factor is this: it was led not by the military (as is customary in Bolivia), but by a vocal coalition of conservative Catholics and *evangélicos* who believed that Morales' government was, quite literally, in the service of Satan. As Morales fled the country, Jeanine Añez, a senator and a politically conservative charismatic Catholic, entered the main government building, hoisting a massive book of Scripture and shouting, "The Bible has returned to the palace!" as she assumed the role of interim president.[41] Though a devout Catholic, Añez enjoyed the strong support of the influential Asociación Nacional de Evangélicos de Bolivia (National Association of Evangelicals of Bolivia), which asserted that Morales had endeavored to "impose contrary beliefs" and "den[ied] us the right to be a church."[42]

Even more importantly, Añez was allied with Luis Fernando Camacho, an ultra-conservative Catholic, whom many believe—and he himself admitted—to be the intellectual author of the coup. It was Camacho who entered the Casa Quemada—Bolivia's equivalent of the White House—with a Bible, a Bolivian flag, and a pre-written resignation letter for Morales tucked under his arm. "God has returned to the palace," he

[39] Anatoly Kurmanaev and María Silvia Trigo, "A Bitter Election. Accusations of Fraud. And Now Second Thoughts," *New York Times*, June 7, 2020, https://www.nytimes.com/2020/06/07/world/americas/bolivia-election-evo-morales.html.

[40] Yascha Mounk, "Evo Morales Finally Went Too Far for Bolivia," *The Atlantic*, November 11, 2019, https://www.theatlantic.com/ideas/archive/2019/11/evo-morales-finally-went-too-far-bolivia/601741/.

[41] Brady McCombs, "Bible vs Indigenous Beliefs at Issue in Bolivia," *Associated Press*, January 24, 2020, https://apnews.com/article/36976d450b3596c2951bd8ed2236311c.

[42] "Bolivia Imposes Animist Worldview on Christian Churches," *Morning Star News*, September 9, 2013.

declared. "To those who did not believe in this struggle, I say God exists and is now going to govern Bolivia for all Bolivians!"[43] A few days later one of Camacho's allies, speaking at a political rally, added, employing the argot of spiritual warfare, "We have tied all the demons of the witchery and thrust them into the abyss. Satan, get out of Bolivia now."[44] In an extraordinary show of ecumenical unity for the shared purpose of building dominion, one of Bolivia's most prominent Pentecostal leaders signaled his endorsement of the ultra-right Catholic Camacho, calling him a fellow "man of faith." Speaking on behalf of other *evangélicos* as well as himself about Camacho, he continued, "It's like Jesus said: 'If these become silent, the stones will cry out.' I believe that he has been used as a stone to elevate the church."

It was only a matter of days before the Dominionist logic of Bolivia's transition of power became overt. From the high altitude of La Paz, Bolivia's most important city, Luis Aruquipa Carlo, an evangelical pastor heading a conservative coalition of Bolivian churches called the National Christian Council, gave Christians' prayers credit for the coup. He claimed that in the hours before Morales' flight for exile to Mexico, the president received a divine command: "Pharaoh, leave Bolivia in peace!" "And I believe that just as He freed Israel from the Pharaoh of Egypt, He freed Bolivia from the Pharaoh Evo," said Aruquipa. "Evo's era is coming to an end. And the era of Christ is being born." He elaborated: "[Under Morales] we were turning into a backwards nation—people wanted to legalize abortion, to legalize gay marriage, they wanted to legalize the *satanistas* (Satanists)!"[45] A female pastor from Santa Cruz, Irene Squillaci, offered similar affirmation. "I see it as a battle between Good and Evil," explained Squillaci. The next task of Bolivia's Christians was to place the government in the hands of "an ally of the principles in which we believe." Bolivia's large indigenous population, many of whom remained loyal to Morales, did not share these Christian Restorationist "principles" and feared they would lose the many advances they had gained under the indigenous president. "They come

---

[43] Tom Phillips, "'Satan, be gone!': Bolivian Christians," *The Guardian*, January 27, 2020, https://www.theguardian.com/world/2020/jan/27/bolivian-christians-evo-morales -indigenous-catholic-protestant.

[44] Anatoly Kurmanaev, "In Bolivia, Interim Leader Sets Conservative, Religious Tone," *New York Times*, November 16, 2019, https://www.nytimes.com/2019/11/16/world/ americas/bolivia-anez-morales.html?action=click&module=RelatedLinks&pgtype= Article.

[45] Phillips, "Satan, be gone!"

here as if it were the colonial era," one indigenous activist protested. "They don't respect our traditions. Just because we have ancestral and cultural traditions does not mean that we are Satanists."[46]

To many it appeared that "apostolic leadership" had already begun, as Añez declared in her plan of government, issued on February 3, 2020, that one of her guiding principles would be one of "renovation" in which "*¡Que Dios ilumine a Bolivia!*" ("May God illuminate Bolivia!").[47] Bolivia was scheduled to hold new presidential elections in May 2020 but did not. This was due to the exigencies of the COVID-19 pandemic, which hit Bolivia extraordinarily hard, thanks to a woefully frail health system and the Añez government's failure to take any meaningful action against the virus.[48] Instead, during the period of peak mortality in July, 2020, the *presidenta*, accompanied by a coalition of evangelical pastors and Catholic clergy, boarded a Bolivian Air Force helicopter to conduct a costly fly-over of major cities and towns. Their purpose: to combat COVID-19 by aerially dispensing "God's blessings and holy water" to heal the affected populations.[49]

Conclusion

For decades now, observers and pundits have posited "the politics of evangelical growth" as Latin America becomes more and more Pentecostal, and many knowledgeable scholars have questioned how long it would take for Latin America's Protestant boom to take an overtly political turn. With the politics of Christian Restoration and Dominion, it appears that the buried giant of Pentecostal political activism has, at last, finally roused itself. Or has it?

It is important to again underscore that many Christians—and even most evangelicals and non-NAR Pentecostals—emphatically do not subscribe to the Restorationist agenda. Even so, its idiom has become more commonplace across the evangelical spectrum, inasmuch as all agree on

[46] "Los ultraderechistas cristianos en Bolivia," *Infórmate Digital*, January 28, 2020, https://elinformatedigital.com/los-ultraderechistas-cristianos-en-bolivia/.
[47] "Programa de Gobierno 2020–2025," https://www.oep.org.bo/wp-content/uploads/2020/02/Programa_Gobierno_JUNTOS_EG_2020.pdf.
[48] María Silvia Trigo, Anatoly Kurmanaev and Allison McCann, "As Politicians Clashed, Bolivia's Pandemic Death Rate Soared," *New York Times*, August 22, 2020, https://www.nytimes.com/2020/08/22/world/americas/virus-bolivia.html.
[49] Fabiola Gutiérrez, "Religiosa y madre de Bolivia: así es el storytelling (costoso) de Jeanine Áñez: sobrevuelos religiosos costaron más de 20 mil," GlobalVoices.org, https://es.globalvoices.org/2020/07/29/religiosa-y-madre-de-bolivia-asi-es-el-storytelling-costoso-de-jeanine-anez/.

certain key issues, such as the efficacy of prayer and the importance of following clear moral guidelines in public and private life.[50] The gist of this chapter is not that the Latin American evangelicals have become politically influential—that is only to be expected, given their advancing numbers. The point is, rather, that a minority movement within Pentecostal Christianity with a clear agenda and methodology, hidden in plain sight, has become a highly influential player within Latin America's political arena. Dominionism, as its proponents and detractors agree, has profound implications for the future.

On October 18, 2020, Bolivia finally held new presidential elections, in which Luis Fernando Camacho, prayer warrior, coup leader, and Restorationist, was one of several leading candidates running against Luis Arce, a Morales surrogate. Camacho lost soundly to Arce, and Bolivians seem, for the moment, to have decisively chosen socialism over Christian nationalism.[51] But Dominionists understand that they are playing a long game: "the wind bloweth where it listeth" (John 3:8, KJV). They might well echo the words of Costa Rica's Fabricio Alvarado, who, after learning he had lost the presidential elections, declared, "It doesn't matter what happened; our praise should go to God. And we are calm [that] our *message* did win the elections."[52]

---

[50] There is no shortage of anti-Dominion screed readily available on websites, blogs, and social media. See, for example, Sandy Simpson, "Dominionism Exposed," Apologetics Coordination Team, February 2, 2006; "La Iglesia offshore de Harold Caballeros," *Plaza Publica*, May 9, 2016, https://www.plazapublica.com.gt/content/la-iglesia-offshore -de-harold-caballeros; and "Harold Caballeros – Abandona Guatemala," *Guatemala Chronicle*, September 25, 2015, https://guatemalachronicle.wordpress.com/2015/09/22/ harold-caballeros-abandona-guatemala/; "Falso Profeta y Apóstol Rony Chavez Denunciado," YouTube video, https://www.youtube.com/watch?v=gTjFmWpleVc (no longer available); and "Falso apóstol y profeta Rony Chaves—El papa de Costa Rica," YouTube video, https://www.youtube.com/watch?v=LvSeTIE-g-0.

[51] Julie Turkewitz, "In Election, Bolivia Confronts Legacy of Ousted Socialist Leader," *New York Times*, October 19, 2020, https://www.nytimes.com/2020/10/18/ world/americas/bolivia-election-evo-morales.html.

[52] Gustavo Fuchs, "Evangelical Uprising: A New Political Opposition in Costa Rica," *New Internationalist: The World Unspun*, April 5, 2018.

4

Fertility and Faith

Latin America and the Limits of Evangelical Growth

Philip Jenkins

No account of contemporary Christianity can fail to take note of the explosive growth of evangelical and Pentecostal churches in Latin America. Scholars and church leaders alike speak of a new Reformation, a new Pentecost, of an outpouring of the Spirit. Were there not at least some quantitative foundations for such claims, there would be no scope for a volume on evangelicalism in Latin America. Yet having said that, few accounts of Latin American Protestantism take account of some crucial social trends that are already having a notable effect on evangelical growth today, and which threaten real constraints in decades to come. Most significant among these factors is demography, and demographic change. Briefly, as I will explain, the fertility levels of a particular society correlate closely with degrees of religiosity. It is open to debate whether one trend influences the other, or vice versa, or if both trends are dependent on some other factor or factors. For present purposes, that really does not matter. The correlation is real, and if that is the case, then the consequences for Latin America are very significant indeed. All countries to some extent are making the historic shift to sub-replacement fertility, and abundant examples worldwide show that this change is very likely to lead to much higher degrees of secularization, measured by membership in organized or institutional churches.[1]

Conventionally, the Protestant story in modern Latin America is presented as a zero-sum game, in which an increase in the Protestant share of the religious marketplace corresponds to a fall in the Catholic share. That may or may not continue to be true. But what is very likely indeed is that the religious marketplace as a whole will contract quite severely with the growth of secular populations.

Fertility and Faith

A direct relationship exists between the fertility rates of a community—the number of children that a typical woman bears during her lifetime—and that society's degree of religious fervor and commitment. High-fertility societies, like most of contemporary Africa, tend to be fervent, devout, and religiously enthusiastic. Conversely, the lower the fertility rate, and the smaller the family size, the greater the tendency to detach from organized or institutional religion. Fertility rates provide an effective gauge for religious behavior and commitment, and rapid changes should serve as an alarm bell about incipient secularization and the decline of institutional religion. As I will explain, the term *secularization* oversimplifies the process substantially, but we may let that stand presently.[2]

Fertility can be measured in different ways. For international comparisons, the most commonly used figure is the Total Fertility Rate (TFR), which is what I will chiefly be using here. The TFR measures the average number of children who would be born to a woman over her lifetime, assuming that she survives to the end of her reproductive life. To take some examples, France's TFR is presently 2.06, while Egypt's is 3.5. In West Africa, the figure for Burkina Faso is 5.7. By itself, the fertility rate does not determine a country's population, which also depends on death rates and infant mortality, but it does have vital consequences, both in

---

[1] Obviously, these themes have attracted a vast literature, which I will only touch on here. For the growth of Latin American Protestantism, see, for instance, Philip Jenkins, *The Next Christendom*, 3rd ed. (New York: Oxford University Press, 2011); David Thomas Orique, Susan Fitzpatrick-Behrens, and Virginia Garrard, eds., *The Oxford Handbook of Latin American Christianity* (New York: Oxford University Press, 2020); and Samuel Rodriguez and Robert Crosby, *When Faith Catches Fire* (New York: WaterBrook, 2017).

[2] The following discussion draws on Philip Jenkins, *Fertility and Faith: The Demographic Revolution and the Transformation of World Religions* (Waco, Tex.: Baylor University Press, 2020).

terms of the overall size of the population and (scarcely less important) its age distribution. If that TFR figure for a particular country is around 2.1 children per woman (roughly the present French situation), then the population will remain broadly stable, and that level is termed *replacement rate*. If the rate is much higher than that, say 4 or 5 per woman, then we will see an expanding population with many young people and young adults, with all the restlessness and turbulence that suggests. A fertility rate below 2.1—what we call *sub-replacement*—results in a contracting population and an aging society.

Since the 1960s societies around the world have been dropping steeply as part of a critical phenomenon called the demographic transition. Initially in Europe, fertility rates fell steeply and suddenly, from 5 or so per woman to replacement, and then substantially below that. Denmark's TFR fell from 2.67 in 1963 to just 1.38 by 1983, although it has now recovered to 1.71. In the Netherlands, the TFR halved between 1962 and 1983. By 1973 the TFR was 2.04, just below replacement, and it bottomed out below 1.5 in the early 1980s. The modern figure is around 1.8. Initially observers explained the twin changes according to strongly local factors, such as the individualism of those historically Protestant nations where the transition became so evident. That interpretation became untenable when Catholic Europe was so strongly affected in the 1970s. By the end of the century, Italy, Spain, Austria, Portugal, and even Ireland were all moving toward Danish-style rates or sinking below them. In 1964 a typical Spanish woman would have three children in her lifetime, a rate that fell to 1.1 by 1997. In the space of a single generation—between 1964 and 1995—Italy's TFR fell from 2.65 to 1.19 (it is now 1.45); the figure for Catholic Austria was comparable. Countries like Spain and Italy acquired TFRs as low as any in recorded history.[3]

Low-fertility societies tend to be older in their demographic profile, a trend that also benefited from medical advances and general prosperity. As people lived much longer, so the median age of societies grew steeply. Today 35 percent of Italians are aged over fifty-five, and the comparable figure for most European nations is around a third. That compares with just 7.5 percent in fertile Nigeria, 7 percent in Kenya, and similar figures across much of Africa. In a ranking of the world's nations by their median age, European nations dominate, taking all but four of the top thirty-three places. Germany, Italy, Austria, and the Baltic nations all stand near the

---

[3]   Jenkins, *Fertility and Faith*, 27–28.

head of the list. Most Western European societies have a median age over 40, and several in the early or midforties: Germany's median age is forty-seven; Italy's is around forty-six; Spain and the Netherlands stand at forty-three. The median age of the whole European Union is forty-four. The comparable figure for the African continent is below twenty, and in many nations it is closer to sixteen.[4]

The significance of the fertility shift is beyond doubt. Central to this transformation was the role of women, in an age of easy contraception and massive expansion of opportunities for higher education and employment. With new aspirations and opportunities in life, with a new commitment to education and career, women determined to postpone childbearing until later in life or even to forego parenthood altogether. A woman who postpones childbearing until her midthirties or later is unlikely to begin a large family on anything like the older model. New social attitudes also meant declining disapproval of couples who chose to live together outside traditional structures of marriage and family, with or without children. For large sections of the population, founding a family and raising children ceased to be the central and defining goal of life, and were replaced by other concepts of personal and career fulfillment. The demographic revolution is above all a gender revolution.[5]

A Secular Revolution

Again at first in Europe, the demographic revolution coincided with an equally sudden drop in religiosity and religious commitment, and a systematic crisis for organized religion of all kinds. By whatever quantitative measure we use for observance, Europeans deserted the churches *en masse* in the 1960s and 1970s, and unlike in the United States, the collapse of mainstream institutions was not compensated by an upsurge of newer denominations. Initially, Protestant countries demonstrated the steepest decline, but Catholic populations soon demonstrated very similar trends. To oversimplify, the resulting changes can often be described through a rough-and-ready "rule of ten." In many standard indices of faith—vocations, ordinations, seminary numbers, monastic

---

[4]   Jenkins, *Fertility and Faith*, 41–42.

[5]   David P. Goldman, *How Civilizations Die (and Why Islam Is Dying Too)* (Washington, D.C.: Regnery, 2011); Jay Winter and Michael Teitelbaum, *The Global Spread of Fertility Decline: Population, Fear, and Uncertainty* (New Haven, Conn.: Yale University Press, 2013); and Darrell Bricker and John Ibbitson, *Empty Planet: The Shock of Global Population Decline* (New York: Random House, 2019).

populations—the levels we find today are often around one-tenth of the scale and intensity of the high-water mark of practice in 1960. Many of Spain's dioceses have reported no seminary admissions for some years, as the numbers of newly ordained priests have collapsed. Even in Ireland, seven of the country's eight seminaries have closed. German vocations have all but vanished. In 2016 the once pivotal Archdiocese of Munich had just one new seminarian. Across once-Catholic Europe, we find an acute shortage of priests and the decline of regular churchgoing.[6]

The Pew Research Center has in recent years done some significant studies, which at first sight offer a paradoxical finding. Looking at Western European nations, a survey published in 2018 found that some 70 percent of the population identified as Christian, with numbers reaching 80 percent in such long-familiar centers of piety as Austria, Ireland, and Italy, and even 41 percent in the Netherlands. But before churches could take comfort in these numbers, the same survey also showed a very low level of actual church attendance on any regular scale, defined as attending monthly or more often. (Those figures take no account of the eternal problem of people overclaiming the amount of their church attendance.) Those reporting as "church-attending Christians" represented just 10 to 15 percent of the population of most of Northern Europe and Scandinavia, 18 percent in Britain and France. The largest proportions of churchgoing Christians were in Ireland, Italy, and Portugal, but not even in those lands did the attending faithful come close to majority status. Applying another criterion for measuring religious attitudes, Western European nations rank very low on a global survey of respondents who agree that religion plays a very important part in their lives. Such religious-oriented individuals constitute just 10 percent of the populations of Britain, Germany, France, and Sweden, and most Western European nations fall below 20 percent.[7]

The drift away from religion is so advanced, and progressing so swiftly, that some scientific surveys project the extinction of faith of all kinds from

6   Marco Tosatti, "Return of the Vocations Crisis," *First Things*, August 10, 2017, https://www.firstthings.com/web-exclusives/2017/08/return-of-the-vocations-crisis; and Jonathan Luxmoore, "Europe's Church Creatively Rethinks as Numbers Plummet," *National Catholic Reporter*, November 15, 2017, https://www.ncronline.org/news/world/europes-church-creatively-rethinks-numbers-plummet.

7   "Religious Identity," in *Being Christian in Western Europe* (Washington, D.C.: Pew Research Center, 2018), 81–94, https://www.pewforum.org/2018/05/29/religious-identity/.

several nations by the end of the present century. A study reported to the American Physical Society in 2011 predicted that by the end of the present century, nine nations would be entirely free of religion. Six of these were European, namely Austria, the Czech Republic, Finland, Ireland, the Netherlands, and Switzerland. Very striking here was the inclusion of nations like Austria and Ireland, where levels of faith are presently holding up relatively well. Actually the study suggested that other nations might well be following a like trajectory, but their official statistics did not permit the kind of analysis that would permit such conclusions. Not included in the list, therefore, was Great Britain, which commonly appears alongside the Netherlands in listings of the world's most secular societies. (The other three nations on the APS listing were all Anglophone members of the former British Empire, namely Australia, New Zealand, and Canada.) Of course, any such long-term projections are tenuous, but the listing of countries is suggestive.[8]

We repeatedly find a potent correlation between fertility and faith, so that a list of the world's nations by fertility rates will be very similar to a ranking of countries by their degree of religious belief and behavior. It is not immediately obvious which change comes first. One path of explanation suggests that religiosity declines first, and that then leads to declining fertility and smaller families. As is commonly noted, larger families do tend to be more connected to religious institutions and more committed to religious practice. Perhaps conservative and traditionalist believers tend to be more family-oriented, more committed to continuity and posterity, and thus they have more children; or else people in large families tend to be more conservative, more vested in traditional religious faith. Indeed, the association between conservative or traditionalist religion and high fertility is often used to explain the relative success of conservative denominations in modern U.S. history, at the expense of liberal mainliners. What separates the winners and losers in the religious economy is not the soundness of their theology but their fertility rates. But now let us imagine conditions changing so that levels of religious belief decline and the number of people with no religion grows; then we would naturally expect a consequent fall in fertility.[9]

---

[8]   Richard Allen Greene, "Organized Religion 'Will Be Driven Toward Extinction' in 9 Countries, Experts Predict," *Belief* (blog), CNN, March 23, 2011, http://religion.blogs.cnn.com/2011/03/23/religion-to-go-extinct-in-9-countries-experts-predict/.

[9]   Callum G. Brown, *Religion and the Demographic Revolution: Women and Secularisation in Canada, Ireland, UK and USA since the 1960s* (Woodbridge: Boydell, 2012);

Alternatively, we might suggest that fertility declines first and that this has its impact on religiosity. We note, for example, that smaller families reduce their ties to organized religious institutions, as there are simply fewer children to put through religious school and first communion classes, or the equivalent training and socialization that exists in other religions. As religious ties diminish, ordinary people increasingly define their values in individualistic and secular terms and are more willing to oppose churches or religious institutions on social and political issues of gender and morality. The availability of contraception, and in many countries, easier access to abortion, allows a social revolution in which sexuality can easily be separated from reproduction. For many people that separation creates more favorable attitudes toward alternative forms of sexuality, especially homosexuality.

Even in once solidly Catholic countries, we see the advance of contraception, abortion, and same-sex marriage, and a precipitous decline in church attendance and participation. In Italy one key sign of a new era occurred in 1974, when a referendum overwhelmingly approved liberalizing divorce laws, by a majority of 59 to 41 percent. The country approved an abortion law in 1978, and in 1981 resisted a repeal attempt with an electoral majority of 68 to 32 percent. Coincidentally or not, the chronology of change faithfully tracks the country's fertility decline: 1976, in fact, marked the first year in which the country reached replacement level, at 2.1, a figure that had by 1981 fallen to 1.6. That is an extreme change within a very few years.[10]

The pace of change was just as rapid in Ireland, long a conservative bastion. Before 1980 Ireland strictly prohibited contraceptive use, and only in 1985 were contraceptives freely available without medical approval. As late as 1995, a referendum approved the legalization of divorce in that country but by a hair's breadth margin of only 0.5 percent of the vote. But moral attitudes then changed quickly. By 2018 the country held a referendum on abortion, which was approved by a crushing margin of 66 to 33. As in Italy, in each case the Roman Catholic Church was critical to the conservative campaigns on the various issues. In many nations, the decline in fertility correlates neatly to the fast-growing acceptance of the practice of same-sex marriage, which was a near-unthinkable concept just a few

and Mary Eberstadt, *How the West Really Lost God: A New Theory of Secularization* (West Conshohocken, Pa.: Templeton, 2013).

[10] Michaela Kreyenfeld and Dirk Konietzka, eds., *Childlessness in Europe: Contexts, Causes, and Consequences* (Cham, Switzerland: Springer International, 2017).

decades ago. In 2015, no fewer than 62 percent of Irish voters approved the constitutional change required to legalize same-sex marriage. Around the world, we regularly see a dependable pattern: as fertility rates fall, so gay rights grow. Low fertility societies become more liberal on issues of sexuality, gender, and reproduction.[11]

It is scarcely necessary to determine an exact sequence of change, as the two factors, fertility and religiosity, work so closely together, and developments occur within a short time span. We might imagine a community that becomes increasingly detached from traditional religious-based concepts of gender roles. That reduces the ideological pressure to define one's role in terms of family, parenthood, and posterity. As women become emancipated from familiar roles, they become more deeply involved in the workforce and do not have time to contemplate the large families of their mothers' generation. That in turn reduces ties to religious institutions. A shift to lower fertility encourages declining religiosity, which in turn would discourage religious enthusiasm, and so on, in a kind of feedback loop. The two factors—family size and religiosity—work intimately together in ways that are difficult to disentangle. If the correlation between fertility and faith is strong and easily demonstrated, the precise nature of causation is not so clear, nor need it be.

Europe and the World

The twin earthquakes—demographic and secular—became strongly apparent in Europe from the 1960s onward, and by the 1980s were attracting intense scholarly commentary and analysis. Soon, the very notion of a European phenomenon collapsed, as European social and demographic patterns spread worldwide, to East Asia, and then to Latin America. In the economically advanced nations of the Organisation for Economic Cooperation and Development (OECD), the average TFR is now 1.7, down from 2.7 in 1970.[12]

In 1968, at the height of concern about a population explosion, the distinguished demographer Philip M. Hauser tried to project what the world would look like fifty years hence. In the then-distant year of 2018, he sug-

---

[11]   Eugenio F. Biagini and Mary E. Daly, eds., *The Cambridge Social History of Modern Ireland* (Cambridge: Cambridge University Press, 2017).

[12]   "Fertility Rates," OECD Data, https://data.oecd.org/pop/fertility-rates.htm. For the rates of the most advanced nations, see Christine Tamir, "G7 Nations Stand Out for Their Low Birth Rates, Aging Populations," *Fact Tank* (blog), Pew Research Center, August 23, 2019, https://www.pewresearch.org/fact-tank/2019/08/23/g7-nations-stand-out-for-their-low-birth-rates-aging-populations/.

gested, global population would rise from its present level of 3.5 billion to 9.7 billion. That estimate was considerably too high, by about 2 billion, and in reality we are unlikely to reach that near-10 billion level much before the 2050s, if ever. But the reason for that error is illuminating. Like most observers at the time, Hauser observed common trends of high fertility in the "third world"—in the three continents of Africa, Asia, and Latin America—and saw no reason to question why those patterns should change. In reality different regions would pursue very different directions, socially, economically, and demographically, and some would hew much closer to the European reality I have identified. That would be especially true in Latin America and large sections of Asia, where Hauser had foreseen the sharpest population growth. Hence those two billion missing humans.[13]

Latin American Populations

Through the twentieth century, Latin America had notched some of the world's highest fertility rates, and particular countries experienced astonishing population growth of six or eight or even tenfold over the course of the century. During that century, Brazil's population swelled from 18 million to over 170 million; Mexico's from 14 million to 100 million; Peru's from 3 million to 27 million. At the end of the century, fertility rates slowed suddenly, and in several countries fell below replacement. Even in the case of those mushrooming nations just mentioned, the rate of growth stabilized markedly around 2000, so that the further huge increases foretold by some experts failed to materialize. In the 1960s Brazil's fertility rate hovered around 6 children per woman, but that figure reached replacement in 2005 and today stands at a very Danish 1.75. Chile's present rate is similar, while Uruguay's is around 1.8. At 2.2, Argentina's is still above replacement, but the rate is falling fast. We are witnessing a social revolution in progress, and a gender revolution.[14]

---

[13] Jill Lepore, "What 2018 Looked Like Fifty Years Ago," *New Yorker*, January 7, 2019, https://www.newyorker.com/magazine/2019/01/07/what-2018-looked-like-fifty-years-ago.

[14] I am drawing these figures from individual country entries in the World Data Atlas at https://knoema.com/atlas. See, for instance, "Chile—Total Fertility Rate," at https://knoema.com/atlas/Chile/topics/Demographics/Fertility/Fertility-rate. For Argentina, see Michele Gragnolati, Rafael Rofman, Ignacio Apella, and Sara Troiano, *As Time Goes By in Argentina: Economic Opportunities and Challenges of a Demographic Transition* (Washington, D.C.: The World Bank Group, 2015). See also Rafael Rofman, Verónica Amarante, and Ignacio Apella, eds., *Demographic Change in Uruguay* (Washington, D.C.: The World Bank Group, 2016).

Economic development is a key driver of demographic change, and the sporadic and patchy nature of growth has produced sharply differentiated patterns of fertility. In Mexico, the country's TFR in the early 1970s was still approaching 7.0, but it then fell to 3.0 by 1995, and by 2018 it stood at just 2.1. But if we break that figure down by states and regions, sharply different patterns emerge. The highest rates still persist in the country's rural and poorly developed southwest, in states like Chiapas and Oaxaca, although even there, fertility today runs above 2.4—in historic terms, a very low level. The closer we come to the United States, in the most advanced regions that profited most from free-trade pacts, globalization, and intensive tourism, the more European the fertility picture appears. Half of Mexico's thirty-one states are already below replacement, and eight have European-looking rates below 1.9.[15]

An Aging Continent

As in Europe, the demographic transformation fundamentally reshapes the age structure of societies. A common stereotype holds that Latin American nations tend to have very young populations, and that youth is reflected in social and religious turmoil and fervor. Although this was true in the population explosion era of the last century, it is no longer so.

High fertility commonly produces a society with a large proportion of the young and very young. In any society teenagers and young adults aged between about 15 and 24—particularly young males—are a source of turbulence and are at the highest risk of involvement in crime. The lower a country's median age, the greater the prospects for instability. A country is likely to be turbulent and politically volatile if the proportion of people aged between 15 and 24 is around 20 percent, and the median age of the population is 22 or less. That "youth bulge" is the normal pattern in most of sub-Saharan Africa, and it contrasts utterly with aging Europe. Normally, when a country's median age reaches 30, it has moved toward a "European" demographic transition, and it is likely to be far more stable socially and politically. The age profile also has critical religious implications. Such egregiously young populations are also singularly open to the appeal of passionate or enthusiastic religion, and fervent revivalism, in a

---

[15] For Mexico's fertility rate, see "Mexico—Total Fertility Rate," World Data Atlas, Knoema, https://knoema.com/atlas/Mexico/Fertility-rate; and "Mexico—Total Fertility Rate," World Data Atlas, Knoema, https://knoema.com/atlas/Mexico/topics/Demographics/Fertility/Fertility-rate.

way that middle-aged and elderly societies are conspicuously not. Age is a major variable in religious behavior and practice.

In the mid- and late twentieth century, Latin American nations definitely fitted that "African" youth bulge model, and their median ages were startlingly young. In 1965 the median for all the nations of Latin America and the Caribbean combined was around 19, rising to barely 21 by 1985. But that figure then rose at a striking rate, to top 25 by 2005, and today it stands at a venerable 31.0.

Most Latin American nations are aging rapidly. If we rank the world's 230 nations by their median ages, then virtually all the fifty youngest societies are African, with a few South Asian and Middle Eastern outliers. The Latin American nation with the youngest age profile is Guatemala, with a median age of 22.1. This places it at number 180 in the list, meaning that there are fifty younger societies in the world. Besides Guatemala, only three Latin American nations have medians at or below 25 years: Belize, Honduras, and Bolivia. Several of the most populous and influential nations have medians above that symbolic landmark of thirty. These include Uruguay (35), Chile (34.4), Brazil (32.6), Argentina (31.7), and Colombia (30.0), with Mexico at 28.3 and Peru at 28.0. All those medians have risen steadily in recent years, and will assuredly continue to do so, moving in what we might call "European" directions. Latin America is a fast-aging society, and its religious patterns will increasingly reflect that reality.[16]

Secularization?

Such figures make nonsense of conventional assumptions about third world fertility rates. Equally discredited is the image of those societies being bastions of simplistic peasant faith—a belittling vision always rooted in Western condescension. In fact religious decline has been a marked feature of Latin American countries in recent decades. This undermines the long dominant narrative of a faithful Catholic society being revolutionized by an upsurge of Protestant and Pentecostal fervor. While there is some truth to such accounts, a great deal more is happening.[17]

The region presents a complex picture, with seemingly strong evidence of continuing passion for religion. Over 480 million Latin Americans are officially described as Catholic, making South America the

[16] Drawing on both CIA and United Nations estimates, conveniently listed at "List of countries by median age," at https://en.wikipedia.org/wiki/List_of_countries_by _median_age.

[17] Philip Jenkins, "A Secular Latin America?" *Christian Century*, March 20, 2013, 45.

world's most Catholic continent. Notionally at least, Brazil and Mexico stand alongside the Philippines at the head of a list of the world's largest Catholic populations. However, many of those notional Catholics participate little in church life, and their faith is at best nominal. The best available survey of religion in the region is a Pew Research Center study published in 2014, which found that 69 percent of the Latin American population identifies as Catholic as against 19 percent Protestant. Those Protestant numbers rise significantly in particular regions, to over a quarter in Brazil. Brazil is home to some spectacularly successful Pentecostal megachurches, which Catholic clergy seek to imitate in order to hold on to believers. New evangelical churches are also booming in the other Latin nations.[18]

But this world is changing. Some observers, in fact, speak of secularization. In the 2014 Pew survey, Catholics and Protestants accounted for 88 percent of people in the region, but that still leaves room for a large and swelling number who followed no religion. Eight percent of Brazilians reported following no religion, and the proportion of unaffiliated—of "nones"—is much higher among the under-twenties. The Pew survey showed the highest proportion of unaffiliated in such developed countries as Chile (16 percent) and Argentina (11 percent), as well as several smaller states of Central America and the Caribbean (El Salvador, Honduras, the Dominican Republic), where the rate runs between 10 and 18 percent. As so often in such classifications, Uruguay emerges as the region's most secular and European-looking country, with almost 40 percent having no religious affiliation. In fact, trends have accelerated in just the few years since the Pew report, and in Chile, the number of Nones is now around 25 percent. That is substantially larger than the well-publicized and highly active Protestant population, which stands at 15 percent.[19]

A similar impression emerges from a 2018 survey that asked people around the world how important religion was to them. The lowest rates were of course found in Western Europe, at 10 to 20 percent of respondents, with Russia and Japan comparable. The United States figure was over 50 percent. But some of the world's lowest rates on the "very important"

[18] *Religion in Latin America: Widespread Change in a Historically Catholic Region* (Washington, D.C.: Pew Research Center, 2014), https://www.pewforum.org/2014/11/13/religion-in-latin-america/.

[19] Pew Research Center, *Religion in Latin America*.

scale were found in Argentina, Chile, and Uruguay, and even the Mexican figure was well below that of the United States.[20]

It should be said here that Nones, people *sin religión*, are anything but a new phenomenon in much of Latin America. From the nineteenth century, many nations had a flourishing tradition of anticlerical and outright antireligious activism, commonly (but not necessarily) connected to Freemasonry. That phenomenon has been reinforced by the growth of highly secular left-wing politics since the 1950s. Some countries, notably Mexico in the 1930s, undertook severe persecutions of the Catholic Church, and those struggles left a legacy of official *laicismo* that survives today. Even so, official Church statistics persisted in counting even determined secularists and anticlericals among its notional adherents. To that extent, part of the secular drift we appear to see in recent years represents new ways of quantifying religious belief, and the surveys undertaken by organizations like Pew. Having said that, recent studies are indeed showing a sizable and easily measurable growth of people who reject religious affiliation, usually not connected with any kind of radical ideology. As in Europe, the trend marks a general movement away from institutional religion.[21]

Legal Change and Social Revolution

In other ways too, many Latin American societies are in the midst of social revolutions familiar from Europe. As I suggested, one of the best indexes of shifting moral attitudes is the legal acceptance of same-sex marriage. The spread of that institution beyond Europe correlates well with other measures of secularization and with very low fertility rates. Where such a measure has been proposed in a Christian context, it has been in the face

[20] *The Age Gap in Religion around the World* (Washington, D.C.: Pew Research Center, 2018).

[21] The most important recent scholarship on people of no religion in Latin America is by Véronique Claire Gauthier De Lecaros. See "Les sans religion en Amérique latine," *Revue des sciences religieuses* 89:1 (2015): 83–104; "Las distintas caras de la secularización en Perú: la fragilidad del encantamiento religioso en la periferia," in Paulo Barrera, ed., *Diversidade religiosa e laicidade no mundo urbano Latino-Americano* (Editora Curitiba, Brazil: CRV, 2016); and "Estudios de recorridos religiosos los desafiliados en context," *Estudos de religiao* 31:3 (2017): 71–90. See also Catalina Romero Romero, and Véronique Claire Gauthier De Lecaros De Cossio, "Quiénes son los 'sin religión' en Lima?" *Estudos de religiao* 31:3 (2017): 111–30. For the anticlerical and secular tradition, see Roberto Di Stefano and José Zanca, eds., *Pasiones anticlericales: un recorrido iberoamericano* (Bernal, Argentina: Universidad Nacional de Quilmes Editorial, 2013).

of stern opposition from both the Catholic Church and from evangeli-cal or Pentecostal churches, who are well organized politically. Even so, such seemingly daunting opposition has not succeeded in preventing the spread of same-sex marriage through most of Latin America's most signif-icant and influential nations. Uruguay passed a national civil union law in 2009 and established full marriage rights in 2013. Brazil approved same-sex unions in 2004, with gay marriages following in 2013, subject to some local discretion. Argentina legalized same-sex marriage in 2010. Mexico has for some years approved the practice according to local jurisdictions, and the states with the more progressive views in this matter are of course the regions with lowest fertility.[22]

Here as elsewhere, it is not that the churches are expelled from the polit-ical arena, but rather that ordinary people do not believe that church views on issues of morality and sexuality should be applied through law. This represents a massive move toward the kind of processes I outlined earlier, of a differentiation that consigns religion to its own particular sphere and a privatization of faith. That entails an emphasis on individual rights and obligations. From this perspective religious attitudes belong strictly within a prescribed realm, with ever less application to regulation over self and fam-ily. Also illustrating this is the broad adoption of contraceptive use, which played so large a role in fertility reduction from the 1970s onward. Across the continent, that revolution occurred despite the strenuous but largely futile campaigning of Catholic authorities. As in Europe, the act of dissi-dence in this particular area encouraged a drift to a great privatization of religion and a willingness to disobey authority in other areas.

Colombia offers a good illustration of recent changes. Traditionally this was a textbook model of a very high-fertility/high-faith society, and during the twentieth century, the country's population exploded from below 4 mil-lion to 40 million—notable even by the standards of Latin America in those years. But the country's TFR fell from 6.8 in 1960 to replacement level in 2001 and 1.85 by 2016. Today its population growth rate places it alongside countries like Ireland or Switzerland. Changes in fertility have had potent consequences for issues of morality and of religious authority. In recent years Colombia has adopted quite progressive policies in matters of gen-der and sexuality, stunningly so for what was long a deeply conservative

[22] Anna-Catherine Brigida, "Latin America Has Become an Unlikely Leader in LGBT Rights," *Quartz*, June 6, 2018, https://qz.com/1288320/despite-its-catholic -roots-latin-america-has-become-an-unlikely-lgbt-rights/.

Catholic country, with an equally moralistic evangelical minority. Even so, the country legalized same-sex marriage in 2016 and moved expeditiously toward full equality for its LGBT population. Just how rapidly those progressive views were advancing has become a source of acute concern to conservative Catholics and especially evangelicals. In 2016 such galvanized religious opposition led to the paper-thin defeat of a historic peace agreement that would have ended the country's long-running guerrilla warfare and brought a much-desired peace. Even so, the country's secular direction in terms of gender and sexual morality is clear.[23]

Abortion laws present a more mixed picture. Uruguay permits abortions through the first trimester, while Brazil grants terminations to safeguard the life of the mother or in cases of rape. After intense debate and massive feminist protests, Argentina in 2020 approved a law allowing terminations up to the fourteenth week of pregnancy. For all its secular orientation on other matters, Chile here stands out as a conservative bastion, with a strict abortion law. Otherwise, though, we witness a consistent trend toward liberalizing morality laws, on issues that both Protestant and Catholic churches hold dear. Over the coming decade, we will see liberal reforms on all these issues triumphing in several more countries, with the churches (of all theological shades) doing little more than fighting rearguard actions.

Scandal

I would argue that the demographic revolution is also likely to produce a significant upsurge in scandals affecting churches or religious groups. At first sight, that linkage might seem bizarre. Surely, we may think, clergy or leaders do something wrong, they are detected, and the public reacts with anger or disgust, and that is a scandal. But the story is more complex. In the Catholic realm, we look, for instance, at the very widespread cases involving child abuse by clergy, and how those *exposés* have tarnished the Church. But we should ask: how far did the abuse scandals drive disaffection from the Catholic Church, as opposed to resulting from it? Of course most such scandals have revealed authentic misconduct, and to

[23] Philip Jenkins, "Brokering Peace in Colombia," *Christian Century*, January 16, 2019, 44–45; "Colombia Legalises Gay Marriage," *BBC News*, April 29, 2016, https://www.bbc.com/news/world-latin-america-36166888; and Ann Farnsworth-Alvear, Marco Palacios, and Ana María Gómez López, eds., *The Colombia Reader* (Durham, N.C.: Duke University Press, 2017).

that extent, the resulting revelations have been necessary and appropriate. Yet without the underlying drift away from the churches in previous years, it is unthinkable that these instances would have been investigated, that the media would have had the courage to take on the powerful churches, or that they would have received mass public support.

In Catholic societies in particular, such revelations simply could not have happened before the 1970s, because of the overwhelming respect and prestige that those churches and their clergy held among believers. For many years before that time, anticlerical and antireligious activists had regularly circulated stories of clerical misdeeds, usually sexual in nature, and Catholics more or less unanimously ignored them as partisan rants. On a practical level, any filmmaker of an earlier generation who might have proposed a project depicting sexual abuse by clergy would have faced implacable opposition from believers both clerical and lay, and the near-certain prospect of effective boycotts would have made any such effort commercially suicidal. Only after the shift in religious attitudes in the last quarter of the century did conditions change to permit a new receptivity to charges and the possibility of airing them.

That correlation between religious decline and scandal is evident in the Latin American context. Across the continent the frequency of scandals in recent years—largely over the past decade—illustrates a fundamental change in public mood and a radical new willingness to challenge clerical structures. Catholic clergy abuse scandals on the familiar Western model have flared in several of the nations that I have touched on, including Brazil, Mexico, and others. By far the most devastating and systematic have occurred in Chile, where, as we have already seen, nonreligious views were already commonplace. Although the details of these cases lie beyond the scope of this book, one key scandal involved a charismatic priest named Fernando Karadima, who was publicly accused of abuse in 2010. Over the decades Karadima had mentored many other priests, some of whom had reached high rank in the hierarchy, and accusations suggested a conspiratorial network of abusers at the heart of the nation's church. The scandal tainted the pope, Francis I, who had promoted some of the accused offenders. In terms of its impact on church prestige, and the loyalties of the faithful, the Chilean story has been quite comparable to what has occurred in Ireland.[24]

---

[24] Linda Pressly, "Chile Church Scandal: 'How I Escaped the Priest Who Abused Me for Decades,'" *BBC News*, September 13, 2018, https://www.bbc.com/news/stories-45486176.

Beyond the news media, tales of clergy abuse have become almost a freestanding genre in Latin American cinema, and that has undoubtedly contributed further to discrediting organized faith. Just to take Chile, one of the most esteemed films from that country in recent years is *The Club* (2015), which has as its setting a remote seaside house that serves as a refuge for disgraced clergy, whose sins are mainly sexual in nature. That same year brought another devastating Chilean study of a serially abusive cleric in *Karadima's Forest*. The Mexican *Perfect Obedience* (2014) likewise describes predatory priests, in a tale inspired by the true-life career of Marcial Maciel, the high-profile founder of the worldwide Legion of Christ movement. Such cultural landmarks demonstrate a shift in popular attitudes toward the church, and they further contribute to the decline of authority structures.

I have spoken here of Catholic scandals, but of course every word applies to Protestant structures, and especially as newer denominations evolve into major churches, with all the institutional power that implies. Of course, Latin American churches have had their scandals and criticisms, but that Catholic pattern might serve as precedent for future years.

Believing and Belonging

I wish to be very careful here in using the concept of "secularization," which is not synonymous with the end of religion, or necessarily a decline of faith or belief. As commonly presented, the secularization idea intermingles two themes that do not necessarily belong together, namely the institutional and the intellectual.

That necessary distinction is illustrated by the work of Grace Davie, whose 1994 work on modern British religious history was subtitled *Believing without Belonging*. That phrase has become popular in the scholarly literature. While fully admitting the massive popular detachment from religious structures—from belonging and participation—Davie argued that religious belief remained widespread. Strictly secularist or irreligious views did and do exist, but they are most advanced among cultural and political elites rather than ordinary people. Davie further suggested that the Christian presence still remains potent through social memory, so that Europe's cultural Christians are "content to let both churches and churchgoers enact a memory on their behalf," secure in the knowledge that Christianity is there if and when they need it. People thus have no problem in defining themselves as Christians, however little that is reflected in actual behavior. Davie's distinction is very important—although we must recall that it applies particularly to countries where churches are intimately allied to states and thus have something of the character of public utilities to provide services as needed, rather than as in the United States, where believers see churches as voluntary associations demanding their support and participation. It also remains an open question how long "believing" can endure without the institutional support and communal reinforcement provided by belonging.[25]

That distinction is crucial for modern Latin America, with its long tradition of state establishment of religion. As in Europe, nobody is seriously predicting the destruction of the Catholic Church or the end of Christianity, and many evangelical churches presently continue to flourish. So do spiritual practices that appeal to individuals and families, and that can be pursued without any commitment to formal adherence to any institution whatever or subscription to any particular code of morals. As an institution, pilgrimage remains as flourishing as ever, and that is especially true in countries like Mexico and Colombia, where churches have suffered grave setbacks. Each year up to ten million attend the pilgrimage of Our Lady of Guadalupe in Mexico City, and comparable throngs visit Brazil's Basilica of Our Lady Aparecida. Far from declining, numbers have actually risen in the past decade. But all this happens against a background of a widespread questioning of the most basic assumptions about the role of the church—of any church—in society. People are happy to believe, but not necessarily to belong.[26]

Demography and Future Trends

Tying this together, I would suggest that tracking demographic change can offer an instructive guide to the religious changes at work in particular societies. Religious leaders and academics alike might well ask how demographic change is relevant to them. In response, I argue that in

---

[25] Grace Davie, *Religion in Britain since 1945: Believing without Belonging* (Cambridge, Mass.: Blackwell, 1994). "Content to let both churches and churchgoers . . ." is quoted from Grace Davie, "Patterns of Religion in Western Europe: An Exceptional Case," in Richard K. Fenn, ed., *The Blackwell Companion to Sociology of Religion* (Oxford: Blackwell, 2003), 272.

[26] For the continuing abundance of grassroots beliefs and practices, often viewed nervously by mainstream churches, see Virginia Garrard, *New Faces of God in Latin America: Emerging Forms of Vernacular Christianity* (New York: Oxford University Press, 2020).

communities where the fertility rate falls substantially below replacement, to "Scandinavian" levels, we might expect to find the following trends:

1. A sharp decline in religious affiliation and involvement in institutions of all kinds.
2. Equally sharp falls in successes reported for mission, evangelism, and church growth.
3. Rapid growth in the numbers of people declaring themselves unaffiliated with organized religion, or rejecting faith as such, in effect becoming Nones.
4. A steep decline in the influence of religious institutions in making law or social policy.
5. The rapid expansion of liberal policies in matters of sexuality and sexual identity, despite the sharp protests of religious institutions. Presently, same-sex marriage provides the best gauge of this trend, but transgender issues will increasingly come to the fore.
6. An upsurge of scandals involving religious leaders or institutions.

Any or all of these trends are essential for understanding the fate of any religious tradition, and especially for the evangelical churches that we are presently discussing. Further, I propose that any consideration of religion in a particular state or society absolutely has to include that demographic dimension, and if it is not, it is missing a crucial part of the puzzle. Hypothetically, let me ask: is it possible to have a "New Reformation" in a country with modern Scandinavian demographics?

If these numbers are not everything, then nor are they nothing.

5

The Historiography of
Latin American Evangelicalism

David C. Kirkpatrick

"About 2 p.m. we heard the roar of furious thousands, and like a river let loose they rushed down on our house. Paving stones were quickly torn up . . . windows and doors were smashed, and about a thousand voices were crying for blood."[1] On October 1, 1902, British Brethren missionary Will Payne confronted the harsh reality of a religious monopoly in Cochabamba, Bolivia. In his diary account, Payne watched helplessly as a "surging mob" easily pushed aside local authorities, wounded the police chief, and breached the Paynes' front door. After the door gave way, Payne recalled, "I was beaten to the ground and dragged by the feet through the patio, while the cry went up, 'To the flames with the Protestant!'" He watched from the floor as the family furniture and book collection were doused in kerosene and lit aflame. "We committed ourselves to the Lord, scarcely expecting to live ten minutes." No sooner had Payne accepted death than the crowd began to scatter as a cavalry regiment charged down the street, provoking panic. Several soldiers slashed at running *campesinos* with their swords. In Payne's engrossing account, his family huddled over the ashes of their household belongings in stunned silence. Payne penned,

---

[1]   Will Payne and Charles T. W. Wilson, *Missionary Pioneering in Bolivia, with Some Account of Work in Argentina*, 2nd ed. (London: H.A. Raymond, 1904), 122.

"The poor children, I was told, were being carried to the flames when some police officer snatched them away."[2]

At first glance, it appears odd to begin with this vivid vignette of violence in a chapter that promises to discuss historiography. The historiography of Latin American evangelicalism, however, is organically connected to the lived experience of evangelical Protestants as religious minorities in the region.[3] Critical questions such as "who is worth writing about?" and "who matters?" are deeply relevant to whose record is written down. Similarly, questions of literacy, as many early converts could not read or write, remain relevant to what counts as historiography and the role of oral history alongside. For most of their history, evangelical communities could never have imagined the political power many wield today in Latin America. Instead, most occupied a place of marginalized, overlooked, and even violently opposed minority.

Beyond simply a window into the lived reality of a religious minority community, Payne's brief account above represents broader realities happening on the ground at the turn of the twentieth century. Of course, Payne wielded the language of his day (bloodthirsty mobs, fanatics, and broader anti-Catholic tropes) to describe these events. But more importantly, a critical transnational angle comes into focus, one that will guide this approach: Britons, Americans, Germans, and others became key interlocutors and agents in this story, as Protestant missionaries entered Latin America in significant number for the first time in the mid-nineteenth century. The Brethren, for example, an evangelical Protestant movement that began in Dublin and southwest England within the period of 1827 to 1831, played an outsized role in this story, especially in the actual writing of this history.

As the nineteenth century progressed, two realities converged: the independence of many Latin American nations from the colonial powers of Spain and Portugal, and the legacy of the Second Great Awakening in the United States, a Protestant revival movement that flourished from the 1790s to the 1830s. Those factors inspired new missionary initiatives from the

---

[2]   Payne and Wilson, *Missionary Pioneering in Bolivia*, 122.

[3]   For more on broader historiography of Latin America, see Steve J. Stern, "Paradigms of Conquest: History, Historiography, and Politics," *Journal of Latin American Studies* 24:1 (1992): 1–34. For more on Central America specifically, see William J. Griffith, "The Historiography of Central America Since 1830," *Hispanic American Historical Review* 40:4 (1960): 548–69. For the historiography of Latin American evangelicals since 1990, see the introduction to this volume.

North and an influx of Protestant missionaries, especially from the United States, into Latin America. As the United States took an increasingly aggressive geopolitical stance, especially toward its Latin American neighbors, its role in the shaping and writing of history mushroomed as well.

This chapter will provide an introductory, while selective, sweep of the historiography of Latin American evangelicals. Even as early as in 1967, Presbyterian American missionary John Sinclair noted 3,115 entries in his *Protestantism in Latin America: A Bibliographical Guide.*[4] In addition, a vast number of relatively small stories abound, such as those highlighted by Pedro Feitoza in his work on missionary writing and the *Imprensa Evangelica* in Brazil, and others who are contributing to this volume.[5] Instead of attempting to be comprehensive, we will pay particular attention to regional nuances, historic turning points, and trends in the literature.

The Place of Evangelical Protestantism in Latin American Christianity

At the turn of the twentieth century, Latin America experienced domestic and foreign policy tumult in the aftermath of the Spanish-American War of 1898 and the resulting Treaty of Paris, which gave the United States temporary control of Cuba, and territorial expansion in Puerto Rico, Guam, and the Philippine Islands.[6] U.S. geopolitical power overlapped with increasing religious fervor across the republic. While the majority of American missionaries remained fixated upon East Asia and Africa, many turned toward a newly "open" mission field of Latin America.

At the turn of the century, in 1901, the year prior to Payne's gripping tale above, Hubert W. Brown gave the "Students' Lectures on Missions" at Princeton Theological Seminary, which he titled "Latin America: The Pagans, the Papists, the Patriots, the Protestants, and the Present Problem." Brown's telling of Latin American history was drawn from his own role in this story as a Presbyterian missionary in Mexico City from the 1880s to 1906.[7] Brown's lectures, which later

---

[4] John H. Sinclair, "Research on Protestantism in Latin America: A Bibliographic Essay," *International Bulletin of Missionary Research* 26:3 (2002): 110–17.

[5] Pedro Feitoza, "Experiments in Missionary Writing: Protestant Missions and the Imprensa Evangelica in Brazil, 1864–1892," *Journal of Ecclesiastical History* 69:3 (2018): 585–605.

[6] The Philippines were given Commonwealth status in 1935 and full independence in 1946.

[7] See the Hubert W. Brown and Wilma Jacobs Brown Papers (Philadelphia: Presbyterian Historical Society), RG 458.

become a multivolume book under the same title, were perhaps the first comprehensive attempt at Latin American Protestant history, broad in geographic scope, including harrowing accounts of violence told by missionaries themselves.[8] This promising start to historiography, especially including Latin America in the broader story of world Christianity, faced significant headwinds.

Careful attention to the *place* of Latin American Protestantism within world Christianity clarifies the particular story, especially *why* historiography on Latin American evangelicalism lagged behind other regions of the world. In June 1910, 1,200 representatives of 160 Protestant mission societies from around the world gathered in Edinburgh, Scotland. The epochal 1910 World Missionary Conference in Edinburgh represents the persistent marginalization of Latin America in the history of Christianity. The region had been dominated by Christianity for over four hundred years, in stark contrast to Africa and Asia, where Christianity remained marginal for much of their history. But for Protestant observers, the nature of Roman Catholic Christianity called into question its inclusion within the boundaries of global Christianity in the Protestant imagination. In other words, Latin America did not fit neatly within the preconceived boxes of Christendom. And, according to Brian Stanley, this is how the majority of delegates thought about the world.[9]

In the planning stages, fierce disagreement erupted over *whether* or *how* to include Latin America in relation to mission work. Since Latin America was thoroughly Roman Catholic, at least in name, was it off-limits to Protestant evangelization? Many Anglo-Catholics argued it was already Christianized, and bitterly contested the work of Protestant evangelical missionaries in the region. As a result, nearly all Protestant statistics in Latin America were excluded from consideration at the conference.[10] This exclusion of Latin American Protestantism and missionary activity, rather than discouraging Protestant advances, motivated U.S. missionary efforts in the region, in particular.

In direct response to the oversight of Edinburgh 1910, six years later North American and Latin American Protestants launched the Congress

---

[8] Hubert W. Brown, *Latin America: The Pagans, the Papists, the Patriots, the Protestants and the Present Problem* (New York: Young People's Missionary Movement of the United States and Canada, 1909).

[9] Brian Stanley, *The World Missionary Conference, Edinburgh, 1910* (Grand Rapids: Eerdmans, 2009), 303.

[10] Stanley, *World Missionary Conference*, 64.

on Christian Work in Latin America, also called the Panama Congress, which in hindsight was a turning point in the history of Christianity in the region. The 1916 congress spurred missionary activity, historiography, and even Protestant political visibility as the president of Panama, Belisario Porras, planned to speak at the congress in the face of significant Roman Catholic opposition.[11] The first commission of the congress, called "survey and occupation," wrote on Latin America's physical, industrial, moral, social, and religious conditions. It also provided a broad description of the history and status of Protestant missions in Latin America.[12] Commission four analyzed the influence of evangelical literature in Latin America with the goal of expanding its circulation.

It is not surprising, then, that Panama inspired some of the most significant historiography of the first half of the twentieth century, in Spanish and English. But this entire discussion of developments in the first half of the twentieth century would surprise many observers. In much of the popular imagination, Protestants did little and wrote little during this time period. But in the words of the Oaxacan writer Gonzalo Báez-Camargo, whom we will highlight below, Latin American Protestants refused to "become permanent outcasts from the ecumenical movement . . . rejected by their brother-Protestants in other countries as something like bastards, with little or no right to exist and breathe the ecumenical air."[13]

One of those who took up this Panama mantle was the Brazilian Presbyterian Erasmo Braga, who represented Brazil at the congress.[14] Braga was a graduate of Mackenzie College in São Paulo (1898), the largest missionary school in Brazil. The year after the congress concluded, Braga wrote *Pan Americanismo: Aspecto religioso*. Braga connected differing backgrounds and approaches to theology across diverse missionary groups and disparate agencies, opening up a crucial dialogue through their shared history.

Overall, the Panama Congress set off a flurry of interdenominational cooperation, especially in publishing and education. Alongside Braga, an

---

[11] Staff, "Porras Overrides Bishop," *New York Times*, February 10, 1916, 4.

[12] Congress on Christian Work in Latin America, 1916, *Christian Work in Latin America*, 1 (New York: Published for the Committee on Cooperation in Latin America, by the Missionary Education Movement, 1916).

[13] Gonzalo Báez-Camargo, "The Place of Latin America in the Ecumenical Movement," *Ecumenical Review* 1:3 (1949): 311–19, at 311.

[14] The Burke Library Archives, Columbia University Libraries, Union Theological Seminary, New York. Committee on Cooperation in Latin America (CCLA) and Congress on Christian Work in Latin America (CCWLA) Records, 1914–1956.

entire generation would be shaped by Panama's ecumenical ethos, especially seminaries in Argentina, Cuba, Puerto Rico, Mexico, and Brazil.[15] Significant historians included the Argentine Methodist Sante Uberto Barbieri, Uruguayan Santiago Canclini, the Chihuahua-born Alberto Rembao with his 1949 *Discurso a la nación evangélica*, and Báez-Camargo, who contributed early analysis of Protestant communities during the Spanish inquisition.[16]

Missionary historians included Webster Browning, Kenneth Grubb, W. Stanley Rycroft, and Reginald Wheeler, who wrote various historical volumes in the 1920s and 1930s on mission work among indigenous South American communities.[17] Thomas S. Goslin would also later write *Los evangélicos en la América Latina, siglo XIX*, a sweeping history of mid- to late-nineteenth-century evangelical work in Latin America.[18]

These missionary and historiographical advances took place within a wider atmosphere of growing anti-Protestant sentiment and anti-American backlash in the region.[19] For example, Catholic bishops at the Constitutional Assembly in Mexico of 1917 equated national identity with Catholicism and questioned the identity, Mexicanness, and even Latin Americanness of Protestants.[20] The Panama Canal had also recently been completed, and broader U.S. interventionism heightened the backlash against Americans,

---

[15] Carlos Mondragón, *Like Leaven in the Dough: Protestant Social Thought in Latin America, 1920–1950*, trans. Daniel Miller and Ben Post (Madison, N.J.: Fairleigh Dickinson University Press, 2010), 114.

[16] Sante Uberto Barbieri, *Spiritual Currents in Spanish America* (Buenos Aires: La Aurora, 1951); and Santiago Canclini, *Escritos de Pablo Besson* (Buenos Aires: Junta de Publicadores de la Convención Evangélica Bautista, 1948). See Sinclair, "Research on Protestantism," 110.

[17] Webster E. Browning, Kenneth G. Grubb, and John Richie, *The West Coast Republics of South America Chile, Peru and Bolivia: Review of 10 Years of Evangelical Progress* (London: World Dominion, 1930); Kenneth G. Grubb, *The Lowland Indians of Amazonia* (London: World Dominion, 1927); *From Pacific to Atlantic: South American Studies* (London: Methuen, 1933); W. Stanley Rycroft, *Sobre este fundamento* (Buenos Aires: La Aurora, 1944); and Reginald Wheeler, *Modern Missions on the Spanish Main: Impressions of Protestant Work in Colombia and Venezuela* (Philadelphia: Westminster, 1925). Cf. Sinclair, "Research on Protestantism," 110.

[18] Thomas S. Goslin, *Los evangélicos en la América Latina, siglo XIX* (Buenos Aires: La Aurora, 1956). Cf. Sinclair, "Research on Protestantism," 110.

[19] See Rosa del Carmen Bruno-Jofre, "Social Gospel, the Committee on Cooperation in Latin America, and the APRA: The Case of the American Methodist Mission, 1920–1930," *Canadian Journal of Latin American and Caribbean Studies* 9:18 (1984): 75–110, at 80.

[20] See Mondragón, *Like Leaven in the Dough*, 114.

and with it Protestant advances. It is not surprising, then, to see various British and non-American missionaries exert outsized influence upon missiological and historiographical trends, given wider wariness against U.S. efforts. Out of this group, which includes many of the Brethren missionaries mentioned below who largely wrote in the first half of the twentieth century, the Scottish Presbyterian John Mackay stands out for providing inspiration and materials for later evangelical intellectual construction.

Transnational Sources and the Latin American Evangelical Left

1916, in this way, became a crucial year for transnational history beyond the Panama Congress. Mackay boarded the SS *Kanuta* that year on a five-week trip from London to South America.[21] At a time when many global evangelical mission organizations fixated on Africa and East Asia, Mackay chose Latin America.[22] Mackay's encounter with Latin American history, culture, and literature convinced him that Christianity in the region lacked local roots. The Christian message retained a foreign accent, and this hindered the acceptance of the gospel. Thus, Mackay wrote his most influential book, *The Other Spanish Christ*, in 1932, as an attempt to diagnose the problems of Latin American Christianity and provide a way forward to an authentically "Latin Christ." In doing so, he recounted the history of Christianity in the region, focusing upon the theme of Christology.[23]

Mackay serves as a natural bridge between the first and second halves of the twentieth century. As a historian, I have consistently been surprised by Mackay's pervasive influence on the next generation of Latin American Protestant evangelicals. In a 2013 interview in his Valencia apartment, the Peruvian evangelical Samuel Escobar was explicit with regard to Mackay's legacy on his generation: "The writings of Latin American ecumenical theologians like Emilio Castro and José Míguez Bonino, or evangelicals like René Padilla and Pedro Arana, show Mackay's pervasive influence."[24] These thinkers would later write some of the most significant

[21] John Mackay Metzger, *The Hand and the Road: The Life and Times of John A. Mackay* (Louisville, Ky.: Westminster John Knox, 2010), 91.

[22] For more, see David C. Kirkpatrick, *A Gospel for the Poor: Global Social Christianity and the Latin American Evangelical Left* (Philadelphia: University of Pennsylvania Press, 2019), 101.

[23] John Mackay, *The Other Spanish Christ: A Study in the Spiritual History of Spain and South America* (London: Student Christian Movement Press, 1932).

[24] Samuel Escobar, interview translated by author, Valencia, October 22, 2013. See also Samuel Escobar, "The Legacy of John Alexander Mackay," *International Bulletin of Missionary Research* 16:3 (1992): 116–22, at 116–17. See also Allen Yeh, "Se hace

contextualized history and theology from within Latin America. The story of these influential evangelicals, whom I call members of the Latin American Evangelical Left, brings us full circle back to the beginning of our chapter—the Brethren movement.

Brethren expertise in publishing—including channels of printing and distribution—played an instrumental role in the later dissemination of Latin American Protestant evangelical history.[25] Because of their lack of hierarchy and practice of robust interchurch negotiation in journals, the Brethren often meted out their own convictions prior to global debates and provided a publishing structure for Latin Americans to later step into their own historiographical and theological construction. Thus, as David Bebbington writes, "because it adhered to its own standards so fiercely, Brethrenism was well placed to act as a ginger group in the evangelical world."[26]

Alec Clifford, the son of British Brethren missionaries in Argentina, served as an important bridge between a British missionary tradition and the Latin American Evangelical Left. Clifford undoubtedly received his passion for publishing from his parents, as his father, James Clifford, began work in Bolivia in 1895 and subsequently pioneered various publishing projects, many of which continue to this day, including *Campo Misionero*, which provided news of the wider Brethren work in Argentina.[27] These were not minuscule denominational publications, either. In 1894 Eglon Harris founded the journal *El Sembrador* (The Sower), which

---

camino al andar: Periphery and Center in the Missiology of Orlando E. Costas" (D.Phil. diss., University of Oxford, 2008), 78, 81. For Escobar, see especially Escobar, "Legacy of John Alexander Mackay." See also Samuel Escobar, "Doing Theology on Christ's Road," in Jeffrey P. Greenman and Gene L. Green, eds., *Global Theology in Evangelical Perspective: Exploring the Contextual Nature of Theology and Mission* (Downers Grove, Ill.: IVP Academic, 2012), 71; and Samuel Escobar, "Heredero de la reforma radical," in C. René Padilla, ed., *Hacia una teología evangélica Latinoamericana: Ensayos en honor de Pedro Savage* (Miami: Editorial Caribe, 1984), 51–72.

[25]   D. W. Bebbington, "The Place of the Brethren Movement in International Evangelicalism," in Neil T. R. Dickson and Tim Grass, eds., *The Growth of the Brethren Movement: National and International Experiences* (Milton Keynes: Paternoster, 2006), 241–60, at 246–47. I also expand on the influence of the Brethren movement on Latin American social Christianity in David C. Kirkpatrick, "Freedom from Fundamentalism: The Surprising Influence of Christian Brethrenism on the Rise of Latin American Social Christianity," *Journal of World Christianity* 7:2 (2017): 211–33.

[26]   Bebbington, "Place of the Brethren Movement," 257.

[27]   Frederick A. Tatford and John Heading, *Dawn over Latin America*, 10 vols. (Bath: Echoes of Service, 1983), 2:67.

at its peak reached a circulation of five hundred thousand copies per bimonthly issue, according to the Brethren journal *Echoes in Service*.[28] In total, more than twelve hundred different tracts and booklets have been published in Brethren circles in Latin America.

In 1962 Clifford helped found the Spanish student magazine *Certeza*, serving as its founding editor; it soon expanded from three issues per year to five in 1963. Each had an average printing of ten thousand copies. While *Certeza* was printed in Buenos Aires, it was also distributed throughout Argentina and in Brazil, Chile, Mexico, Peru, Venezuela, Bolivia, Colombia, Ecuador, and "the countries of Central America and the Caribbean."[29] Its highest circulation was in Argentina, most likely due to Clifford's Brethren networks across the country and later aided by Samuel Escobar's own.

The International Fellowship of Evangelical Students (IFES) at that time was under the leadership of Brethren Australian General Secretary Stacey Woods, who also founded the InterVarsity Christian Fellowship (IVCF) in Canada and the United States. IFES is the worldwide representative body that arose out of the InterVarsity Fellowship (IVF), later known as the Universities and Colleges Christian Fellowship (UCCF) in Britain and InterVarsity Christian Fellowship–USA (IVCF). Together, they are some of the largest Christian university student ministries in the world. As with Woods, Clifford refused to create a dependent ministry based upon his expertise. In 1965 the executive committee of the IFES met with the topic of inquiry "How can we help indigenous writing?"[30] Clifford mentored younger Latin Americans in publishing work, namely, Peruvian Samuel Escobar and Ecuadorian René Padilla, who were both staff members with the IFES.[31] Samuel Escobar had moved to Argentina from Peru in 1960 and befriended Clifford that year. There, Escobar recalled, his own "horizon continued to grow." Padilla later assumed the position of editor, later expanding into his own publishing house, Ediciones Kairos, which

---

[28]   A. Pulleng, "Opportunities Today in Central America and in South America," *Echoes Quarterly Review* 25:1 (1973): 19–20.

[29]   Correspondence: Literature Committee Association General Secretary for Literature, Box 162, SC 49, Billy Graham Center Archives (BGCA), Wheaton College, Wheaton, Ill. Special thanks go to Dr. Daniel Bourdanne for access to this restricted file.

[30]   Correspondence: Literature Committee Association General Secretary for Literature, BGCA.

[31]   See especially David C. Kirkpatrick, "C. René Padilla and the Origins of Integral Mission in Post-war Latin America," *Journal of Ecclesiastical History* 67:1 (2016): 351–71.

specializes in publishing Spanish-language history and theology—many from first-time authors. IFES, of course, was not alone in its Spanish-language publications. Other key publications include *Pensamiento Cristiano* of the Latin America Mission, which was also founded by Clifford in 1953; *Editorial Caribe;* and others. By 1974 IFES claimed that *Certeza* had become "the interdenominational magazine with the widest circulation in Latin America."[32]

In these Spanish-language journals and magazines, we see some of the most significant contextual history and theology at a time when wider English-language writing was focused almost exclusively on Catholic stories such as theologies of liberation and later on Pentecostalism.[33] This is a key point, and one I want to clarify. This chapter does not seek to export credit for Latin American evangelical history to northern sources. Rather, my argument is much narrower: forward-thinking missionaries, especially in the Brethren tradition, provided the structure for strategic publication, including historiography. In other words, the content and agency were thoroughly Latin American, while the structures were transnational in origin.

Power, Pentecostals, and the Present Day

The broader structures of Latin American religion and politics also faced significant pressure during this time—structural shifts that ushered in the present era of evangelical growth, influence, and a surge of historiographical writing. This generation just discussed came of age during significant political and religious upheaval that I have written about at length elsewhere—the Cuban Revolution, the Second Vatican Council of the Catholic Church, and other monumental shifts across the region. Less visible to Western observers were migration trends that laid a foundation for Protestant evangelical demographic growth, visibility, and an explosion of historiography that we see in the present day. In other words, demographic shifts led to *significant* historiographical shifts. The postwar period ushered in tremendous change for Latin American Protestants and the writing of their history alongside, as many major cities witnessed doubling and tripling of size over a few decades through movement from rural regions to cities.[34]

---

[32] "IFES Information Sheet 1974," International Fellowship of Evangelical Students Papers, IFES Headquarters, Oxford, UK.

[33] Examples include early issues of *Certeza* magazine, such as the 1966 issue on Marxism and Christianity, contiguous with or earlier than Catholic discussions on the topic.

[34] See Kirkpatrick, *A Gospel for the Poor*, 33–53.

Observers from the north noted and often cheered theologies of liberation and the political environment that gave rise to them. But during this time, many observers and historians failed to note the significant trends shifting across the religious landscape. After World War II, Protestantism began to gain a foothold in Latin America, as urbanization provided a new social context for religious life. Protestant churches found acceptance at the margins of this new urban environment, growing in places that traditional Roman Catholic structures largely struggled to reach.

The Evangelical Left arose in the shadow of the Cuban Revolution, but this time period also witnessed a significant expansion of Pentecostal efforts in the region. Much of the scholarship on the Pentecostals lagged quite significantly, but became increasingly difficult to ignore as they flexed political muscles. It would not be until the late 1980s and early 1990s when multiple monographs signaled a wider turn toward Latin American Protestant evangelicalism and Pentecostalism within the academic study of religion especially.[35] We should note English-language writings such as Sheldon Annis' *God and Production in a Guatemalan Town* (1987) and Edward Cleary and Hannah Stewart-Gambino's *Power, Politics, and Pentecostals in Latin America* (1997). Significant denominational Spanish work was done by Juan Sepúlveda of the Iglesia Misión Pentecostal (Chile) and Manuel Gaxiola of the Iglesia Apostólica de México.[36] In more recent times, Rubén Ruiz Guerra, Virginia Garrard, Arlene Sanchez-Walsh, Carlos Mondragón, Daniel Salinas, Todd Hartch, Daniel Ramirez, Erika Helgen, and many others have contributed mightily to our understanding in both Spanish and English.[37] Garrard, for example,

[35] David Stoll, *Is Latin America Turning Protestant? The Politics of Evangelical Growth* (Berkeley: University of California Press, 1990); David Martin, *Tongues of Fire: The Explosion of Protestantism in Latin America* (Oxford: Blackwell, 1990); and Virginia Garrard-Burnett and David Stoll, eds., *Rethinking Protestantism in Latin America* (Philadelphia: Temple University Press, 1993).

[36] Juan Sepúlveda, "The Perspective of Chilean Pentecostalism," *Journal of Pentecostal Studies* 4 (1994): 41–49; Juan Sepúlveda, "Another Way of Being Pentecostal," in Calvin Smith, ed., *Pentecostal Power* (Leiden: Brill, 2011), 37–61; and Manuel Gaxiola, *Nacimiento del movimiento pentecostal, 1901–1916* (México, DF: Cerlam, AC, 1998).

[37] Rubén Ruiz Guerra, *Hombres Nuevos: Metodismo y Modernización, 1873–1930* (Mexico City: CUPSA, 1992); Virginia Garrard-Burnett, *Protestantism in Guatemala: Living in the New Jerusalem* (Austin: University of Texas Press, 1998); Arlene M. Sánchez-Walsh, *Latino Pentecostal Identity: Evangelical Faith, Self, and Society* (New York: Columbia University Press, 2003); Carlos Mondragón, *Leudar la masa: el pensamiento social de los protestantes en América Latina, 1920–1950* (Buenos Aires: Kairos, 2005); Carlos Mondragón and Carlos Olivier Toledo, eds., *Minorías religiosas:*

filled a tremendous gap in our understanding of Guatemala, perhaps the most demographically successful country for Protestantism. Hartch's *The Rebirth of Latin American Christianity* (2014) provides a clearer picture of the wider ecclesial context of both Roman Catholic and Protestant Christianity. Hartch argued that growing Protestant competition in the religious marketplace revitalized Roman Catholicism in the second half of the twentieth century, rather than weakened it. This larger argument follows the pattern of recent studies such as Roman Catholic priest Edward Cleary's *How Latin America Saved the Soul of the Catholic Church*.[38] Hartch's constructive use of history is at once accessible and worth considering. Anthropologists, such as Kevin O'Neill, Andrew Chesnut, and Casey High, have also sometimes outpaced historians of Latin American Christianity, providing interdisciplinary encouragement we would be wise to heed.[39] Today we continue to see historiographical lacunae particularly within the history of non-charismatic Protestantism, but strong strides have been made here in recent books by Daniel Salinas, Carlos Mondragón, and others.[40]

We are at a crucial moment for historiography on Latin American evangelicalism. Evangelical and Pentecostal Protestants have gained political power in many parts of Latin America. But historians must resist the simple, prepackaged, politically convenient categories that often plague

---

el Protestantismo en América Latina (Mexico City: Universidad Nacional Autónoma de México, 2013); Daniel Salinas, *Latin American Evangelical Theology in the 1970s: The Golden Decade* (Leiden: Brill, 2009); Todd Hartch, *The Rebirth of Latin American Christianity* (Oxford: Oxford University Press, 2014); Daniel Ramírez, *Migrating Faith: Pentecostalism in the United States and Mexico in the Twentieth* Century (Chapel Hill: University of North Carolina Press, 2015); Erika Helgen, *Religious Conflict in Brazil: Protestants, Catholics, and the Rise of Religious Pluralism in the Early Twentieth Century* (New Haven, Conn.: Yale University Press, 2020). For discussion of the recent historiography, see the introduction of this book.

[38] Edward L. Cleary, *How Latin America Saved the Soul of the Catholic Church* (New York: Paulist, 2009).

[39] Kevin O'Neill, *City of God: Christian Citizenship in Postwar Guatemala* (Berkeley: University of California Press, 2010); Andrew Chesnut, *Born Again in Brazil: The Pentecostal Boom and the Pathogens of Poverty* (New Brunswick, N.J.: Rutgers University Press, 1997), and *Competitive Spirits: Latin America's New Religious Economy* (Oxford: Oxford University Press, 2003); and Casey High, *Victims and Warriors: Violence, History, and Memory in Amazonia* (Urbana: University of Illinois Press, 2015).

[40] J. Daniel Salinas, *Taking Up the Mantle: Latin American Evangelical Theology in the 20th Century* (Carlisle: Langham Global Library, 2017); Mondragón, *Leudar la masa*; Kirkpatrick, *A Gospel for the Poor*.

the study of evangelicals in the United States. While acknowledging shared streams and sources, historians must allow Latin American evangelicalism to display its own agency—one of negotiation, resistance, adoption, and local construction.

II
Particular Lands

6

Evangelical Conceptions of History, Racial Difference, and Social Change in Brazil, 1900–1940

Pedro Feitoza

Brazil has long been home to a broad variety of expressions of evangelical Christianity.[1] Throughout the nineteenth and early twentieth centuries, immigrants and missionaries representing a wide array of denominations and Protestant organizations entered the country, from German-speaking Lutheran migrants to Pentecostals, from Episcopalians to the Open Brethren. Most of these groups sought to expand their reach and congregations through evangelism, the creation of networks of convert families, the training of their own personnel, and the circulation of Bibles and Christian literature. Some groups, such as the Presbyterians, Methodists, and Baptists, founded institutions of primary, secondary, and higher education that over time evolved into respectable organizations and trained some of the country's leading linguists, artists, and educators. The encounters of missionaries and converts with traditional societies and a Catholic Church undergoing a process of institutional expansion and devotional renewal led to the rise of distinctive religious practices and beliefs, and

[1] Research for this chapter was financially supported by the São Paulo Research Foundation (FAPESP), grant #2019/14369–2.

even encouraged movements of independence from foreign mission bodies among Presbyterians and Baptists.[2]

In spite of all such diversity of ecclesial models, beliefs, and religious practice, the thinking and ideologies of Brazilian evangelicals up until the post-World War II era have been frequently dismissed as imitative, shallow, and little concerned with the pressing social situation of the country. The rise of theologies of liberation and integral mission in Latin America during the Cold War, with their disparate but self-conscious perception of the social and political realities of the continent, exerted some fascination among Western scholars, who then began to view previous Catholic and evangelical expressions as culturally inauthentic and socially alienated. For influential commentators, including historians, theologians, and social scientists, Brazilian ministers and knowledgeable converts embraced the conservative dogmatism of "Old School" American Presbyterianism and reproduced in its communities traces of North American civil religion, which deepened the gap between Brazilian believers and their own society.[3] In a contribution to the *Fundamentalism Project*, Paraguayan historian Pablo A. Deiros claimed that in Latin America "evangelical Protestantism is fundamentally conservative and firmly committed to zealous proselytism in the name of the gospel." This theological conservatism translated into social conservatism, as converts practiced a "vertical" spirituality concerned with inward personal transformation that alienated believers from their social surroundings and legitimized the status quo.[4] In an influential book on the introduction of Protestantism in late nineteenth-century Brazil, sociologist Antônio G. Mendonça asserted that Protestant individualism, pietism, and theological rigidity isolated believers and ministers from broader movements of social change

---

[2]   For a general history of Protestantism in Brazil, see Émile Léonard, *O Protestantismo Brasileiro: Estudo de eclesiologia e história social*, 3rd ed. (São Paulo: ASTE, 2002 [1963]); and for a shorter summary, see Pedro Feitoza, "Historical Trajectories of Protestantism in Brazil, 1810–1960," in Eric Miller and Ronald J. Morgan, eds., *Brazilian Evangelicalism in the Twenty-First Century: An Inside and Outside Look* (Cham, Switzerland: Palgrave Macmillan, 2019), 31–63.

[3]   Paul Pierson, *A Younger Church in Search of Maturity: Presbyterianism in Brazil from 1910–1959* (San Antonio, Tex.: Trinity University Press, 1974), 94–98, 102–3; and Antônio Gouvêa Mendonça and Prócoro Velasques Filho, *Introdução ao Protestantismo no Brasil* (São Paulo: Edições Loyola, 1990), 14, 31–34, 133–44.

[4]   Pablo A. Deiros, "Protestant Fundamentalism in Latin America," in Martin Marty and R. Scott Appleby, eds., *Fundamentalisms Observed* (Chicago: University of Chicago Press, 1991), 149–52, 171–73.

and cultural renewal.[5] Some scholars, on the other hand, have sought to locate the precise moments in which Latin American Protestants abandoned their dependence on North American theological conservatism and developed an "authentic" local theology. For some it happened in the 1950s, when ministers and foreign missionaries began to deploy categories of analysis arising from European sociology to comprehend the social and economic situation in Brazil.[6] Others situated such renewal in the 1930s and 1940s, when Brazilian pastors and professors encountered the German theology of Karl Barth and Dietrich Bonhoeffer, and American versions of the social gospel.[7]

Carlos Mondragón's important book *Like Leaven in the Dough* offers a timely remedy to such generalizations. In it, Mondragón showed how Latin American Protestant ministers and intellectuals projected themselves into local social and political debates on democracy, religious liberty, and the rise of fascism and communism in the interwar era through a periodical called *La Nueva Democracia* (The New Democracy). Contributors such as Mexican Congregationalist Alberto Rembao, Argentine Methodist Jorge Howard, and Mexican writer Gonzalo Báez-Camargo followed closely the social and political debates of their respective contexts and wove Protestant thinking into them. They claimed that a personal religious experience, which produced participatory and responsible individuals, was key to understanding the principles of democracy, and recovered the image of Jesus Christ as a manual worker to bring evangelical Christianity closer to working-class mobilizations.[8] Evangelicals translated central tenets of Anglophone Protestant theology into local idioms and images, navigating across multiple cultural landscapes and domesticating religion along the way.[9]

[5]   Antônio G. Mendonça, *O celeste porvir: A inserção do Protestantismo no Brasil*, 3rd ed. (São Paulo: EDUSP, 2008), 362.

[6]   Rubem Alves, *Protestantism and Repression: A Brazilian Case Study*, trans. John Drury (London: SCM Press, 1985).

[7]   Silas Luiz de Souza, *Pensamento social e político no Protestantismo Brasileiro* (São Paulo: Editora Mackenzie, 2005).

[8]   Carlos Mondragón, *Like Leaven in the Dough: Protestant Social Thought in Latin America, 1920–1950*, trans. Daniel Miller and Ben Post (Madison, N.J.: Fairleigh Dickinson University Press, 2011).

[9]   David Maxwell, "Historical Perspectives on Christianity Worldwide: Connections, Comparisons and Consciousness," in Joel Cabrita, David Maxwell, and Emma Wild-Wood, eds., *Relocating World Christianity: Interdisciplinary Studies in Universal and Local Expressions of the Christian Faith* (Leiden: Brill, 2017), 47–69.

Instead of locating the thinking of Brazilian ministers and converts into specific theological schools and fixed positions of the ideological spectrum, this chapter situates their writings in the religious and social debates of their own age. Since the very beginnings of the Protestant missionary enterprise in Brazil, missionaries and converts started to engage with the social and political issues of the day, discussing the broader implications of their status as religious minorities and advocating the legitimacy of evangelical propaganda in the country. Of course, they did so through the specific political and social concepts of their era, mobilizing the predominant intellectual, cultural, and linguistic vocabulary. This chapter examines the ways in which Brazilian evangelicals channeled conceptions of national history, racial difference, and social change into the religious and social debates circulating in the Brazilian public sphere throughout the first decades of the twentieth century. Its protagonists are the Presbyterian ministers and writers who offered new interpretations of the history of Brazil since the late nineteenth century and took part in the Congress on Christian Work in Latin America in Panama City, 1916. First, this chapter will look at the historiographical work of Brazilian evangelicals, analyzing their attempts to "invent" a deep Protestant past that served to legitimize their missionary efforts in modern Brazil. The second part of the chapter focuses on two Presbyterian ministers, the Revs. Eduardo Carlos Pereira and Erasmo Braga, and their involvement on debates about racialist thinking and social change.

Brazil and the Global Circuits of the Reformation

In the nineteenth and twentieth centuries, the expansion and consolidation of a world-system of nation states reshaped modern religious sensibilities and practice. The relationship between nationalisms of different kinds and world religions in this period was often conflictive and ambiguous. Religious solidarity, pilgrimage, and education could both fragment a drive for national determination and lay the cultural groundwork for the rise of nationalist sentiments and identity.[10] In many places, nationalist politicians and writers questioned the civil loyalty of religious minorities. Ultramontane Catholics in Britain, for instance, were accused of being

[10] Christopher Bayly, *The Birth of the Modern World, 1780–1914: Global Connections and Comparisons* (Oxford: Blackwell, 2004), 361–63; Brian Stanley, *A World History of Christianity in the Twentieth Century* (Princeton, N.J.: Princeton University Press, 2018), 36–38; and Benedict Anderson, *Imagined Communities: Reflections on the Origin and Spread of Nationalism*, revised ed. (London: Verso, 2006).

disloyal to the monarchy, whereas conversion to Christianity in India and China was often deemed antinational.[11]

In early twentieth-century Brazil, evangelicals were among such embattled religious minorities. Catholic priests, conservative writers, and nationalist intellectuals objected to the expansion of evangelical propaganda in the country for a number of reasons. First, Catholic polemicists such as Father Agnelo Rossi claimed that the Protestant Reformation broke away from the unity of Christendom, and consequently its modern missionary enterprise had a similar potential to fragment the unity of the nation.[12] Second, for writers such as Jackson de Figueiredo and Father Leonel Franca, evangelical Christianity waged war against the hierarchy and order inscribed by God in nature, disaggregating social bonds, fomenting social division, and sowing the seeds of anarchy.[13] Following a somewhat similar line, the traditionalist thinker Gilberto Freyre affirmed in his 1933 classical work *The Masters and the Slaves* that in colonial Brazil, Catholicism served as a cement of social unity, purging the Portuguese colonial endeavor of the divisive experience of the French and the English.[14] Third, nationalist writers viewed the Protestant missionary enterprise in Brazil as a tool of North American imperialism, a soft instrument of cultural and ideological penetration.[15] Decades later, this argument was picked up by Marxist intellectuals.[16]

In the face of such a set of accusations, Christian minorities sought to advocate the historical rootedness of their religion, a resource deployed in order both to counter the notion that they threatened the foundations of nationality and to situate themselves in a chain of events meaningful for the nationalist imagination.[17] For instance, Bengali Christian writers in the nineteenth century discussed evidence of St.

[11] Peter van der Veer, "Religion and Nationalism," in John Breuilly, ed., *The Oxford Handbook of the History of Nationalism* (Oxford: Oxford University Press, 2013), 660.

[12] Riolando Azzi, *A Neocristandade: Um projeto restaurador* (São Paulo: Paulus, 1994), 80.

[13] Leonel Franca, *A Igreja, a reforma e a civilização*, 5th ed. (Rio de Janeiro: Agir, 1948 [1922]); and Francisco Iglésias, *História e ideologia* (São Paulo: Perspectiva, 1971), 109–59.

[14] Gilberto Freyre, *Casa grande & senzala: Formação da família Brasileira sob o regime da economia patriarcal*, 48th ed. (São Paulo: Global, 2003 [1933]), 91–92.

[15] Azzi, *A Neocristandade*, 81–82.

[16] L. A. Moniz Bandeira, *Presença dos Estados Unidos no Brasil (Dois séculos de história)* (Rio de Janeiro: Civilização Brasileira, 1978), 124.

[17] van der Veer, "Religion," 660.

Thomas' travel to India in order to locate their religious communities into a lineage that could be traced to the apostolic tradition and thus dismiss the idea of the foreignness of Christianity in the region.[18] And in nineteenth-century West Africa, Yoruba converts built upon the religious repertory of *orisa* religion to claim that Christian teachings were a fulfillment of their earlier practices, writing Christianity providentially into Yoruba history.[19] In Latin America the issue at stake was the thin historical anchorage of evangelical Christianity in the region. Whereas Catholic clerics claimed that religious change would erode the cultural and spiritual foundations of their nations, Protestant writers embarked on a different endeavor. In the 1930s and 1940s, a Mexican Congregationalist called Alberto Rembao linked the origins of the Protestant Reformation to sixteenth-century Spanish Christian mystics and argued that modern Latin American Protestantism was firmly rooted in Iberian early modern humanist and reformist traditions. For Rembao, these histories would help Mexican converts to "de-Saxonize" Protestantism and universalize it.[20]

In a similar fashion, Brazilian evangelicals devised a set of different discursive strategies to counter the accusations of Catholic and nationalist writers since the second half of the nineteenth century. In the 1870s, in the midst of a bitter conflict pitting the Brazilian Empire against members of the Catholic hierarchy, Presbyterian pastors based in Rio de Janeiro published a translation of William Gladstone's critique of Ultramontane Catholicism, claiming that the decrees of Pope Pius IX condemning the "errors" of modern civilization were in stark opposition to the values of the modern world.[21] Decades later, the missionary and bureaucratic expansion of the Catholic Church during the First Republic (1889–1930) gave leverage to Protestant criticism of the status of the Church after the overthrow of the Brazilian Empire. In this period, the Church managed to expand its administrative and institutional presence in the country with the aid of foreign religious orders, such as French and Belgian Vincentians and American

---

[18] Shinjini Das, "An Imperial Apostle? St Paul, Protestant Conversion, and South Asian Christianity," *Historical Journal* 61:1 (2018): 103–30, at 125–26.

[19] John D. Y. Peel, *Religious Encounter and the Making of the Yoruba* (Bloomington: Indiana University Press, 2000), 299–300.

[20] Mondragón, *Like Leaven in the Dough*, 105–8.

[21] William Gladstone, *Os decretos do Vaticano em suas relações com a lealdade civil: Discussão política* (Rio de Janeiro: Typographia Universal de Laemmert, 1875).

Maryknoll missionaries.[22] At the same time, laypeople and members of the Catholic clergy protested against religious disestablishment and the creation of civil registrations of marriages and births. Brazilian Protestants and foreign missionaries compared the increasing denationalization of the Catholic clergy to the rise of a local evangelical leadership in the country, and claimed that the Catholic resentment with constitutional clauses on religious liberty showed their enmity toward the Brazilian Republic.[23]

But besides this, Protestants sought to locate evangelical Christianity in the depths of Brazilian history, demonstrating that their religion was not alien to the soul of the nation. This move started in the mid-nineteenth century, when Methodist missionary Daniel Kidder and Presbyterian chaplain James Fletcher recovered the history of an invasion of French Huguenots in sixteenth-century Rio de Janeiro in their book *Brazil and the Brazilians*. In this best seller, widely read by the American missionaries who embarked for Brazil, Kidder and Fletcher reminded their readers that it was on the Guanabara Bay, that iconic site in Rio de Janeiro, that the "banner of the Reformation was first unfurled" in the American continent.[24] According to the authors, it was there, in a colony founded by the French admiral Nicolas de Villegagnon in 1555, with the purpose of offering asylum for persecuted Huguenots, that "these French Puritans offered their prayers and sang their hymns of praise nearly threescore years and ten before a Pilgrim placed his foot on Plymouth rock, and more than half a century before the Book of Common Prayer was borne to the banks of the James River."[25] In their narrative, the French colony soon attracted the interest of the Reformed Church of Geneva, from where ministers, students, and colonists were recruited and sent to Rio de Janeiro. Kidder and Fletcher asserted that this initiative, carried out when the Reformation was in its infancy and Calvin, Farel, and Beza were still alive, consisted

---

[22]   Ralph Della Cava, "Catholicism and Society in Twentieth-Century Brazil," *Latin American Research Review*, 11:2 (1976): 7–50; Kenneth P. Serbin, *Needs of the Heart: A Social and Cultural History of Brazil's Clergy and Seminaries* (Notre Dame, Ind.: University of Notre Dame Press, 2006), 58–59, 70–72; and Sergio Miceli, *A elite Eclesiástica Brasileira: 1890–1930*, 2nd ed. (São Paulo: Companhia das Letras, 2009).

[23]   Philippe Landes, *Dom Aquino: Imperialismo e Protestantismo* (Cuiabá: Typ. d'A Penna Evangelica, 1928).

[24]   Daniel P. Kidder and James C. Fletcher, *Brazil and the Brazilians, Portrayed in Historical and Descriptive Sketches* (Philadelphia: Childs & Peterson, 1857), 46; this sentence was repeated almost verbatim on 59.

[25]   Kidder and Fletcher, *Brazil*, 54.

of the first missionary endeavor carried out by Protestants.[26] But it was also a short-lived experience. Villegagnon soon betrayed his Protestant compatriots and sent them back to France in poorly equipped vessels; the Portuguese set out to recover the territory, starting a war against the French; and the Jesuits, headed by the priests Manuel da Nóbrega and José de Anchieta, wiped away the Protestant presence in Rio de Janeiro. The religious experience of these French Calvinists, however, sowed the seeds of something deeper that, in the narrative of Kidder and Fletcher, did not die easily. For them, the "faithful prayers" of those "pious Huguenots" and the "mysterious dealings of Providence" enabled modern Brazilians to benefit, three centuries later, from a tolerant constitution in religious matters, a good government, and some material prosperity in comparison to their South American neighbors.[27]

Decades later, in the midst of a series of commemorations of historical events that shaped Brazilian and world history, evangelical ministers and writers elaborated some of the details related to these events and carried further the historical anchorage of Protestantism in Brazilian history. In 1896 when city councilors of the state of São Paulo planned to erect a statue in honor of the Jesuit priest José de Anchieta, one of the founders of the city, a Protestant pastor objected vehemently, recalling the history of the French colony and the violence surrounding its dissolution. The Presbyterian Rev. Álvaro Reis wrote two tracts addressing the republican press of São Paulo and the governor of the state and raising a plethora of arguments against Anchieta's statue. For Reis, building such a monument with public money would violate the principle of church-state separation consecrated by the republican constitution of 1891. But more than that, such a statue would perpetually praise the life and deeds of a man, Anchieta, and an organization, the Jesuits, who stood in stark opposition to the "enlightened" values of the republic and the tolerant spirit of the age. Reis depicted Father Anchieta as an uneducated and selfish priest, who fueled animosities between the Indians and the first inhabitants of São Paulo, a relationship that was once amicable. More specifically, Reis claimed that José de Anchieta acted as an executioner to Jean de Balleur, referred to in Brazil as João de Bolés, one of the Protestant survivors of the French colony.[28] For Reis, the specter of Jesuitism was irreconcilably opposed to

---

[26] Kidder and Fletcher, *Brazil*, 54.

[27] Kidder and Fletcher, *Brazil*, 60.

[28] Álvaro Reis, *Anchieta, o carrasco de Bolés á luz da historia patria* (São Paulo: n.p., 1896); and Álvaro Reis, *José de Anchieta á luz da historia patria* (São Paulo: n.p., 1896).

the progress of the Brazilian republic, and he used these stories to build an argument that emphasized the antiquity and ubiquity of Catholic violence in the history of the nation, representing the Jesuits as antipatriotic and antirepublican.

It was in 1900, however, that the most elaborate and wide-ranging evangelical interpretation of Brazilian history appeared. To commemorate the four hundredth anniversary of the arrival of the Portuguese in Brazil, a group of writers and scientists edited a monumental collection of essays examining various aspects of Brazilian history since 1500, including literature, agriculture, sciences, the arts, mining, industry, and religion. The book on Catholicism, written by the influential priest Júlio Maria, claimed that the Catholic Church played a pivotal role in constructing a sense of Brazilianness. For him, the first mass, the Jesuits, and their missionary enterprise brought the various ethnic and social groups that formed colonial society together, civilizing the New World under the sign of the cross.[29] The response to Júlio Maria's book came from the influential journalist and Protestant convert José Carlos Rodrigues, who was then editor of *Jornal do Comércio*, South America's most widely circulated paper. His book, titled *Non-Catholic Religions in Brazil*, was included in the collection and republished separately in 1904.

Drawing from a collection of rare books and papers kept in his vast personal library, Rodrigues reconstructed in detail the history of the sixteenth-century French settlement of Rio de Janeiro. He represented Nicolas de Villegagnon as a restless and authoritarian man, who aimed at creating a "mystical community" in Brazil separate from the Catholic Church but equally distinct from the Lutheran and Calvinist reformations.[30] But Rodrigues also stressed that there were direct links connecting the French colony of Rio de Janeiro to the European Reformation. He argued that the ministers sent to Brazil were handpicked in Geneva by John Calvin, and that they zealously evangelized the first French colonists and the Indian tribes.[31] In Rodrigues' narrative, Villegagnon turned against the community of Calvinists and expelled them from Brazil, putting three of them to death. The failure of the colony, however, did not erase the Protestant principle from Brazil. According

[29] Júlio Maria, "A religião, ordens religiosas, instituições pias e beneficentes no Brasil," in *O Livro do Centenário (1500–1900)* (Rio de Janeiro: Imprensa Nacional, 1900).
[30] José Carlos Rodrigues, *Religiões acatholicas no Brazil, 1500–1900* (Rio de Janeiro: Jornal do Commercio, 1904), 12, 20.
[31] Rodrigues, *Religiões*, 15–17.

to Rodrigues, the original inhabitants of Rio de Janeiro held the French colonists and ministers in higher esteem compared to the Portuguese, treating them generously and embracing some of their doctrines. He reproduced excerpts from the reports of Jesuit priests and missionaries claiming that the "Lutheran and Calvinist poison" could be found among Indian groups of Rio de Janeiro up to the mid-seventeenth century.[32] And he made a similar point regarding the evangelistic efforts of the Dutch missionaries that entered the region of Pernambuco in 1630. Again, Rodrigues affirmed that even after the departure of the Reformed Dutch, Catholic priests encountered Calvinist and Lutheran "heresies" among some Indians of Pernambuco, who mocked the doctrines of the Jesuits as "the folly of priests" and their Church as false.[33] With this work, José Carlos Rodrigues intended to show that in spite of the failure of these Protestant settlements in colonial Brazil, the religious legacy of the French and Dutch Protestants lived on. Their doctrines penetrated indigenous tribes and made the Portuguese effort to reconquer the land physically and spiritually even harder. Like his friend Álvaro Reis, Rodrigues also stressed the socially disaggregating effects of Jesuit violence, which dissolved harmonious social relations, drove away the economically dynamic Protestants and Jews, and consequently shattered the progress of the colony.[34]

But besides situating the Catholic-Protestant struggles of the early modern era in the origins of the nation, Brazilian evangelicals also sought to locate these historical experiences in the transnational circuits of the Reformation in the sixteenth century. In 1917, when Brazilian congregations commemorated the four hundredth anniversary of the Lutheran Reformation, an elder of the Presbyterian Church of Rio de Janeiro called Domingos Ribeiro translated into Portuguese an excerpt of the martyrology written by the French Calvinist Jean Crespin. In it, the author recounted the execution of the French Huguenots Jean du Bourdel, Matthieu Verneuil, and Pierre Bourdon in Rio de Janeiro under Villegagnon, and Ribeiro portrayed them as the "proto-martyrs" of evangelical Christianity in Brazil.[35] The last part of this tract included the so-called

---

[32] Rodrigues, *Religiões*, 26–37.

[33] Rodrigues, *Religiões*, 80–81.

[34] Rodrigues, *Religiões*, 38–72, 82–94.

[35] Jean Crespin, *A Tragedia de Guanabara, ou historia dos protomartyres do Christianismo no Brasil*, trans. Domingos Ribeiro (Rio de Janeiro: Typ. Pimenta de Mello & C., 1917).

Guanabara Faith Confession, a document written by these French Calvinists alongside André de la Fon. In the same year, a short book published by the Independent Presbyterian Church of São Paulo to commemorate the Reformation also recalled the violence surrounding the religious transformations of the early modern era. The opening chapter, written by the Independent Church's founder, the Rev. Eduardo Carlos Pereira, deployed dramatic words to describe the political and religious repression against Protestantism in Europe. And here he incorporated the experience of the Huguenot martyrs of Rio de Janeiro into the bloodshed characteristic of the era, linking them to English martyrs such as Hugh Latimer and Thomas Cranmer.[36]

In recovering such histories in the early twentieth century, Brazilian Protestants attempted to formulate some arguments. By calling the French Huguenots who died in Rio de Janeiro under Villegagnon "proto-martyrs" of the evangelical cause, they sought to locate their own religious communities in a longer historical lineage and show that the evangelical missionary enterprise in modern Brazil was an echo of a distant past. Numerous evangelical writers since the late nineteenth century referred to Villegagnon as the "Cain of the Americas,"[37] as if his role in the execution of his Calvinist compatriots represented a sort of primordial sin in Brazilian lands. Furthermore, these evangelical descriptions of the Jesuits consolidated among Brazilian Protestants a historiographical trend, albeit inaccurate, with roots in the sixteenth century depicting Ignatius of Loyola as an antithesis of Luther and Calvin, and the Company of Jesus as a papal army bent on stopping the spread of Protestantism.[38] In the early decades of the Brazilian republic, these associations were particularly significant. Protestants represented themselves as faithful, patriotic citizens of the regime, committed to the moral and social progress of their nation, while representing the Jesuits as archaic, disruptive, and the local representatives of a foreign potentate based in Rome.

---

[36] *A commemoração do 4º centenário da reforma—31 de Outubro de 1917* (São Paulo: Typographia d'O Estandarte, 1917), 16–17.

[37] Reis, *Anchieta*, 23, 25; Rodrigues, *Religiões*, 24–25; Erasmo Braga, *Pan-Americanismo: Aspecto religioso* (New York: The Missionary Education Movement, 1917), 25; and Eduardo C. Pereira, *O problema religioso da America Latina: Estudo dogmatico-historico* (São Paulo: Imprensa Methodista, 1920), 58.

[38] Robert A. Markys, "Introduction: Protestants and Early Jesuits," in Jorge Cañizares-Esguerra, Robert A. Markys, and R. P. Hsia, eds., *Encounters between Jesuits and Protestants in Asia and the Americas* (Leiden: Brill, 2018), 1–8.

Evangelical Interpretations of Race and
Social Change after Panama 1916

At the same time when Protestants began to crystallize such interpretations of Brazilian history that influenced the evangelical imagination for a long period, a missionary conference channeled the attention of some leading Brazilian pastors to different concerns. This was the Congress on Christian Work in Latin America, gathered in Panama City in February 1916. Known as the Panama Congress, this event was the first and most important early twentieth-century missionary conference dedicated to analyzing the promises and difficulties surrounding Protestant missionary work in Latin America. It was an offspring of the remarkable World Missionary Conference of Edinburgh, 1910, which also served as an operational and missiological inspiration to organizers of the Panama Congress.[39] Among the 235 official delegates, who represented forty-four evangelical organizations, only twenty-seven were Latin Americans, and the official language of the meeting was English, even though participants spoke in Spanish and Portuguese in between plenary meetings. One of the goals of the Panama Congress was to bring together the various evangelical institutions, mission societies, and denominations operating in the continent to Christianize Latin American culture through their evangelistic, educational, literary, and social efforts.[40] Although Latin American participants were the minority, they were the key agents who mediated between the goals of the conference and their own cultures, translating their core principles to wider publics. This section will investigate how two Brazilian participants at the Panama Congress, the Revs. Eduardo Carlos Pereira and Erasmo Braga, built upon ideas picked up at the conference to take part in debates on racial difference and social change in Brazil.

In the period ranging from 1870 to 1930, theories of racial difference, scientific racism, and their variations became nearly ubiquitous explanations for Brazil's social problems and prospects for the future. The intellectual influences that shaped racialist thinking in Brazil came from different sources. Physical anthropologists, for instance, claimed that the various

[39] William R. Hogg, *Ecumenical Foundations: A History of the International Missionary Council and its Nineteenth-Century Background* (Eugene, Ore.: Wipf and Stock, 2002 [1972]), 173. On the Edinburgh Conference, see Brian Stanley, *The World Missionary Conference, Edinburgh, 1910* (Grand Rapids: Eerdmans, 2009).

[40] Jean-Pierre Bastian, *Protestantismos y modernidad Latinoamericana: historia de unas minorías religiosas activas en América Latina* (Mexico, DF: Fondo de Cultura Económica, 1994), 154–56.

races that formed humankind had different origins, and sought to analyze human behavior in the light of the "laws" of nature and biology. Even those who did not go so far as to assert that differences between human races were insurmountable also believed in forms of environmental or climatic determinism.[41] For Brazilian scientists and men of letters, the indictments of racial theories were particularly agonizing. Brazil was the last country of the Americas to abolish slavery, and at the dawn of the twentieth century its population was composed mostly of Blacks and mestizos. Influential writers such as Euclides da Cunha and Silvio Romero sought to counter the prevailing pessimism by arguing that racial mixture would eventually whiten Brazilian society, paving its way to "civilization." Others, such as the physician Raimundo Nina Rodrigues, held negative views of miscegenation, and believed it would condemn the country to permanent inferiority.[42] Variations of racial theories were equally pervasive in Brazilian social thought. The idea of degeneration, for instance, extrapolated the boundaries of racial thinking into the domains of individual behavior and healthcare: it was believed that alcoholism, laziness, inappropriate education, and diseases could "degenerate" humans, and such behavioral traces could be transmitted to their offspring.[43] Despite the relative optimism or pessimism of most Brazilian intellectuals, the idea that race determined the pace of modernization shaped conceptions of progress.

The establishment of communities of foreign Protestant immigrants in nineteenth-century Brazil was closely connected to policies influenced by racialist thinking. Throughout this era, influential politicians and political advisors believed that white Protestant immigrants from Germany and Switzerland would help Brazilian society replace its Black slaves with a "civilizing" workforce.[44] And one of the elements that attracted

[41] Lilia M. Schwarcz, *The Spectacle of the Races: Scientists, Institutions, and the Race Question in Brazil, 1870-1930*, trans. Leland Guyer (New York: Hill and Wang, 1999), 48–51; and Charles A. Hale, "Political and Social Ideas in Latin America, 1870–1930," in Leslie Bethell, ed., *The Cambridge History of Latin America. Vol IV: c. 1870–1930* (Cambridge: Cambridge University Press, 1986), 397–99.

[42] Thomas Skidmore, *Black into White: Race and Nationality in Brazilian Thought* (New York: Oxford University Press, 1974), 48–64.

[43] Dain Borges, "'Puffy, Ugly, Slothful and Inert': Degeneration in Brazilian Social Thought, 1880-1940," *Journal of Latin American Studies* 25:2 (1993): 235–56.

[44] Emília Viotti da Costa, *The Brazilian Empire: Myths and Histories* (Chicago: University of Chicago Press, 1985), 94; and João Klug, "Imigração no Sul do Brasil," in Keila Grinberg and Ricardo Salles, eds., *O Brasil imperial, vol. III—1870–1889* (Rio de Janeiro: Civilização Brasileira, 2009), 206–7, 217–19.

Confederate immigrants fleeing from the Civil War in the United States to São Paulo was the persistence of African slavery in Brazil.[45] Modern missiologists and Brazilian evangelicals, however, held theories of racial difference in suspicion. In contrast to the polygenists, who believed in innate distinctions between the human races, Protestant mission theorists insisted on the biblical narrative of the unity of mankind.[46] In Brazil, local ministers and foreign missionaries envisioned conversion and education as the main drivers of individual and social improvement, replacing the dictates of environmental and racial determinism with a loosely defined religious determinism. The most influential text that shaped conceptions of race among Brazilian evangelicals was a tract written by Émile de Laveleye, a Belgian Catholic economist, titled *The Future of Catholic Peoples*. Translated into Portuguese in 1875 by the Presbyterians in Rio de Janeiro, this tract popularized the idea that it was religious practice and worship that determined the progress of societies, not race. For Laveleye, religious confessions produced unequal social and behavioral impulses. Protestantism, with its work ethic and attachment to the written word, nourished positive attitudes toward education, trade, agriculture, and the arts, whereas the centralized and hierarchical structures of the Catholic Church collapsed into despotism and ignorance. Picking examples from Switzerland, Laveleye affirmed that the Latin cantons of Neuchâtel and Vaud developed at a faster rate than the German cantons of Lucerne and Valois: "the first are Latin, but Protestants; the latter are German, but subject to Rome. Worship and not race is, therefore, the cause of the first's superiority."[47] For the influential Brazilian theologian and writer Rubem Alves, the attachment of Brazilian Protestants to Laveleye's explanation of the decay of Catholic nations illustrated their difficulties in dealing with elaborate categories of social analysis and expressed their inclination to spiritualize structural problems.[48] Alves' explanation, however, misses the

---

[45] Cyrus Dawsey and James Dawsey, eds., *The Confederados: Old South Immigrants in Brazil* (Tuscaloosa: University of Alabama Press, 1995).

[46] Brian Stanley, "Christian Missions, Antislavery and the Claims of Humanity, c. 1813–1873," in Sheridan Gilley and Brian Stanley, eds., *The Cambridge History of Christianity: World Christianities, c. 1815–c. 1914* (New York: Cambridge University Press, 2006), 449–54.

[47] Émile de Laveleye, *Do futuro dos povos Catholicos: Estudo de economia social*, trans. Miguel Vieira Ferreira (Rio de Janeiro: Typographia Universal de E. & H. Laemmert, 1875), 9–10.

[48] Rubem Alves, *Protestantism and Repression: A Brazilian Case Study*, trans. John Drury (London: SCM Press, 1985), 163.

point. Although apparently unsophisticated, Laveleye's arguments had particular appeal and significance when racial theories were in vogue.

In the context of the Panama Congress of 1916, Brazilian Protestant ministers deployed Émile de Laveleye's thesis in different ways and redefined the concept of race. At least since the mid-nineteenth century, when Latin American nations were still in their infancy, writers and politicians were suspicious of the economic and military expansion of the United States in the continent, fearing that their hard-won independence from European powers could give way to new forms of external control over their nations. This diplomatic and commercial wariness was often interpreted along the lines of racial divides, opposing the Anglo-Saxon and the Latin races of the Americas.[49] But Brazilian participants at Panama 1916 experienced it differently. For them, the congress was a friendly, amiable encounter of the dominant races of the Americas, whose representatives engaged in sincere friendship and dreamt about the union of the continent.[50] In other global evangelical missionary conferences throughout the twentieth century, participants also described how on such occasions Christian fellowship displaced racial divisions and encouraged them to reimagine their belonging to the "Universal Church."[51] In the case of the Panama Congress, the Great War in Europe exacerbated such sentiments, which not only challenged the image of Europe as an embodiment of Christian civilization,[52] but also activated the enthusiasm of Protestants in the Americas with the future of their own continent. Brazilian participants at the congress compared the "fratricidal war" in Europe to the fraternal encounter of the Anglo-Saxon and the Latin peoples in Panama City.[53]

[49]   Mauricio Tenorio-Trillo, *Latin America: The Allure and Power of an Idea* (Chicago: University of Chicago Press, 2017); and Michel Gobat, "The Invention of Latin America: A Transnational History of Anti-imperialism, Democracy, and Race," *American Historical Review* 118:5 (2013): 1345–75.

[50]   Braga, *Pan-Americanismo*, 50, 62, 87–88, 92–94, 181–82; and Pereira, *O problema*, 144–45, 175.

[51]   That was the impression Zimbabwean Methodist leader Thomson Samkange had of the Tambaram Conference in India, 1928: Terence Ranger, *Are We Not Also Men? The Samkange Family & African Politics in Zimbabwe, 1920–64* (Harare: Baobab, 1995), 70–74.

[52]   Brian Stanley, *Christianity in the Twentieth Century: A World History* (Princeton, N.J.: Princeton University Press, 2018), 17.

[53]   Pedro Feitoza, "Protestants and the Public Sphere in Brazil, c. 1870-c. 1930" (PhD diss., University of Cambridge, 2019), 178–80.

The Brazilian delegates at Panama 1916, examining the significance of the event for the religious and social life of Latin America, modified the concept of race without eschewing it altogether. Erasmo Braga, for instance, asserted that in order to depict an accurate portrait of the social features of American societies, analysts should concentrate on the spiritual and intellectual elements that formed the races of the Americas, instead of focusing on ethnic factors. In his argument, distinct historical and religious trajectories determined the unequal development of the Anglo-Saxon and Latin races in the continent, and he made reference to "Laveleye's law" when claiming that civil liberty and social progress prevailed in places where evangelical Christianity made greater inroads.[54] The elements that differentiated the Anglo-Saxon from the Latin peoples in Europe and the Americas, then, were their history and religion: the former founded religious communities of dissidents centered on the principles of the free examination of the Scriptures and religious liberty; the latter repressed their compatriots with the bonfires of the Inquisition and a centralized religious and political structure.[55] Even though Braga's description of the significance of Panama 1916 reinforced some origin myths that circulated in the American continent at that time, he did not naturalize racial difference, claiming that it was not a fruit of biological determinism, but of history.

Eduardo Carlos Pereira, on the other hand, propounded a broader, provocative interpretation of Christian universalism that redefined the concept of race in his long work of religious controversy titled *The Religious Problem of Latin America* of 1920, partly based on his experience at the Panama Congress. Like Braga, Pereira too claimed that Émile de Laveleye's explanation for the decadence of Latin peoples was validated by the scientific method.[56] He too praised the universal fraternity fostered at the congress. But he affirmed explicitly that the concept of race was "anthropologically uncertain and historically confused," and rejected the cephalic index, widely used by physical anthropologists and craniologists to measure "racial degeneration," as a valid tool for the assessment of racial differences.[57] For Pereira, the "monogenism of

[54] Braga, *Pan-Americanismo*, 3–8, 48–50.
[55] Braga, *Pan-Americanismo*, 5–8.
[56] Pereira, *O problema*, 119–24.
[57] On the uses of craniology in Brazil, see Schwarcz, *Spectacle*, 260–62; and Robert Levine, *Vale of Tears: Revisiting the Canudos Massacre in Northeastern Brazil, 1893–1897* (Berkeley: University of California Press, 1992), 207–8.

the human species," the belief that all races had a common origin, had been firmly determined in the domains of science by recent findings. In his arguments, Charles Darwin's evolutionary theory had proved that mankind derived from a common biological origin, and in the modern world no one could oppose the idea "that all human races were conceived as varieties of one only primitive family, headed by the biblical patriarch." After Darwin,

> the polygenism of the human species must have entered into a coma, and contemporary science, hand in hand with Christian religion, proclaimed the fraternity of all races, the original equality of all branches of the human family. . . . In fact, there is no absolute physiological and psychological distinction between the various ethnic groupings that we call races. In the individuals of all of them there are the same organs and functions, the same moral and intellectual faculties, the same thoughts and essential sentiments."[58]

Pereira brought together the traditional evangelical emphasis on the authority of the Bible with the scientific confidence characteristic of his era to challenge prevailing racial theories. Merging evolutionary science into evangelical conceptions of Christian universalism was not unusual at that time. Protestant missionaries in the Pacific also embraced certain elements of Darwinian science to produce a "theological anthropology" that stressed human universality.[59] Furthermore, although such appropriations of scientific discourse may sound eccentric, Pereira regarded himself as an orthodox evangelical who believed in the supreme authority of the Bible and in the universal priesthood of believers, and who was an enthusiast for the operations of mission and Bible societies. Like Braga, Pereira did not obliterate racial differences. Instead, he affirmed that specific behavioral traces distinguished the human races. In his classification, Anglo-Saxons were individualistic and pragmatic, a people who sacrificed aesthetics in favor of comfort, and possessed analytical aptitudes. Latin peoples, on the other hand, were collectivist, sympathetic, and communicative, preferring synthesis and generalizations over the particularity of facts.[60]

---

[58] Pereira, *O problema*, 147–49.
[59] Jane Samson, *Race and Redemption: British Missionaries Encounter Pacific Peoples, 1797–1920* (Grand Rapids: Eerdmans, 2017).
[60] Pereira, *O problema*, 149–53.

It was also during the Panama Congress that Brazilian evangelicals came into direct contact with the social gospel.[61] In fact, foreign missionaries and Brazilian ministers had started to mobilize around public issues and social causes such as educational reform and the abolition of slavery since the last decades of the nineteenth century.[62] But their embrace of the social gospel as a self-conscious doctrine came in 1916, when the Methodist American Bishop Francis McConnell gave an address at the congress titled *Christian Faith in an Age of Doubt*. For McConnell, one of the leading exponents of the social gospel in the United States, the struggles between faith and science that characterized the religious experience of the nineteenth century had given way to reconciliation and cooperation in his age. This reciprocal relationship between the Christian and the scientific spirits had potential to alleviate the anxieties of mankind in an era of wars and industrialization, overcoming the forces of poverty and hunger and affirming the supremacy of human values in the world.[63] McConnell's address exerted a profound impact on Eduardo C. Pereira and Erasmo Braga, as both of them cited and meditated upon the speech at some length in their books. Pereira, for instance, stressed that the reciprocity between religion and science could, besides solving "the urgent problems of health and pauperism," reconcile evangelical Christianity with the Brazilian intelligentsia, which he described as swayed by the winds of incredulity and agnosticism.[64]

But it was Erasmo Braga who became the key advocate of the principles of the social gospel in Brazil. He, too, called attention to McConnell's address at the Panama Congress and summarized the lecture in his report of the conference.[65] But whereas Eduardo Pereira's appreciation of McConnell's speech was inserted in a major work of religious controversy that was highly critical of Catholicism and attributed many of the country's

[61] This was also true for other parts of Latin America: José Míguez Bonino, *Rostros del Protestantismo Latinoamericano* (Buenos Aires: Nueva Creacíon, 1995), 26–27; and Carlos Mondragón, *Like Leaven in the Dough*, chap. 3.

[62] José Carlos Barbosa, *Slavery and Protestant Missions in Imperial Brazil*, trans. F. MacHaffie and R. Danford (Lanham, Md.: University Press of America, 2008); and Fernando de Azevedo, *A cultura Brasileira: Introdução ao estudo da cultura no Brasil*, tomo terceiro, 3rd ed. (São Paulo: Edições Melhoramentos, 1958 [1943]), 127–29, 140.

[63] *Christian Work in Latin America*, vol. 3 (New York: Missionary Education Movement, 1917), 297–304.

[64] Pereira, *O problema*, 168–71.

[65] Braga, *Pan-Americanismo*, 99–100.

social ills to its influence on culture and education, Erasmo Braga's critique of the Catholic Church was milder. Braga was a second-generation evangelical who thus did not experience religious change in terms of a strong rupture with his pre-convert cultural and social worlds. In missionary fields, it was common for the second and third generation of believers to reconcile with some elements of their parents' former culture.[66] In Braga's arguments, it was the social ills of the country that demanded the intensification of evangelical missionary efforts in Brazil, not simply the widespread influence of Catholicism. And these social problems included the high rates of illiteracy; outbreaks of diseases such as syphilis, tuberculosis, and malaria; popular addiction to *cachaça*, a sort of white rum; lack of basic sanitation in cities; and the effects of rapid industrialization.[67] The consequences of the dissemination of evangelical Christianity in Brazil could be best noticed in their impact upon the refashioning of individual behavior and subjectivities, not numerical growth. In a remarkable passage of his report of the Panama Congress, Braga claimed that it was in the domestic intimacy of rural and urban families, in which the "vivifying energy of the Gospel" penetrated and produced "great spiritual struggles," that observers could see how processes of religious change became embodied in fairer work relations, fostered sexual hygiene among the youth, and led converts into electoral honesty.[68]

During a conference on comparative religions organized by the Spiritualist Crusade in Rio de Janeiro in 1928, Erasmo Braga best showed his commitment to the social gospel, weaving some of its principles into the modern missionary emphasis on cross-denominational cooperation. In his long address, Braga compared the contemporary movement toward evangelical cooperation to the Reformation in the sixteenth century. Both had been animated by an impulse of "reversion to primitive Christianity." And as the best sources of this move were the life and deeds of Jesus Christ registered in the Gospels, evangelical Christians became "propagandists of the book," agents of literacy, and enthusiasts

---

[66] On the importance of tracing religious change across generational lines, see David Maxwell, "Continuity and Change in the Luba Christian Movement, Katanga, Belgian Congo, c. 1915–50," *Journal of Ecclesiastical History* 69:2 (2018): 326–44.

[67] Erasmo Braga and Kenneth G. Grubb, *The Republic of Brazil: A Survey of the Religious Situation* (London: World Dominion, 1932), 8–10, 14, 27; Braga, *Pan-Americanismo*, 106.

[68] Braga, *Pan-Americanismo*, 52–54.

of universal education.[69] Braga also explained the meaning of Protestant individualism to the critics of evangelical Christianity as a process of self-discovery and moral liberation, by which men and women reconciled their consciousness with God. This process produced "incoercible" individuals, who did not negotiate a single line of their renewed conscience under the pressures of their moral surroundings. And such individualism projected itself into social life, as evangelical Christians expressed their unease with present-day iniquities. In the address, Braga enumerated a set of social problems that haunted the modern world, including the industrialization of human relations, class and racial conflicts over the world, distance between capital and labor, secret diplomacy, the strong nationalisms of the interwar era, and pornography. Only a united body of committed Christians, he claimed, could overcome the factional divisions created since the Reformation, coordinate their efforts, and Christianize the social order.[70] And here he acknowledged his intellectual debts to Tommy Fallot, Francis McConnell, and Walter Rauschenbusch, precursors and exponents of the social gospel. Braga began to embrace the social gospel in the 1910s and 1920s, at the same time when public authorities and independent associations launched anti-alcohol and sanitation campaigns in Brazil.[71] In some writings, Braga expressed his enthusiasm for such campaigns, representing advances in public health and temperance as signs of the expansion of the kingdom of God on earth.[72] Evangelical concerns with hygiene and sobriety, then, were by no means a mere expression of evangelical conservatism in this period, as some have argued.[73] Instead, they merged together international theological discourses, evangelical notions of individual respectability and self-reliance, and local secular concerns.

---

[69] Erasmo Braga, *Religião e cultura* (São Paulo: União Cultural Editora, n.d.), 70–72. The same address was published in Gustavo Macedo, ed., *Religiões comparadas* (Rio de Janeiro: Roland Rohe & Cia, 1929).

[70] Braga, *Religião e cultura*, 93–98.

[71] Skidmore, *Black*, 179–84; and Nicolau Sevcenko, *Orfeu extático na Metrópole: São Paulo, sociedade e cultura nos frementes anos 20* (São Paulo: Companhia das Letras, 1992), 84–85.

[72] Braga and Grubb, *Republic*, 8–9, 27–29; and Braga, *Pan-Americanismo*, 150–54.

[73] Pierson, *Younger Church*, 94–104; Alves, *Protestantism*, chap. 6.

Conclusion

This chapter has shown how Brazilian evangelical ministers and writers built upon a vast repertoire of theological, philosophical, and scientific ideas to forge their own interpretations of national history, racial difference, and social change. Instead of isolating themselves into the closely guarded boundaries of theological dogmatism, the protagonists of the previous pages actively took part in the historical and ideological discourses of their age, engaging with the public debates of the day from their own religious perspectives. In recovering the history of the French colony founded in sixteenth-century Rio de Janeiro, Brazilian Protestants situated their country in the transnational networks of the Protestant Reformation, inscribing evangelical Christianity deep into the Brazilian past. In the first decades of the twentieth century, they claimed that the designs of divine providence enabled that distant historical echo to resonate soundly in contemporary Brazil through the evangelistic efforts of churches and congregations, which produced their own patriotic citizens faithful to the laws of the republic. At roughly the same time, ministers and scholars such as Erasmo Braga and Eduardo Carlos Pereira resorted to a variety of theological and philosophical concepts to modify the idea of race and eschew key principles of scientific racism. They also appropriated the concerns of the social gospel and channeled them into the sweeping transformations of Brazilian society in the interwar era. In the light of this, it may be useful to situate the rise of public theologies in Brazil and Latin America in a longer historical lineage, punctuated by continuities and ruptures, that does not start in the post-World War II era, but can be traced back at least to the early twentieth century. Brazilian evangelicals mediated between multiple theological and cultural frameworks, integrating them by means of a creative process of intellectual production.

7

Indigenization and Believers' Accounts of Pentecostal Faith in Chile, 1910–1920

Joseph Florez

> In one of the meetings, two little girls were ecstatic. They saw our Savior surrounded by angels; the most wonderful thing was that they both had the same vision at the same moment. Glory to God! He is manifesting Himself to us so that we prepare to go out to meet him.
>
> Inocencio Gómez[1]

Testimonies like the one above began circulating in Chile's evangelical newsletters as early as September 1909. As revivalists recounted their experiences in the pages of the movement's weekly newspapers, *Chile Evangélico* and later *Chile Pentecostal*, Pentecostalism spread on a wave of enthusiastic reports of charismatic practices. Willis C. Hoover (1858–1936), an American Methodist preacher originally from Freeport, Illinois, recalled that the great revival began with "laughter, weeping, shouts, singing, strange tongues, visions, ecstasies in which people fell to the floor and felt themselves transported to other places."[2] Seized by the Holy Spirit, believers described speaking with the Lord, with angels, or

---

[1] Inocencio Gómez, "Gorbea," *Chile Evangélico*, December 17, 1909.
[2] Willis C. Hoover, *The History of the Pentecostal Revival in Chile*, trans. Mario G. Hoover (Santiago: Imprenta Eben-Ezer, 2000), 33.

with the devil.[3] During the movement's earliest decades, the press, both secular and sacred, was essential in disseminating and documenting these stories, making it instrumental in Pentecostalism's early formation and growth in Chile. And while the testimonies and descriptions of faith and practice that appeared in those pages have seldom been investigated, they present scholars with a unique lens through which to view the character of belief among the movement's earliest adherents and shed light on their understanding of the doctrinal and cultural issues that were shaping Pentecostalism more broadly.

While scholars have discussed the impact of Pentecostalism in Latin America at great length, they have painted a far more disjointed picture of the early spread of the movement and its relation to local cultures. Many argue that Pentecostalism consistently reproduces its doctrines and canons, structures, and rituals wherever it takes root.[4] Simply put, Pentecostalism looks surprisingly similar in different social, political, and economic contexts. Other observers, however, conclude that the growth of Pentecostalism over the last century owes no small part of its success to its ability to fragment and rearticulate itself according to the local cultures and customs of the people who join it—a process of indigenization and contextualization.[5] To be sure, the emergence of an aggressively expansionist

---

[3]   F. Jorquera R., "Ven y ve," *Chile Evangélico*, October 29, 1909. Juan Rodriguez Ortiz presents a rich depiction of the diversity of the early movement through graphic and written sources in his work *Chile Evangélico, 1909–1910: Testimonio gráfico del origen del Movimiento Pentecostal Chileno*, 2nd ed. (Santiago: Parousia Editorial, 2015).

[4]   See Christian Lalive d'Epinay, *Haven of the Masses: A Study of the Pentecostal Movement in Chile*, trans. Marjorie Sandle (London: Lutterworth, 1969); and David Lehmann, *Struggle for the Spirit: Religious Transformations of Popular Culture in Brazil and Latin America* (Cambridge: Polity, 1996). Discussions about Pentecostalism's impact on Latin American society and politics began in the 1960s with the publication of Lalive d'Epinay's *Haven of the Masses* and Emilio Willems' *Followers of the New Faith: Culture Change and the Rise of Protestantism in Brazil and Chile* (1967) and continue today. Other studies include those by Jean-Pierre Bastian, *Los disidentes: Sociedades protestantes y revolución en México* (México City: Fondo de Cultura Económica, 1989); David Stoll, *Is Latin America Turning Protestant? The Politics of Evangelical Growth* (Berkeley: University of California Press, 1990); and David Martin, *Tongues of Fire: The Explosion of Protestantism in Latin America* (Oxford: Basil Blackwell, 1990).

[5]   See, for example: Juan Sepúlveda, "Indigenous Pentecostalism and the Chilean Experience," in Allan Anderson and Walter Hollenweger, eds., *Pentecostals after a Century: Global Perspectives on a Movement in Transition* (Sheffield: Sheffield Academic Press, 1999); José Míguez Bonino, *Faces of Latin American Protestantism: 1993 Carnahan Lectures*, trans. Eugene Stockwell (Grand Rapids: Eerdmans, 1997);

religious movement in what was a heavily entrenched Catholic society in the midst of great social, political, and economic transformation is a problem to be explained, but not an inevitable process to be traced from the first planting of revivalism on Latin American shores to its flowering decades later. This chapter suggests that the nature of that transformation can be more fruitfully explored through the experiences and narratives of converts recounted in the pages of early Chilean Pentecostal periodicals and circulars.

Given the impact and reach of the Azusa Street Revival (1906–1909) on the global spread of the movement, our usual perspective on early Pentecostalism in Chile faces inward: religious fervor flowed from the United States and Europe across the oceans, finding their way to Latin America, and eventually to Chile. Frameworks of "conversion" and "mission" dominate notions of the spread of the movement rather than ideas like "indigenization" and "revival." Essentially, the "master narrative" of early Pentecostalism in Chile remains import-focused. While Chileans made contributions to Pentecostal culture and assumed leadership of the movement, they are often portrayed as supporting actors in the world's fastest growing religious transformation in the last century. But if we shift our perspective to try to view the spread of Pentecostalism in a way that faces outward from local religious experiences, revivalism may take on a very different appearance. Native believers become the drivers of change, and Pentecostalism enters from distant lands. Autochthonous religious practices are now the primary interlocuters and Pentecostalism the background noise. Chile, the country at the heart of this study, becomes the site of religious reconfiguration, connected to, but also distinct from, the global spread of a new religious movement. Local epistemologies and contexts rather than broad understandings of faith formulated across the world move to the forefront of historical inquiry.[6]

This chapter addresses ongoing discussions about the character of Pentecostals' belief and worship during the movement's first years in Chile. First, it lays out the hotly debated concept of "indigenization" and its implications for studying Pentecostalism's origins in the country. Second, it attempts to approach the study of early believers' interpretation

---

and Jean-Pierre Bastian, "Metamorphosis of Latin American Protestant Groups: A Sociohistorical Perspective," *Latin American Research Review* 28:2 (1993): 33–61.

[6] Daniel Richter proposes a similar approach in his influential study of Indigenous history in North America. See Daniel K. Richter, *Facing East from Indian Country: A Native History of Early America* (Cambridge, Mass.: Harvard University Press, 2001).

and transformation of their faith through the accounts they published in Pentecostal periodicals including *Chile Pentecostal* and *Chile Evangélico* between 1910 and 1920. I aim to show that the pneumatological vision of Chile's first Pentecostals demonstrated that the methods and styles of worship were not centered on attempts to understand an imported religious worldview, but rather, on continuous efforts to shape that worldview in terms of local ways of knowing and expression. Believers' own accounts reveal a patchwork narrative of Pentecostal belief that oscillated between resisting and accepting the logics of both traditional religious structures and revivalistic impulses.

The Origins of Pentecostalism in Chile

It is generally considered that the famous revival of Azusa Street in 1906 is the cradle of modern Pentecostalism. But scholarly accounts of Pentecostalism's early growth in Chile suggest its emergence hinged just as much on a search for a new mystical experience rooted in local concerns as it did on the wider religious currents that were sweeping the globe. Perhaps the most important founding figure in the history of Chilean Pentecostalism was actually the North American Methodist pastor Willis Collins Hoover. He graduated as a doctor from a university in Chicago in 1884, but after five years gave up medicine and applied to William Taylor's self-supporting Methodist mission in Chile.[7] From 1889 to 1902 he lived in northern Chile, serving as a teacher and later a pastor, eventually forming two congregations outside the city of Iquique.[8] During a trip to the United States in 1895, he visited a "pre-Pentecostal" congregation in Chicago and was impressed by the "constant state of revival" in which that church

---

[7]   Sepúlveda, "Indigenous Pentecostalism," 113. Under the direction of American missionary William Taylor, the first Methodist church in Chile was founded in 1878 and soon turned out to have some appeal among the masses. Although Taylor began his ministry in Baltimore, Maryland, where he was highly influenced by the Holiness Movement, his career spanned continents. He was instrumental in establishing churches in India, Mozambique, the Democratic Republic of Congo, and Peru. In Chile, Taylor advanced a program of self-supporting missions whereby missionaries earned their living from working in Methodist schools rather than receiving salaries from the missionary board in the United States. On the life and work of William Taylor see Goodsil F. Arms, *History of the William Taylor Self-Supporting Missions in South America* (New York: Methodist Book Concern, 1921); and William Taylor, *Ten Years of Self-Supporting Missions in India* (New York: Phillips & Hunt, 1882).

[8]   J. B. A. Kessler, *A Study of the Older Protestant Missions and Churches in Peru and Chile* (Goes: Oosterbaan & Le Cointre, 1967), 101, 108.

was living. In 1902, Hoover was transferred to the Methodist Episcopal Church of Valparaíso where he soon formed the impression that the congregants had only vague ideas of the meaning of sanctification. With this in mind, Hoover conducted a series of studies on the Acts of the Apostles in Sunday school with the aim of "becoming like the early Church." According to Hoover, members were "taken by an intense spirit of prayer" and "had such a manifestation of Spirit that cries were heard from afar."[9] These experiences laid the foundation for the rise of a genuine search for a new type of religious experience in Chile.

The Pentecostal movement has been expansionist from the very beginning. Ideas of global spiritual conquest were driven by an eschatological vision that all of the world's inhabitants must be converted before Christ's return. This led hundreds of Pentecostal missionaries to set out from North America and Western Europe within the first years of the phenomenon, reaching as many as forty different nations within its first decade of existence.[10] But the movement also moved across less formal pathways including local contacts, personal correspondence, and pamphlets. Both were true in the case of Chile. In 1907 Mary Ann Hoover (Willis' wife) received a copy of Minnie Abrams' booklet *The Baptism of the Holy Ghost and Fire*. Abrams, who had studied with Mrs. Hoover in the United States, described a Christian revival in Mukti, India, where people had been baptized by the Holy Spirit, spoken in other tongues, fallen to the floor, and had various visions. After this the Hoovers began corresponding with other religious leaders in India, Venezuela, and Norway, which had all documented similar experiences. In Hoover's own words "a hunger was awakened in us for possessing all that which God had stored for us."[11]

With Hoover's support, lay members of the congregation in Valparaíso began daily prayer groups and all-night watch services every Saturday to improve their spiritual wellbeing. The charismatic meetings that often spilled out into the streets quickly attracted the derision of Methodist and secular leaders alike. Denunciations circulated in Chile's most prominent newspapers, describing the revivalists as "fanatics" engaged in "acts of fanatical exaltation" where they "pretend to have visions, healing, and

---

[9]   Hoover, *Pentecostal Revival in Chile*, 4–5.

[10]   Allan Anderson, *To the Ends of the Earth: Pentecostalism and the Transformation of World Christianity* (Oxford: Oxford University Press, 2013), 61–63.

[11]   Hoover, *Pentecostal Revival in Chile*, 28.

everything that is usual in mental infirmities."[12] It was also claimed that Pentecostals participated in strange rituals that involved sheep blood, trances, demonic expulsion, apparitions, and other delirious acts. One unnamed observer in an article in *El Mercurio* (Chile's oldest periodical) opined: "The authority would do well to intervene and put an end to these scandals . . . To prevent the exploitation of poor people and aggravation of the illness of a few hysterics."[13]

Authorities of the Methodist Church responded with equal disdain. The charismatic displays of devotion expressed by revivalists were considered contrary to the Scriptures, irrational, and anti-Methodist. Following a particularly tense episode in the Second Methodist Church in Santiago in September 1909, where a young revivalist woman, Nellie Laidlaw, known for her gift of prophecy, was not given permission from the pastor to speak to the congregation, lay members decided to hold separate services in private homes.[14] While Hoover counseled disgruntled members to wait to present their case at the next annual Methodist Conference to be held in February 1910, church officials decided to sever all relations with the people who had withdrawn and continued to hold separate meetings in "scandalous opposition."[15] At the annual conference the next year, a disciplinary commission leveled complaints against Hoover of "teaching and publicly and privately disseminating false and anti-Methodist doctrines." To ease the denunciation, the conference agreed to withdraw the charges against him if he would return to his home country, to which he agreed. A separate resolution was passed, however, that declared that the baptism of the Holy Spirit through the gift of tongues, visions, healings, or other manifestations was contrary to the doctrines of the Scriptures and the Methodist Church.

The two groups in Santiago, which had been virtually excommunicated, understood that the conference's resolution was a denunciation of the revival movement as a whole. Unsurprisingly, their reaction was to orga-

[12] "Fanatismo enfermizo," *El Mercurio*, Santiago, Chile, November 3, 1909.

[13] "Fanatismo enfermizo."

[14] As Juan Sepúlveda points out, this episode is generally regarded as the start of Pentecostalism in Chile as it is the first occasion that members of the First and Second Methodist Churches in Santiago held independent services. Nellie Laidlaw is described in Juan Kessler's work, *A Study of the Older Protestant Missions and Churches in Peru and Chile*, as a recent convert with a history of drunkenness, drug use, and prostitution (117–21).

[15] Sepúlveda, "Indigenous Pentecostalism," 117; and Kessler, *Study of the Older Protestant Missions*, 122.

nize themselves as a separate church with the name of the *Iglesia Metodista Nacional* (National Methodist Church). The Valparaíso congregation soon followed suit. Motivated by the actions of his congregants, Hoover resigned from the mission. In his letter, which was read out in front of his congregation, he made clear he was not separating himself from the doctrines of John Wesley or the Methodist Church, "but from the Church's government, by reason of conscience." Soon after, the groups in Santiago invited him to act as their superintendent. He agreed but suggested the name of the new church should be *Iglesia Metodista Pentecostal* ([IMP] Pentecostal Methodist Church) to emphasize that the schism was not the result of nationalistic tendencies.

The timing and unfolding of the events in Valparaíso and Santiago have led Chilean scholars like Juan Sepúlveda and Luis Orellana to argue that the revival occurred independently of Azusa Street.[16] In particular, Sepúlveda suggests that the implications of that timing carry important theological distinctions for the movement in Chile. So much was that so, in fact, that Valparaíso must be recognized as the source of an alternative vision and expression of Pentecostal identity—one that was not completely detached from its roots within the Wesleyan-Holiness movement or the Methodist Church. Specifically, Sepúlveda questions the influence of Charles Parham's doctrine of speaking in tongues as the initial evidence of the Holy Spirit in the Chilean revival. "Strange tongues," he argues, constituted but one among many manifestations of the Holy Spirit and were not given any priority (above the others) in Hoover's account of the revival. In an article published in 1928 to defend the movement from its local detractors, Hoover described the differences between Pentecostals and other traditions as follows:

> What distinguishes the Pentecostals from other denominations—and at the same time startles and offends some strangers who attend the services—is that fact that the Spirit of God is manifested among them, according to the promise of the Word of God. The manner of the manifestation neither is sought by the person who receive[s] it, nor by the one who leads the service. Some services pass with no manifestation;

[16] Juan Sepúlveda, "The Power of the Spirit and the Indigenization of the Church: A Latin American Perspective" in Néstor Medina and Sammy Alfaro, eds., *Pentecostals and Charismatics in Latin America and Latino Communities* (New York: Palgrave Macmillan, 2015), 17–25; and Luis Orellana, *El fuego y la nieve: Historia del movimiento pentecostal en Chile: 1909–1932* (Concepción: Centro Evangélico de Estudios Pentecostales, 2006).

some persons don't ever experience them, or if they do, it happens only rarely. Sometimes there is laughter, there is crying, there is shouting, there is dancing. But these things come something like that "rushing mighty wind" on the Day of Pentecost.[17]

Analyzing the quotation above, Sepúlveda notes that Hoover does not specifically mention tongues or other charismatic practices that were often associated with Azusa Street. Instead, he speaks of manifestations—being Pentecostal meant allowing the Holy Spirit the freedom to work without any preconceptions of how it would do so, or whether such manifestations are voluble, expressive, or even perceptible. It was people's openness to the gifts of the Spirit that allowed them to be touched by God's transforming power to become new persons and Christ's witnesses. The pneumatological understanding of the revival in Chile, then, was not defined by a complete break with the Wesleyan Holiness movement, but rather, to use Sepúlveda's own words, "a widening of this tradition to encompass an emphasis upon the experience of the transforming power of the Holy Spirit, but in keeping with the Wesleyan tradition refused to promote any or all such manifestations as the single evidence of baptism of the Holy Spirit."[18] Hoover emphasized the restoration of the signs and wonders that accompanied the outpouring of the Holy Spirit in apostolic times but, following the Wesleyan tradition, he rejected the notion that proof of the presence of the Holy Spirit could only be found in such charismatic displays. It is here that Sepúlveda locates the indigenization of early Chilean Pentecostalism.

Without underestimating the impact of Hoover's particular conception of Pentecostal pneumatology on the movement in Chile, it is clear that his shadow looms large over scholarly work that attempts to document the contours of the early believers' understanding of their new faith. Despite ample evidence of patterns of charismatic worship and unscripted, egalitarian experiences of the Spirit documented in Hoover's accounts, we actually know very little about how new converts and lay believers experienced the movement or understood the revival more

---

[17] Hoover, *Pentecostal Revival in Chile*, 167.
[18] Sepúlveda, "Power of the Spirit," 24. Sepúlveda responds to Cecil Robeck's claim that the Valparaíso revival was influenced (albeit indirectly) by the Azusa Street Revival. See Cecil Robeck, "Pentecostal Origins from a Global Perspective," in Harold Hunter and Peter Hocken, eds., *All Together in One Place: Theological Papers from the Brighton Conference on World Evangelicalism* (Sheffield: Sheffield Academic Press, 1993), 168–82.

generally. Furthermore, it is difficult to get a firm grasp on the relative importance they placed on the particular experience of Spirit baptism. The historical record has barely touched on believers' own discernment of spiritual forces and the meaning they placed on certain manifestations. With few exceptions, past arguments have drawn their evidence from the leaders of Chile's earliest Pentecostal churches, principally Willis Hoover himself.[19] However, the driving questions behind this chapter—namely, what might revival look like when viewed from the inside out, and how can we understand the forces of "indigenization" that shaped the movement—require us to consider the perspective of the believers themselves.

Indigenization

The concept of "indigenization" has generated a considerable amount of scholarly debate. The term was first used by the Assemblies of God missiologist Melvin Hodges in his widely influential book *The Indigenous Church* (1953). His work emphasized creating "indigenous churches" and stressed church planting as a fundamental principle of Pentecostal mission strategy. Hodges claimed that the aim of all mission activity was to build indigenous churches.[20] He also stressed that the foundation for indigenization was the Holy Spirit.

> There is no place on earth where, if the gospel seed be properly planted, it will not produce an indigenous church. The Holy Spirit can work in one country as well as in another. To proceed on the assumption that the infant church in any land must always be cared for and provided for by the mother mission is an unconscious insult to the people that we endeavour to serve, and is evidence of a lack of faith in God and in the power of the gospel.[21]

For Hodges, the reason for the movement's continued growth was the "personal infilling of the Holy Spirit" that "produces believers and workers with unusual zeal and power" capable of expanding indigenous churches all over the world.[22] Yet, as Allan Anderson points out, Hodges was still a product of his own context, seeing "missions" as originating in developed

[19]   One notable exception is Orellana's *El fuego y la nieve*.
[20]   Melvin L. Hodges, *The Indigenous Church* (Springfield, Mo.: Gospel Publishing House, 1953), 10–11.
[21]   Hodges, *Indigenous Church*, 14.
[22]   Hodges, *Indigenous Church*, 132.

nations slowly moving to the rest of the world.[23] Indigenization, then, only signified the transference of governance to native converts. Led by the Holy Spirit, local congregations were to become self-supporting and self-propagating, but the heart of Pentecostal ministry, under the tutelage of Western missionaries, would remain the same. This view of Pentecostalism's growth in Latin America is also reflected in studies of the movement's relationship with local cultures.

David Lehmann, for example, claims that Pentecostal churches are "notoriously uniform across the globe" and that they display a "radical similarity of practice" despite the great "dissimilarity" of the local cultures in which they grow.[24] If viewed from this perspective, the nature of early Chilean believers' understanding of the movement would hinge on implicit assumptions about the way Pentecostalism engaged local ontologies. To begin, it suggests that the Pentecostal message remained the same, although its guidance and application were placed in the hands of local believers. Any change in Pentecostalism that occurred was simply the result of the shift of administration of churches to local peoples. As a concept, indigenization then becomes a broad placeholder for missiological reflection based on church planting and expansion. It also assumes that Latin American Pentecostalism in general, and the experiences of early Chilean Pentecostals in particular, can be adequately described solely through the framework of global Pentecostalism. Other scholars, mostly from Latin America, have found such analyses lacking. They focus on Pentecostalism's ability to reorient itself according to different cultures. These works usually highlight converts' indigenization of the movement's worship styles, canons, and rituals as evidence of Pentecostalism's ability to transform itself to local meanings and cultural contexts. Douglas Peterson, for example, asserts that "the role of North American churches and their missionaries can best be described as catalytic, providing mod-

[23] Allan Anderson, "Toward a Pentecostal Missiology for the Majority World" (lecture, International Symposium on Pentecostal Missiology, Asia-Pacific Theological Seminary, Baguio City, Philippines, January 29, 2003).

[24] David Lehmann, "Review of David Martin, *Pentecostalism: The World Their Parish*," *Journal of Religion in Africa* 33:1 (2003): 120–22, quoted in Joel Robbins, "The Globalization of Pentecostal Charismatic Christianity," *Annual Review of Anthropology* 33 (2004): 118. See also Lalive d'Epinay, *Haven of the Masses*; Simon Coleman, *The Globalisation of Charismatic Christianity: Spreading the Gospel of Prosperity* (Cambridge: Cambridge University Press, 2000); and David Lehmann, *Struggle for the Spirit: Religious Transformation and Popular Culture in Brazil and Latin America* (Oxford: Polity, 1996).

els which Latin American Pentecostals adapted to their own situations."[25] According to these scholars, Pentecostalism in Latin America was shaped and influenced by local concerns from the outset. What this suggests, I believe, is that Pentecostalism indigenizes itself not by fitting into local cultures through some sort of transformation of its guiding principles, but by allowing local worldviews and the challenges represented therein to guide its implementation. While there existed great diversity of practice and worship among early believers, the movement's contours sprang from the indigenizing force of Pentecostalism.[26] As will become clear, early Chilean Pentecostal narratives support both sides of this debate, suggesting that the believers' own understandings of the movement reflect a paradoxically "radically antisyncretic" and "profoundly localized" worldview.[27]

The testimonies of early Chilean Pentecostals demonstrate a transformation that followed a path between, and often crossed, the two processes of indigenization and heterodoxy. What is needed, I believe, is a conception that views early Chilean Pentecostalism and its forms and expressions as the starting point for an authentic religious and social expression in the context of Latin America with a constant eye to the system of beliefs that guided the movement more broadly. Parham's emphasis on speaking in tongues as evidence of Spirit baptism, for example, was a dominant theological paradigm across the movement in Chile, but its practice and importance varied considerably among believers. The first converts in Chile demonstrated great diversity of thought and did not always conform to such narrow theological boundaries. In fact, at times they adopted a more expansive pneumatology. For this reason, early Pentecostalism in Chile should not be singularly defined by the ecstatic experience of Spirit baptism nor by the characteristics of local traditions. It was both. Many converts appeared to hold the initial evidence of glossolalia as the substance of their faith, while others considered Spirit baptism not as an end in and of itself. Their accounts describe instances when the line between these two interpretations was indiscernible. The diverse pneumatological focus of early Pentecostals in Chile suggests that they attempted to hold the doctrines and styles that dominated the global spread of the movement

[25] Douglas Peterson, *Not by Might, Nor by Power: A Pentecostal Theology of Social Concern in Latin America* (Oxford: Regnum, 1996), 5.
[26] Sepúlveda, "Power of the Spirit," 17. See also José Míguez Bonino, *Faces of Latin American Protestantism: 1993 Carnahan Lectures*, trans. Eugene Stockwell (Grand Rapids: Eerdmans, 1997).
[27] Robbins, "Globalization," 118.

in tandem with a translation (but not a rejection) of the Protestant faith and expressions of local culture.

Pentecostal Print Culture and Baptism of the Holy Spirit

Scholars of Pentecostalism have long recognized the importance of periodicals to the growth and spread of the movement. Historian Grant Wacker concludes that they "constituted by far the most important technique for sustaining national and world consciousness."[28] Circulars and newspapers depicted the dramatic growth of Pentecostalism during its critical first few years. The newly formed Pentecostal churches in Chile published periodicals with the intention to spread news of the revival throughout the country and the world. They believed that the revival marked the point of the return of Pentecost and the outpouring of spiritual gifts to God's people. They also served many critical purposes for the fledgling movement in Chile. They relayed news of the revival at home and abroad, served as a spiritual extension for those who could not physically attend meetings, and functioned as a medium of exchange among the small but growing community of believers. Most importantly, though, these weekly conveyors of an "imagined community" of Pentecostals, to use Benedict Anderson's ubiquitous expression, depicted the importance that new converts placed on the links between baptism of the Holy Spirit and evidence of the gifts bestowed on those who experienced it.[29] These narratives and recounted experiences provide a rich source for historical analysis. They give us a small glimpse of the importance believers placed on evidence of baptism of the Holy Spirit as it aligned with the framework of the Pentecostal movement around the world, or conversely, as certain practices were set aside in the search for a religious experience that was uniquely suited to the context of Chile.

Chile Evangélico remains one of the critical but underutilized sources for understanding the early years of the movement. Within its pages are hundreds of testimonies, sermons, letters, and reports from the revival

---

[28] Grant Wacker, *Heaven Below: Early Pentecostals and American Culture* (Cambridge, Mass.: Harvard University Press, 2001), 264. See also Allan Anderson, *An Introduction to Pentecostalism: Global Charismatic Christianity* (Cambridge: Cambridge University Press, 2013); and Edith Blumhofer, *Restoring the Faith: The Assemblies of God, Pentecostalism, and American Culture*, 2 vols. (Chicago: University of Illinois Press, 1993).

[29] Benedict Anderson, *Imagined Communities: Reflections on the Origins and Spread of Nationalism* (London: Verso, 2006).

across the globe. The periodical first appeared in September 1909 as the official voice of the *Iglesia Evangélica Presbiteriana* (Presbyterian Evangelical Church) in Concepción just as the revival was taking off in Santiago. During its first year the periodical was produced weekly under the direction of Pastor Tulio Rojas, and later by lay member Enrique Koppman, who owned the press.[30] When it was renamed *Chile Pentecostal* in November 1910, its circulation became quarterly.[31] The periodical was published in Concepción until 1915, when it was moved to Valparaíso and placed under the direct supervision of Hoover.[32] Although similar to other Pentecostal periodicals in content and format, *Chile Evangélico* adopted its own pattern in both physical layout and appearance. During its first year, the periodical was produced in a larger format with only four pages. After nearly forty editions, the size was reduced, but the length extended to sixteen pages.[33] The funding for the paper came from the sale of subscriptions and donations from members. By 1927 *Chile Pentecostal* circulated three thousand copies annually to over ninety congregations including groups in Argentina, Bolivia, and Peru.[34] Directly underneath the title of *Chile Evangélico*'s first several editions appeared their constant challenge: "Until we all reach unity in the faith and in the knowledge of the Son of God and become mature, attaining the whole measure of the fullness of Christ—Ephesians 4:13." The summons to spread the gospel perfectly encapsulated the theme of the paper throughout its run. In a very concrete sense, the movement's periodicals were an extension of the revival itself.

The content of *Chile Evangélico* and *Chile Pentecostal* remained remarkably consistent in the first years of the movement. Each issue included testimonies, missionary reports, letters, sermons, spiritual statements,

---

[30] Orellana, *El fuego y la nieve*, 37. In Concepción, a group of nearly forty members of the Presbyterian Church, like the groups in Santiago and Valparaíso, abandoned the Church after a crisis with North American missionaries to form an independent organization in January 1910. The separatist church was characterized by its desire to be self-sustainable and free of the presence of foreign missionaries. These revivalists published *Chile Evangélico*.

[31] The name was changed again in 1928 to *Fuego de Pentecostés*.

[32] Miguel Ángel Mansilla, *La cruz y la esperanza: La cultural del pentecostalismo chileno en la primera mitad del sigo XX* (Santiago: Editorial Universidad Bolivariana, 2009), 48.

[33] Ortiz, *Chile evangélico, 1909-1910*, 15-16. Unfortunately, the first seven editions of *Chile Evangélico* have not been located. A very special thanks is in order to Corporación SENDAS in Santiago, which has undertaken the laborious task of digitizing every remaining edition of both *Chile Evangélico* and *Chile Pentecostal*.

[34] Mansilla, *La cruz y la esperanza*, 48.

and theological musings. The longest entries were the testimonies. Published conversion stories and personal accounts frequently stressed Spirit baptism. As the cornerstone of the doctrine of the Pentecostal experience, it is not surprising that editors chose to highlight these accounts. Nearly every page of the paper contained a story of someone who had received the gifts of the Spirit. These descriptions signified that the gifts were not simply a singular event but also an intimate experience to be had by those who sought them out among the community of believers. While accounts of indigenization in the early movement have usually been told through the perspectives of leaders (like Willis), individual testimonies served as the cornerstone of the paper. These were the witnesses whose accounts fueled interest in the movement and offered affirmation of the leaders' declarations. Through the paper believers exchanged spiritual experiences and in doing so, revealed how lay members and everyday converts really understood the unfolding of Pentecostalism in the country.

Chilean Pentecostalism has deep roots in the "collective culture of the *bajo pueblo*" and no doubt found most of its congregants in the popular sectors. Historians Gabriel Salazar and Julio Pinto use the phrase to describe not only those individuals who were preoccupied with daily survival but also the "dense fabric of marginal networks . . . that churned against the dominant system."[35] Pentecostals not only spread their message along these expansive social networks, but used their shared experiences of social, economic, political, and religious marginality to add meaning and force to their discourse. Like their counterparts across the world, they championed the need to be born again, the belief in the embodied power of prayer, a focus on praise and worship, the democratic exercise of gifts of the Spirit, and the admiration of ritual spontaneity over hierarchical authority even as they reoriented that script to fit the particularities of their personal contexts. The power of the Pentecostal message resonated at the intersection of the hope for a radical personal change and the anxieties and pressures that dogged and shaped the lives of Chile's marginalized sectors. Their efforts were an attempt to realize the spiritual and physical possibilities in their own context. Two themes were dominant in the construction of early Chilean Pentecostals' religious conversion experience: poverty and Catholicism.

[35] Gabriel Salazar and Julio Pinto, *Historia contemporánea de Chile IV: Hombría y feminidad* (Santiago: LOM Ediciones, 2002), 42.

Throughout the periodicals, accounts express reception of the gifts of the Holy Spirit as providing a counterweight or solution to experiences of economic precarity in which most believers found themselves. The testimony of a voluntary lay preacher who lived in rural southern Chile is descriptive:

> This year, as I suppose it must have been there, there has been great need. We give glory to the Father for His Son Jesus, because we have not lacked, despite having spent some time with nowhere to go or something to eat some days . . . One day I left my house and, on my return, I knew that there was nothing to eat for my children. On the way Satan came and told me: Will you wait for something to eat? What are you going to give? His plan made me sad, but I also felt a voice that penetrated deep in my heart and it was the voice of the Master when he said: Whence shall we buy bread, that these may eat? With these words of my Lord I was so full of confidence that I thought I did not need anything. When I arrived home the Lord had complied with his word. Glory to His name! He had provided us with bread. Like that, we have learned to walk with our Master.[36]

It is clear that Pentecostal practice and discourse were informed by a direct, sometimes all-encompassing relationship with God and that these understandings and physical expressions were in tension with many aspects of traditional Chilean culture. Accounts like the one above suggest that the appeal of Pentecostalism can be explained in terms of the movement's reformist character, both spiritually and physically. At the same time, Pentecostalism was also understood to be an experiential belief system where physical trials and hardship tested and shored up one's faith. Poverty, then, was a trial and the "bread" was the reward for trusting in the words of the Lord. In their everyday experiences, Pentecostals found both the reasons and *manna*, to use a biblical term, for the continuance of their belief; their faith was both informed and extended by their context. Pentecostalism entwined itself in the lived reality of life at the margins, finding meaning and significance at the crossroads of local circumstances and threats against which one must struggle.

Converts also railed against the rigid structures and stagnant worship styles of the Catholic Church that represented a site of human ignorance

---

[36] Narciso Castro, "Pailahueque, octubre 16 de 1914," *Chile Pentecostal*, November 15, 1914.

that stunted believers' spirituality. One convert described the tension in the pages of *Chile Evangélico* in 1910 as follows:

> When I look at my brothers who are determined to deny the glorious truth of the ministry of the Holy Spirit in the Church of Christ, I feel great compassion for them, because the words that are spirit and life for many, mean nothing to them, they are dead letters and without real value; they want a routine formality to win the world and the Lord rejects it, it is a corpse twice dead; they want a church without initiative or enthusiasm and the Lord has filled us with his Spirit and our nation will become closer for the development that the Lord's work is directing to our hearing, they want to keep us in a prolonged childhood . . . [37]

Though Catholic and Protestant observers ridiculed Pentecostal religiosity as exotic, strange, and a form of "collective psychosis," Pentecostals welcomed and embraced the charismatic ardor they found in their new relationship with God.[38] In their new faith, Pentecostals found a more effective medium for the work of the Spirit than the "dead letters" and "routine formality" of the Catholic Church.

For some time, scholars have argued that we can understand Pentecostal accounts like those above as an alternative system of knowledge and practice to the dominant culture, or a systematic counterculture explicitly associated with those removed from the circles of power and control.[39] Key to scholars' claims of indigenization, however, is the opinion that revivalists in Chile did not simply adopt Pentecostalism as a transplanted system of beliefs, but that they reinterpreted the movement's dominant impulses in light of a preexisting push for transformation within the Methodist Church. It did not do away with the practices and canons of the mother church completely. Chilean theologian Daniel Godoy suggests it is more effective to view the eventual schism as a shift in religious practice.[40] While believers searched for new experiences of the gift of the Holy

---

[37] Laura Ester Contreras, "¿Por que buscáis entre los muertos al que vive?" *Chile Evangélico*, February 17, 1910.

[38] "Fanatismo enfermizo"; and Ignacio Vergara, *El Protestantismo en Chile* (Santiago de Chile: Editorial del Pacífico, 1962), 126.

[39] See, for example, Jean Comaroff, *Body of Power, Spirit of Resistance: The Culture and History of a South African People* (Chicago: University of Chicago Press, 1985); and Lehmann, *Struggle for the Spirit*.

[40] Daniel Godoy, "El Espíritu Santo . . . con los pobres: Cien años de pentecostalismo chileno," *Teología en Comunidad: Revista de Estudios Teológicos y Pastorales* 12:18 (2009–2010): 91.

Spirit, they did not always believe it required direct evidence. For example, in a word of caution about placing undue significance on the gift of the tongues, one unnamed observer in *Chile Pentecostal* opined thus:

> For many months we have been learning by experience. Although a blessed company of the faithful has experienced its blessing because of this, we want to pass on these words of admonition to others, with the request that the one who gave the experience, also bless it and use it. Let us honor the Holy Comforter more than his gifts, even the most wonderful.
>
> We have heard very solemn and useful messages on occasion when the Spirit has come with power over someone who prayed. With frequency we hear the message: "Jesus coming quickly"; but in some parts the enemy has entered with false prophecies, trapping many that were not firm in their faith.
>
> The operations of the unconscious mind are very profound, and although those who prophesied may have been sincere, it would be better if they consulted other Spirit-filled workers before putting the prophecies into effect. For example, long and useless journeys have been made, and the money destined for the work of God has been spent without profit, in some cases. Prophecies, being from God, will surely be fulfilled.
>
> We must speak much more of Him than of "tongues" (however we thank God for the sign of tongues). Frequent use of these experiences makes them lose their power when the occasion comes. There is a danger here that willful or stubborn people may (even without knowing it) use the words: "The Lord has shown me" or "The Holy Spirit says, through me," to achieve their own ends. To such we must say: "The Spirit must confirm it personally," or "I have to be guided by the clear Word of God."[41]

Speaking in tongues was (and is) seen as physical proof of the baptism of the Spirit. It was understood as a tangible gift from God and concrete expression of a direct relationship with the Divine. And yet, if the passage above is any indication, Chilean Pentecostal pneumatology, however charismatic, was tempered by warnings of misuse and depravity; the emphasis on the hackneyed deployment of tongues runs counter to the unconstrained, impromptu expressions of the Holy Spirit that characterized the movement in other parts of the world.

On the other hand there is clear evidence that early Pentecostals placed greater importance on a personal and individual experience of Spirit

---

[41] "El bautismo pentecostal: Consejor papar obreros y otros," *Chile Evangélico*, June 30, 1910.

baptism than has been documented in scholarly reflections. Believers' desire to achieve a new relationship with God, in which the individual's praise and prayers reached him unmediated even by language and traditional religious authority is a defining element of Pentecostalism across the world.[42] Even though revivalists in Chile believed their charismatic expressions were renewing the Methodist Church from within, they were not convinced that it could be done. Highlighting the importance of the miraculous manifestations of the Holy Spirit over and above institutional belonging, one convert claimed the following:

> No one asked the Lord to teach us to speak a foreign language, but the truth is that many among us sing and pray in an unknown language. If this is precisely what the Methodist Church rejects, the Lord accepts it because it is his own work.[43]

Pentecostals viewed their actions as an expansion of their lost religious heritage. To believers, their charismatic experiences were the work of the Spirit of God and his immanent presence in the world. It was a return to a more personal relationship with God, but not a denial of the Methodist faith—at least initially. One revivalist wrote, "[W]e are not following the impulses of an 'enlightened' or 'prophetic' individual, nor are we demonic, spiritualists, fanatics, deceivers . . . we are and will be Methodists and we are and will be Christians."[44] Members were convinced that their work was the manifestation of the power and mercy of God in a changing world.

This is not to say that the experience of *being* Pentecostal was not dramatic, intense, and spontaneous or that individuals' interpretations fell in line with Hoover's theological discourse. The absence of a foreign ecclesiastical hierarchy meant that Pentecostals were free to develop new configurations of worship and governing systems. The most distinctive departure of the first Pentecostal services was the irruption among congregants of speaking in tongues or glossolalia. That particular gift of the Spirit was one of the most distinctive elements of Chilean and worldwide Pentecostalism at the beginning of the twentieth century. Pentecostal pneumatology was rooted in the Bible with a particular emphasis on accounts of

[42] André Corten and Ruth Marshall-Fratani, "Introduction," in André Corten and Ruth Marshall-Fratani, eds., *Between Babel and Pentecost: Transnational Pentecostalism in Africa and Latin America* (Bloomington: Indiana University Press, 2001), 5.

[43] Laura Ester Contreras, "Ecos de la conferencia metodista," *Chile Evangélico*, March 3, 1910.

[44] Enrique J. Ortiz, "Ecos del despertamiento en Santiago," *Chile Evangélico*, November 19, 1909.

Pentecost in the book of Acts and the descent of the Holy Spirit upon individuals. Numerous testimonies in *Chile Evangélico* and *Chile Pentecostal* reveal that early Pentecostals understood glossolalia as clear evidence of Spirit baptism. "It was a blessing so big that it raised the souls praising Christ in strange tongues, as if the Spirit gave to them what they were speaking, it was a wonder bigger than anything we had seen before," wrote one convert.[45] Generally, this occurred during the congregational chants and with more frequency during vigils. It was understood as an expression of a direct relationship with the Divine as well as a cultural resource that gave practitioners a mechanism to project their faith in a physical way. Pentecostals viewed the experience as an embodied reaffirmation of their belief and the transcendent manifestation of inner sanctification.

Other gifts of the Holy Spirit were also deemed important. Prophecy, for instance, expressed itself in free and unencumbered forms. Early accounts revealed prophetic dreams, visions, and inspiration. Pentecostalism's priesthood of all believers meant that the person relating the prophecy could be a man or a woman, a new convert or an older member of the congregation, an upstanding husband or rehabilitated convict. One member from the island of Chiloé recalled the following:

> In almost all meetings there are strange tongues with interpretation. It is always a great blessing for the Church. At times, the Spirit is speaking to the Church and other times speaking to those that are not saved . . . My wife has received the gift of prophecy and the Holy Spirit prophesied through her many things concerning the work.[46]

Just like glossolalia, prophecy manifested itself in private moments and public worship like prolonged vigils or weekend services. Prophecies dealt mainly with the work of evangelization, but in some cases foretold a coming calamity. Such practices were central to evangelism and conversion; without them, believers considered worship to be devoid of meaning. They focused on themes of salvation, hardship, sickness, and healing, which were conveyed by those living in the midst of the same social situations and facing similar problems. It is not surprising that this message reverberated among individuals struggling to provide for families, living in abject conditions, or feeling socially marginalized. Through subjective testimonies, Pentecostalism demonstrated a unique ability to personalize its message and mobilize collective groups for spiritual change.

---

[45] María Rudolph, *Chile Pentecostal*, November 15, 1914.
[46] "Chiloé, Huillinco, agosto de 1913," *Chile Pentecostal*, August 15, 1913.

Conclusion

Various themes have emerged from the examination of Pentecostals' testimonies as they searched for renewed religious experience in Chile at the beginning of the twentieth century. Based on their accounts in periodicals like *Chile Evangélico* and *Chile Pentecostal*, many believers concluded that their search for an authentic and personal experience of the Holy Spirit necessitated new forms of worship and practice, even when and where they stood apart from the prescribed doctrines of the Methodist Church. Many of the justifications they provided for the eventual schism with their established religious traditions focused on a desire to renew the church from within. However, we should not overlook the nature of the process that led to their separation nor the importance and emphasis they laid on the elements of the broader Pentecostal movement that sustained and carried them forth.

The value of periodicals and newsletters to the spread and growth of Pentecostalism throughout Chile (and the world) cannot be denied. And yet they remain an underused resource for historians and scholars of the movement in Chile. They provide unique insights into the beliefs of early Pentecostals and a wealth of information about how Chilean Pentecostals understood the contours of the movement that would shape the country's religious landscape for the next one hundred years. As Miguel Mansilla notes, "the various investigations of Chilean Pentecostalism have not considered them a source of information for analysis" even though they are an integral part of the movement's memory and heritage and could be used to "fill the historical void" that exists around early believers' interpretations of their faith.[47]

More broadly, the aim of this chapter has been to revisit questions about the indigenization of Chilean Pentecostalism using the experiences of early converts' narratives as our guide. Whereas Latin American Pentecostalism is often viewed through the lens of an imported religion, believers' letters and statements made in periodicals portrayed a very nuanced process in which local religious concerns and contexts played a crucial role in shaping Pentecostal religious worldviews. At the same time, revivalists

---

[47] Mansilla, *La cruz y la esperanza*, 49. In addition to the thorough work of Miguel Mansilla, two excellent studies that analyze early believers' experiences using periodicals are Orellana, *El fuego y la nieve;* and Juan Sepúlveda, *De peregrinos a ciudadanos: Breve historia del cristianismo evangélico en Chile* (Santiago: Fundación Konrad Adenauer, 1999).

consistently emphasized the power of the Holy Spirit, even as they developed it within the existing frameworks of their religious lives. Shifting the historical narrative to the perspective of the believers themselves begins to turn our view outward from religious experiences, and revivalism begins to look more like a complex weaving of indigenization and conformity rather than one of simple acceptance or rejection. In Chile, existing religious and cultural traditions were the bases from which the global spread of Pentecostalism developed. But what came out of the process looked less and less like the institution that gave it birth. As early Pentecostals themselves expressed in their testimonies, their journey through revivalism was as much a reaction to the formalism in established churches in the nineteenth century as it was a genuine search for a new type of religious experience; believers held both of these forces in tandem. Their traditional faith and revivalist vigor moved together, rather than running contrary to one another.

8

The Creation of the Argentine Evangelical Identity

Matt Marostica

This chapter is based on participant/observer fieldwork that I began twenty-eight years ago. My family and I arrived in Buenos Aires early in October of 1992. The proposed subject matter of my research was the growth and possible political impact of evangelical churches in Argentina. I can admit now that the topic was slightly fanciful. In the early 1990s, Argentina was not known to have experienced significant church growth; it was not Brazil, Chile, or Guatemala. I had chosen to study the evangelical movement in Argentina because I had already lived in Buenos Aires and loved it. To the extent that the evangelical church had grown in and around Buenos Aires, I knew that most of the growth would be centered in the poor outer-ring municipalities of Greater Buenos Aires such as General Sarmiento and Malvinas Argentinas. I had lived in and knew my way around those difficult neighborhoods; my life experience had prepared me to conduct participant/observer research alongside Argentines in the popular sector. However, given that Argentina was not recognized as one of the centers of evangelical activity in Latin America, there was some risk that there would not be enough happening on the ground to make a viable dissertation project even with my comparative advantages as an ethnographer.

It is a truism that fieldwork never goes exactly as one expects. In my case, by pure happenstance, Argentina's two most important and internationally influential evangelists saw their ministries flourish in 1992. In fact, Claudio Freidzon's mass ministry began in 1992 just as I was arriving in the country. Similarly, though perhaps somewhat less dramatically, Carlos Annacondia conducted three large crusades around Buenos Aires during my time there. Though he had been actively ministering on a mass scale for seven years, his popularity, energy, and enthusiasm continued to draw thousands of people, and his influence within the evangelical church became more pronounced. Now, so many years later, it turns out that these two men had a profound effect on evangelical churches not only in Argentina, but also around the world. Claudio Freidzon famously spurred a large, vibrant revival in Toronto in 1994. Carlos Annacondia is a justly renowned senior figure in the international Pentecostal movement. I ended up being in the right place at the right time.

There is general agreement within the community of researchers who study the evangelical church in Argentina that something momentous occurred in the decade that followed the collapse of the military dictatorship in 1983. In my view, it was not primarily that the church grew—it did. Measured as a percentage of the population, the best estimates show tremendous growth. Semán and Wynarczyk show that in the city of Buenos Aires, the number of Pentecostals increased by 30 percent from 1980 to 1992,[1] while Frigerio and Wynarczyk estimate that between 1960 and 1990, the percentage of evangelicals in Argentina increased from 2.6 percent to 9 percent of the population.[2] Measured by the number of Pentecostal churches registered with the state—880 in 1983 to 1550 in 1991[3]—there was tremendous growth. Nor was it just that the church became much more visible to society than it had been during the dictatorship—it did that, too. In fact, church growth generated a moral panic centered on the perception that cults were invading

---

[1]   Hilario Wynarczyk and Pablo Semán, "Campo evangélico y pentecostalismo en Argentina," in Cesár Ceriani Cernadas and Mariana Espinosa, eds., *Argentina evangélica. Estudios socioantropológicos sobre misiones e iglesias* (Santiago del Estero: Bellas Artes, 2018), 31–54.

[2]   Alejandro Frigerio and Hilario Wynarczyk, "Diversidad no es lo mismo que pluralismo: Cambios en el campo religioso argentino (1985–2000) y lucha de los evangélicos por sus derechos religiosos," in Cernadas and Espinosa, eds., *Argentina evangélica*, 399–425.

[3]   Daniel Míguez, "El Protestantismo popular en la Argentina: las lógicas de expansión del pentecostalismo durante el siglo XX," in Cernadas and Espinosa, eds., *Argentina evangélica*, 51–109.

Argentina.[4] In addition, the evangelical church was transformed from a collection of mutually antagonistic missionary and immigrant denominations into a coherent social movement with recognized leaders and a shared identity.

A Symbolic Coming Out: The Bonnke Crusade of Fire

The transformation of the evangelical church that occurred in the first decade after the dictatorship was put on public display for the first time in the Reinhardt Bonnke crusade that took place in Buenos Aires over the period of a week in late 1992. Bonnke, a German-born evangelist who passed away in 2019, was invited to bring his "Crusade of Fire" to Argentina in a quixotic attempt to evangelize and "forever change" the seat of Argentine power and wealth—the Recoleta neighborhood of Buenos Aires. To that end, evangelicals came from across greater Buenos Aires to the neighborhood of Argentina's traditional elite to make themselves heard. What was announced as a crusade to capture the city's center became, instead, an affirmation of the new identity of *la Iglesia Evangélica Argentina*. It is unlikely that this evangelical celebration resulted in a single convert from La Recoleta. It did, however, serve to affirm a sense of identity and common purpose in those in attendance.

To start the crusade, the Baptist pastor and principal organizer of the event, Eduardo Lorenzo, prayed, "Oh God, we are holding this crusade in a neighborhood that is associated historically with those that have oppressed our country economically; with [military coups]. . . . We, the people of God will not be oppressed any longer . . . we are sending a message to those in office that we will no longer stand for their corruption and oppression."[5] As a resident of the Recoleta, I walked down to the crusade every evening; I attended all six nights of the Bonnke crusade. Every night, thousands of people from the outer-ring suburbs descended on the neighborhood in rented buses naming their church and place of origin. The event's organizers announced crowds of 60,000 on weekday nights and 130,000 on the weekends. The United Nations Plaza where the event was held was covered with stands selling evangelical publications, music, and musical instruments, as well as food. An excellent sound system allowed a number of the better Christian music groups to show off their talents

---

[4]   Alejandro Frigerio, "La invasión de las sectas: El debate sobre nuevos movimientos religiosos en los medios de comunicación en Argentina," *Sociedad y religion* 10:11 (1993): 24–51.

[5]   Author's notes, November 29, 1992.

(though the musical highlight was the world-famous guitarist, Cacho Tirao, a believer, but decidedly not a Christian musician). Each night also featured an hour of musical worship in which the crowd sang the music of popular Christian artists (predominantly the songs of the German Mexican minister and musician, Marcos Witt)—all of which made this event a fun, upbeat evangelical party.

The same sense of coming together as a people of God and the sheer joy of being part of something larger than a local church that was manifest in the Bonnke crusade was evident in each of the forty or so mass evangelistic events that I attended in 1992 and 1993. In addition to Bonnke, these included a series of concerts by Marcos Witt; crusades by Carlos Annacondia; meetings in Claudio Freidzon's church; his crusades in two large indoor arenas (Luna Park and Obras Sanitarias); and his massive outdoor event that filled the Velez Sarsfield soccer stadium. In all of these, the crowds knew the songs and the codes of conduct, and recognized each other as brothers and sisters in Christ.

Only ten years before, as the country emerged from the brutal Catholic nationalist dictatorship, there was no sense of belonging to something bigger than the believer's local church; no interdenominational organizations or publications; no sense of common purpose; no shared practices. So, what happened?

The argument that I will make here is that Carlos Annacondia drove the creation of a new, unified national identity for the vast majority of Argentina's evangelical Christians. He created a new way of being evangelical in Argentina. Believers embraced this new identity and rejected the old denominational models established by the missionary and immigrant founders of their churches. To put it in classical Weberian terms, Annacondia, a charismatic leader, brought about a transformation in the evangelical population of Argentina. As Weber put it, "charisma, in its most potent forms, disrupts rational rule as well as tradition altogether and overturns all notions of sanctity."[6] Annacondia disrupted tradition and overturned accepted notions of sanctity within the evangelical churches. He overturned the accepted teachings of the missionary founders of Pentecostal denominations by introducing new charismatic practices (charismatic in the religious, not Weberian, sense), and by demanding wide participation in his crusades. In doing so, Annacondia drove the creation of a new evangelical identity based on believers' shared experiences in his crusades.

[6] Max Weber, *Economy and Society* (Berkeley: University of California Press, 1978), 1117.

At the close of the first decade following the dictatorship, Claudio Freidzon consolidated that new evangelical identity by appealing directly to the believers who had been transformed through Annacondia's charisma. In his ministry, Freidzon offered the evangelical church a "new anointing" and provided "fresh" access to the Holy Spirit. Freidzon's brilliance lay in his recognition of the power and opportunities that had been created through Annacondia's work unifying the evangelical community. Freidzon appealed directly to the new evangelicals who had emerged united through a decade of experience in sponsoring and attending Annacondia's crusades. Freidzon helped the church to embrace its new shared identity openly and joyfully.

Background: Missionary Churches

Argentina is a nation of immigrants, a Catholic country with a historically diverse array of alternative religious practices recognized by the federal government: Judaism and Islam as well as Protestant alternatives to Catholicism have been present in Argentina nearly since its founding. However, as Daniel Míguez notes, the Protestant churches were state-sponsored denominations serving immigrant populations; they did not proselytize. The evangelical church on which I focus here "is characterized by a zeal to seek converts and a tendency to create doctrines and practices that incentivize and symbolize conversion."[7]

The Argentine evangelical church defined in this way is overwhelmingly, though not exclusively, Pentecostal. The emergence of Pentecostalism in Argentina is primarily a product of missions from North America and northern Europe. These missionary churches, established in the 1920s through the 1950s, remained closely tied to the teachings and practices set out by their particular missionary founders from the time of their establishment until the end of the military dictatorship. The evangelist Marfa Cabrera, the most prominent woman with a sustained ministry in the history of the Argentine church, explained the lasting effect of the missionary teachings to me in this way: "The organizations that they created here held on to those teachings. They remained stuck in time. Anything new was extremely suspect."[8] Holding on to the missionary teachings meant, in practice, that denominational identities were strong and that each church stuck jealously to its own.

The mechanism that sustained the missionary teachings even after the actual missionaries had returned to their countries of origin was known within the evangelical community as the "myth of the missionary." The

7   Míguez, "El Protestantismo popular en la Argentina," 55.
8   Interview by author, May 23, 1993.

missionaries had taught the gospel, so everything that they taught must be true and should be adhered to precisely as it was received. The missionaries grounded their teachings on strict biblical foundations. Restrictions on makeup, dancing, the separation of men and women in church, the rejection of political activity, and the rest of their teachings rested on verses from the Bible. Even with the missionaries gone, their denominations had the Bible and knew the verses which substantiated the things that the missionaries had taught. The strength of those biblical foundations was reinforced by the books and pamphlets that the missionaries left after their departure and new materials which continued to flow from denominational headquarters. Jorge Guilles, a pastor from one of the first denominations started by Argentines (The Pentecostal Christian Missionary Church), explained the persistence of the missionary teachings to me, saying, "Those of us that were outside of the missionary denominations always used to say, 'they have the manual.' The missionaries, when they did leave, also left behind materials, like manuals, which told the churches how to act and what to believe."[9]

Forced into isolation during the military dictatorship, pastors in the missionary denominations held on to the teaching of the missionaries in the face of the military's assault on nearly all actors in civil society. From 1976 through 1983 there was no public sphere, no room for collaboration or cooperation. Fear of the military kept individuals and social actors, including churches, separated and internally focused. The dictatorship's sudden collapse created space for a rapid opening of civil society that resulted in political, cultural, and religious innovation. Many social and cultural entrepreneurs emerged. Foremost among the religious innovators was Carlos Annacondia, whose commitment to preach to marginal sectors of Argentine society produced lasting change in the church as well as in the poorer neighborhoods beyond the city limits of Buenos Aires.

Carlos Annacondia

I am making the strongest possible claim regarding the impact of Carlos Annacondia on the church. He transformed it. Others had a hand in laying the groundwork and in creating institutions that supported the new evangelical movement. Some evangelists built large, vibrant churches. Annacondia, however, did not set out to create a church or to attract followers.

---

[9] Interview by author, March 4, 1995.

He wanted to transform people's lives by teaching them about the power of believing in Jesus. In doing so, he attacked fifty years of denominationalism and overturned the dominance of the missionary as the central figure of the evangelical community. He supplanted the myth of the missionary with a new identity, a new set of practices, and a new central figure.

Annacondia was a powerful cultural entrepreneur in great part because he was not dependent on his crusades for his livelihood. At the time of his conversion from Catholicism, Annacondia was a successful small businessman who owned a specialized tool and die manufacturing company with about thirty employees. The evangelistic enterprise that he developed, Message of Salvation, began as an independent church formed by Annacondia, his family, and his employees, all of whom became converted following Annacondia's personal conversion through a Panamanian evangelist. Within a year of his conversion (and still during the dictatorship), Annacondia began to see visions of himself preaching in a squatter settlement. In August 1981, he started preaching in just such a *villa miseria* in Bernal in Greater Buenos Aires. Of that experience, he says, "God protected me. He gave me authority over that place—I cast the demons out of those people and out of that place. And, one day, God took me out of that place and put me in a better neighborhood. And, I used the same message to convert the rich as I had used to convert the poor."[10]

Annacondia's message was straightforward: God and the devil exist and are in permanent battle with each other. By accepting Christ, individuals gain access to the divine power they need to overcome Satan. This power is open to anyone, and anyone can join in the fight. As Annacondia puts it, "The mission of the devil is to rob, murder, and destroy. Christ's mission is to save and give life. My mission is to confront Satan."[11] With this message, which he repeated in every crusade, Annacondia gave the evangelical community a potent new grammar that connected the problems of life in the Argentine popular sector to Satan and his demons and offered the power of Christ as a solution.

As Monica Tarducci and Pablo Semán both point out, Annacondia's impact is not only evident at the mass scale of his crusades but also within the smallest local churches. Tarducci interviewed women in one small congregation, all of whom reported coming to Pentecostalism through Annacondia. They also reported using Annacondia's message regarding

[10] Interview by author, June 21, 1993.
[11] Interview, June 21, 1993.

the power of Christ over demons to curb their husbands' destructive behaviors.[12] In a brilliant study of the diffusion of Pentecostalism in the poorest neighborhoods of an already poor suburb of Buenos Aires, Semán discovered that unschooled pastors felt that they could open churches in their garages or living rooms by recreating the practices of an Annacondia crusade in their homes. He notes that Annacondia's crusades "showed a different way of doing Pentecostal worship . . ."[13] Rather than going to a seminary to become a pastor, these pastors of local minichurches were taught to fight for Christ and against Satan in Annacondia's crusades.

The two practices in the crusades which had the greatest impact on those present were spiritual liberation and healing. When Annacondia liberated those possessed by demons, he paced the stage naming different demons, his voice rising to add emphasis to the battle he was fighting: "Out, out, out! Every demon of *Macumba*, of black magic, of red magic, of spiritualism, of Judo, of Karate, of the New Age! Let go of them, let go of them, let go of them! Out, out! Every demon of *Umbanda*, Out! All unholy spirits. Out!"[14] As he continued to reproach the demons, people would begin falling to the ground, some as if fainting, others writhing and shaking. Teams of two men would carry those that fell to the "liberation tent" where they would be ministered to by pastors and other workers who had been trained by Annacondia's team in the techniques of spiritual liberation. While the crusade continued, those who had been liberated remained in the tent receiving comfort and prayers.

Fabian, a young man who was converted in an Annacondia crusade, related his personal experience of liberation as follows:

> When I was sixteen, I began playing around with some friends, one of whom practiced *Macumba* [Afro-Brazilian spiritualism]. One night my friend got me to drink a bit of unholy blood. After that I began to feel terribly sick in my heart—rebellious. I started to fight with my mother all the time. I had thoughts of killing her. She started going to Annacondia's crusade in San Martín [May-June 1985] and she became converted. She told me I should go and that made me furious. One night my friends and I decided to go, just to make fun of all the crazy people. When I

---

[12] Monica Tarducci, "Las mujeres en el movimiento Pentecostal: Sumisión ó liberación," in Cernadas and Espinosa, eds., *Argentina evangélica*, 373–95.

[13] Pablo Semán, "De a poco mucho: Las pequeñas Iglesias pentecostales y crecimiento Pentecostal. Conclusiones de un estudio de caso" *Revista Cultura & Religión* 4:1 (2010): 25.

[14] Author's notes from many crusades.

stepped onto the field where they were holding the crusade, I fell down, completely overcome. When I woke up, it was six hours later—3:00 a.m. They explained to me that I had been possessed by an evil spirit and they wanted to know what type of spirit it could be so that they could help me more. I told them about the blood . . . Since then my mother and I never fight. My brother is now a believer. I haven't left the way of the Lord since.[15]

Fabian's statement is typical of the testimonies I heard regularly repeated in Annacondia's meetings during "testimony" time. His experience appears to be typical of the mass of new believers that entered the churches through Annacondia's crusades in the mid-1980s.

Spiritual healing also figured prominently in Annacondia crusades. Healing was and continues to be one of his primary attractions. The testimonies of people who feel themselves to be healed rival those of the people who have received spiritual liberation. One of the most common of these testimonies is the recurring claim that cavities in their teeth became filled with "heavenly material in the shape of a cross or of a dove."[16] Annacondia explained to me that these heavenly dental fillings provide "an undeniable testimony to doubting Thomases."[17]

Spiritual liberation and healing added two new practices to the repertoire of the evangelical pastors and believers who participated in Annacondia's crusades. As previously noted, belief in demons that afflict the lives of those in the popular sector is widespread. The possibility of overcoming those afflictions through Christ and without paying a traditional healer created a powerful incentive to visit Annacondia's crusades. Bad health is, not surprisingly, a regular feature of the lives of the poor in Greater Buenos Aires. The once well-regarded public health system has been in steady decline since at least the 1960s, so the possibility of an instant cure to long-standing and ill-attended health problems is very appealing. There is a long history in Argentina of appeals to saints and other popular religious icons (such as the *Difunta Correa*—the deceased woman Correa—who is believed to have breastfed her baby for days after her death) for the blessing of health. The transfer of the expectation of an immediate health blessing from a saint to a flesh-and-blood faith-healer appears to have been an easy one.

---

[15] Interview by author, January 19, 1993.
[16] Author's notes from many crusades.
[17] Interview, June 21, 1993.

Annacondia brought an innovative combination of beliefs and practices to the evangelical church. This new way of being evangelical replaced the old package of missionary teachings and exploded the myth of the missionary. He brought a new general diagnosis of the problems confronting the church (demons) and a new remedy (spiritual warfare and healing). In doing so he served as a charismatic figure around whom a new evangelical identity would be created.

Annacondia and Unity

When Annacondia began his ministry, he was new to the church and did not join an existing denomination. He worshipped with his family and his employees. He was an outsider who was not bound by any particular set of teachings nor by a denominational identity. Thus, when he started to become known as an evangelist after the collapse of the dictatorship, he had not been exposed to the missionary identities that had kept most Pentecostal churches "stuck in time." As he explained to me, "When I was converted . . . I was converted without a pastor. Those of us in my business were converted and we started to pray. . . . We said, well there can only be one church of Jesus Christ; we could not comprehend that serious divisions could exist."[18] When he began to understand "that the Pentecostals and the Baptists could not stand each other [*no se podían ni ver*], I knew that it was a human defect; that the devil had insinuated himself into the Church. So, when I started to be noticed, I made one rule regarding my participation in crusades: I always invited all of the churches in the area to join the campaign. If the pastors had a problem with that, I would not preach in that area until they could resolve their differences."[19]

How are we to understand Annacondia's ability to demand unity from churches that were historically and doctrinally committed to strict denominationalism? Annacondia, himself, gives a very material explanation: "Since my ministry worked in their interest, the churches were forced to comply. The Pentecostals had no choice other than to invite the Baptists."[20] What interested the churches were the fruits which Annacondia's campaigns were creating—thousands of decisions for Christ. Annacondia further notes that the very act of working together to organize and

18 Interview, June 21, 1993.
19 Interview, June 21, 1993.
20 Interview, June 21, 1993.

promote the campaign taught the participating churches that "they had the same doctrine, the same love. That's where unity really started."[21]

Annacondia's brilliant evocation of the concerns of the Argentine popular sector, his charisma, and the changes he produced in the lives of so many new converts demolished fifty years of intense denominationalism. His presence as a new Argentine man of God displaced the missionary as the central figure of the evangelical church. His crusades provided the milieu for innovation in which the new evangelical identity was developed.

Annacondia's crusades had the power to demolish the old missionary model in great part because they were extremely intense. As he says, when he enters a place, he goes there to do "battle" and he expects the same aggressiveness of the churches that participate in the crusade. The pastors are required to work nightly, and their churches are expected to contribute workers who seek out those who are ready to commit to Christ as well as carry off and minister to those who are overcome by the Spirit and liberated from demons.

One night in Ciudadela, I experienced the intensity and aggressiveness of the crusade firsthand. Taking notes toward the end of the night (around midnight), I looked up and realized that I was surrounded by eight to ten people who started to ask me why I was writing instead of succumbing to the power of the Holy Spirit. I started down the path of explaining that I was a sociologist studying the community and that the notes were critical to my ability to write my thesis when I returned to the United States. I also explained that I had been to many Annacondia crusades and that I admired him and found him appealing. Actually, I said, "I like Annacondia's crusades." That did not go over well. An Annacondia crusade is lifechanging, they told me. It's not something that you "like." They then asked me why I did not want to be healed. This was mystifying to me. I was young and healthy. They explained to me that, no, I was not healthy—I wore glasses. Brother Annacondia, they told me, had the power to heal the sickness in my eyes. I told them that I liked my glasses. They insisted that I could be cured, but then went on to the more important issue—they asked if I was a believer. I told them that I believed in God, but did not declare myself to be a *creyente evangélico*. As with all of my previous responses, this also went over badly. In their eyes I had not embraced the power of the Holy Spirit, nor had I allowed myself to be liberated from the demons that were controlling me. Still surrounded, I began to feel panicked.

---

[21] Interview, June 21, 1993.

I was saved by an Armenian evangelical pastor, Edgardo Surenian, who sensed my predicament and came to my rescue. He escorted me away from the group, bought me a hot dog and a soda, and told me which bus line to take to get back to Buenos Aires. After I had settled down, Surenian explained how he came to be a sponsor of the Annacondia crusade. He said, "Can you really imagine how we all feel about Annacondia and his effect in our churches? Look at me. I'm from the serious, quiet Armenian church. Here I am, vice-president of this crusade. I have thirty people from my church working here every night and look at what's going on here. People falling down, speaking in tongues, shaking all over from demons. This is the extreme end of the Pentecostal spectrum, and here we are supporting it."[22]

Surenian, a journalist as well as a pastor, noted that the gifts of the Spirit on offer in an Annacondia crusade were now also uniformly spread across all evangelical churches. The "extreme end of the Pentecostal spectrum" had been normalized and spread throughout the evangelical church. This observation by a pastor with a critical eye and the ability to recognize a sociologist who had gotten in over his head captured as much as any of my informants the profound change that Annacondia produced in the church.

Institutional Supports

Thus far, I have made a "strong man" argument that Carlos Annacondia transformed the evangelical churches of Argentina from a conglomeration of often mutually antagonistic missionary denominations into a new social movement with a coherent identity and shared religious practices. Unsurprisingly, there were also more institutional forces at work. These included interdenominational organizations such as the primarily Baptist-led ACIERA (Christian Alliance of the Evangelical Churches of Argentina, est. 1983) and the Pentecostal CEP (Confederation of Pentecostal Evangelicals, est. 1983). Rogelio Nonini, President of ACIERA, explained to me, "The convergence driven by Annacondia has two sides. The new charismatic practices of the formerly subdued churches, and the acceptance of formal studies and discipline by the more extreme elements of Pentecostalism. This communion and mutual respect have made it possible for us [ACIERA and CEP] to enter a new era together. An era that has made it possible for us to program things together, events like . . .

---

[22] Interview by author, February 17, 1993, at 3:00 a.m.

Bonnke . . . and activities, like the meeting next month . . . regarding the new law on religious liberty."[23]

In addition to organizing the Bonnke event and mobilizing collective action regarding the new law seeking increased religious liberty, these two organizations also pursued the creation of a national council of pastors that would have the authority to sanction those that deviated from accepted norms and to resolve disputes in the community. When they announced this new initiative, Rogelio Nonini set out the concerns that drove this institutional cooperation, saying, "We need to reach a unity in our ethical concepts, which would ensure that the character and conduct of Christians be in conformity with the Gospel that we preach." He made this statement in the March 1993 issue of the broadly accepted community publication, *El Puente.*[24]

Even more critical than the interdenominational organizations in the development of a new evangelical identity was the monthly newspaper, *El Puente* (The Bridge). Available at nearly every church and in every crusade, *El Puente* aimed expressly and through its very name to bring evangelicals together. The fortunes of *El Puente* were closely tied to the success of the Annacondia crusades of the mid-1980s. As its founder, Marcelo Lafitte, explained to me, "Before *El Puente* there was nothing interdenominational in the country, no media whatsoever. *El Puente* was born together with the Annacondia crusades of 1985 and the revival that accompanied those events. My idea was to provide a bridge that would unite the Church. What does a bridge do? It brings the two banks of the river together. It is unity, but a unity that allows everyone to return to their own side."[25]

El Puente served as more than just a bridge. It became the informational nexus of the entire evangelical movement. The interdenominational organizations used it to make their positions known. When the government acted in ways that affected the church, it was reported there. The life of the movement was transmitted to believers in and through the monthly edition of *El Puente.*

El Puente and *el fenómeno Freidzon*

When Claudio Freidzon's ministry suddenly exploded into the church, it was covered, debated, and normalized in *El Puente*. Between December 1992 and April 1993, there were sixteen articles on *el fenómeno Freidzon*.

---

[23] Interview by author, June 2, 1993.
[24] *El Puente*, March 1993, 5.
[25] Interview by author, May 5, 1993.

The January 1993 issue is typical. There were four articles whose headings and basic thrust were as follows:

1. We interview Pastor Claudio Freidzon: "I only ask that you let some time go by and look at the fruits." The article states the commitment of *El Puente* to objectively present the facts regarding a phenomenon that "cannot be ignored" (20).
2. This has happened before, which can "Confirm that it comes from God." The author is supportive of Freidzon, noting that the phenomenon of "falling in the Spirit" has happened in previous revivals (René Padilla, noted activist and theologian, 21).
3. Rector of the Baptist Seminary, "All experiences need a biblical base." The author is highly critical of Freidzon. He argues that Freidzon's use of the term "anointing" is "unbiblical" (Dr. Stanley D. Clark, 31).
4. Point and counterpoint: A reporter from *El Puente* interviews various pastors who conclude that the Freidzon phenomenon is probably a mix of "the Holy Spirit, the flesh, and the Devil" (José Caballero, executive editor of *El Puente*, 31).

The *fenómeno Freidzon* continued to be debated between pastors and on the pages of *El Puente* from January through April 1993. It became settled only after Freidzon led a five-hour mass meeting at the Velez Sarsfield soccer stadium in April of 1993. In that meeting Carlos Annacondia not only preached, but also expressed his strong support for Freidzon and the work that the Holy Spirit was doing through him. Annacondia lent his personal charisma and weight as the central figure of the new evangelical movement to legitimize Freidzon's ministry.

Freidzon's Appeal to Believers

Claudio Freidzon's "Crusade of Miracles" ministry was based on the experience of what he called the "new anointing" or the "fresh anointing" of the Holy Spirit, which is said to expand and renovate believers' experience of God's power in their lives. Those who receive the "fresh anointing" develop a heightened sensitivity to and awareness of the influence of the Holy Spirit. The outward manifestations that accompany this spiritual gift include falling in the Spirit, "drunkenness in the Spirit," uncontrolled laughter, and "crying with joy."

I was present when this blessing was far from routinized, and certainly before all of the modes of interaction between Freidzon and those seeking the spiritual blessing he offered had been defined. The result was unpredictability. No one, including Freidzon, knew what would happen when he came together with large groups of believers. Once word spread that the Holy Spirit was being manifest in new and powerful ways, any meeting that Freidzon attended was overwhelmed by those seeking his blessing. In November 1992 I attended a seminar on "spiritual warfare" in the Obras Sanitarias arena (filled to capacity with 6,600 believers). Freidzon had been invited to preach. His service began at 1:00 p.m. and was scheduled to end at 3:00 p.m. He spent the entire afternoon inviting pastors onto the stage where he would blow into the microphone, throw his suit jacket, or simply wave his arms at people. The result was always the same: they would fall to the ground laughing and praising God. Those that struggled to their feet would be smitten by another wave of Freidzon's arms and fall to the ground again. The meeting finally let out at 9:00 p.m. with everyone simply too exhausted to laugh, sing, or fall down anymore.

Freidzon's ministry, unlike Annacondia's, was not directed toward "the unconverted." The new anointing, as the name suggests, was directed primarily at those who had already experienced a *first* anointing. In order for Freidzon to succeed on a mass level, it was essential that a large group of believers with a shared identity should already exist. Freidzon himself was well aware of the process that made this ministry possible. Regarding the changes that made this pool of believers with a shared identity available, he told me, "With the arrival of Carlos Annacondia, it was as if the Argentine people was awakened to what God can do outside of a religious liturgy, outside of the normal life of a church. Carlos Annacondia came and threw down some of the preconceptions that we had regarding God's actions, and the people began to realize that God was showing us a power that we had not been seeing before. For God, this power is not new, but, rather, our experience of it is new."[26]

Carlos Annacondia's stature came from his ability to attract new adherents to the evangelical church in his mass crusades. Freidzon developed a mass ministry because he offered a message that reconfirmed to existing believers the importance of their beliefs and practices. Freidzon reflected to his followers the charismatic identity that they had developed over the preceding decade. Freidzon's ministry functioned as a reaffirmation

---

[26] Interview by author, January 29, 1993.

of the new evangelical identity. Believers from all of the churches in the movement thronged to his crusades seeking what Freidzon calls "more" of God's power. This was a power that they had first discovered and grown to expect in the crusades of Carlos Annacondia. The earlier preacher, as Freidzon understood, gave evangelicals a way of accessing God's power. Freidzon, by appealing directly to that new, shared sensitivity to the Holy Spirit, drew the community together in fresh and unexpected ways.

In addition to making believers feel renewed enthusiasm about being part of the church, Freidzon broadened membership in the evangelical community by bringing the new anointing to sectors of the historical Protestant churches that had not taken part in the Annacondia crusades. These churches had not embraced the charismatic revolution of the previous decade. In a meeting that I attended in Freidzon's church, an Anglican bishop was among the featured recipients of the fresh anointing. Laughing and falling, the bishop assured Freidzon that he would carry the new anointing back to his church.[27] Similarly, Freidzon brought the new anointing to the Central Baptist Church of the respected theologian and former Princeton professor, Pablo Deiros.

Conclusion

I first lived in Argentina from 1979 through 1981. This was the period in which the military dictatorship was at its most dominant. By the time that I arrived in late 1979, the military had killed or jailed most of the "subversives," which it perceived as threats to Argentina and to the Argentine Catholic Church. As a result of this assault, the military had succeeded in pushing civil society into hiding and in convincing Argentine citizens to retreat into their homes. Argentine civil society was quiescent. People stuck to themselves and their immediate families. I witnessed this quiescence firsthand. People avoided the police and the military. They walked to the other side of the street if they saw a green Ford Falcon—the preferred vehicle for kidnapping people off the sidewalks of Buenos Aires. Argentines were justifiably terrified of the regime, and it showed.

The emergence of a new evangelical identity in Argentina must be understood against the background of this Catholic nationalist military regime and its assault on Argentine civil society. Under the military, evangelicals were not permitted to hold large-scale meetings and particularly not large-scale outdoor meetings—the very type of meeting that Carlos

---

[27] Meeting at Freidzon's church in the Belgrano neighborhood of Buenos Aires, May 20, 1993.

Annacondia used to mobilize believers after the fall of the dictatorship. The restriction on large-scale meetings was galling to the evangelicals since their central goal is to evangelize. The military's religious registration system further limited the ability of the evangelicals to mobilize collectively because pastors were required to register their ministry, regardless of denominational affiliation, with the Foreign Office.

The collapse of the dictatorship was followed by a period of wild exuberance. People tried new things. Carlos Annacondia, an outsider to organized Pentecostalism and a believer without church or pastor, played a key role in this social experimentation by offering a new way to find God. Annacondia's new way was rooted in Pentecostal behavior and in popular Catholicism. The new set of charismatic practices that he created exploded through the poorer suburbs of Buenos Aires. People loved coming together and worshipping without fear of being jailed or of disappearing. They loved exuberantly embracing Jesus Christ and throwing off the social isolation imposed by the military.

Looking back on the evidence presented here, all of the evangelical activists whom I interviewed in doing my fieldwork attributed the profound changes in the church in the first decade after the dictatorship directly to the crusades of Carlos Annacondia. The key change in the church, I have argued, can best be understood as a shift from the denominational identities established by founding missionaries to the new evangelical identity. Annacondia pushed this change by introducing a novel message that resonated in the popular sector, by bringing the practices of demonic liberation and spiritual healing to the entire evangelical community, and by demanding unity in support of his crusades. At the end of the decade, Claudio Freidzon began the revival of the "fresh anointing" by recognizing and drawing on the power that lay in the unity of the church and the shared identity of Argentine evangelical Christians.

9

Evangelicals in Peruvian Politics

From Impossible Theocracy to
Political Influencers, 1990–2019

Véronique Lecaros

Many Peruvians became conscious of the presence of evangelicals in their society for the first time during the political campaign of Alberto Fujimori in 1990.[1] At the time, evangelicals represented around 5 percent of the population, but many of them publicly and enthusiastically supported "Brother Fujimori" (Hermano Fujimori) and his promise of sweeping changes.[2] This enthusiasm was hiding a great deal of improvisation, like most of Fujimori's political planning in 1990.

Since 1990, evangelicals have become part of the political landscape. Several renowned pastors have consistently developed public and political strategies mainly to promote an agenda of ethics in which sexual morality plays an important role. (Ex)pastors are by now spread across the whole political spectrum. It has reached the point where party leaders feel obliged to include some (ex)pastor in their congressional candidates list.

---

[1]   In this chapter, following the Latin American usage, I shall apply the term "evangelical" to all Christians who are not Catholic.

[2]   Although Fujimori is Catholic, he was content without denying it to be treated as an evangelical. Véronique Lecaros, *L'Église catholique face aux évangéliques, le cas du Pérou* (Paris: L'Harmattan, 2012), 67. Spanish version: *La Iglesia Católica y el desafío de los grupos evangélicos, el caso del Perú en América Latina* (Lima: Prensas Universitarias Universidad Antonio Ruiz de Montoya, 2016).

This situation confronts us with many challenging questions. I shall focus in this chapter on three main points:

1. What is the origin of evangelical political power? What makes the movement so effective? Is it voting discipline or a more subtle combination of factors?
2. How has evangelical involvement in politics changed the equilibrium of power between churches and the state? Could we consider it a reversal from the evolution toward secularization in the political sphere, which has been underway since the beginning of the twentieth century?
3. The evangelical population is fragmented into a countless number of varied churches. Among them, who is involved in politics? How? Is it possible to distinguish, in spite of this apparent diversity, a common perspective?

Before dealing with these topics, I shall present a brief and panoramic chronology of evangelical political involvement during the past thirty years.

Evangelicals in Politics: A Successful Conquest of Power?

Before 1990, evangelical involvement in politics remained very discreet, related mainly to religious self-interest. The Presbyterian pastor Pedro Arana, a candidate for APRA (a leftist party at the time), was elected in the constituent congress of 1979, capitalizing on the support of evangelical churches by promising to defend their cause in the writing of the constitution. As he related in a personal interview, to promote his candidacy, he simply wrote to the pastors of the main evangelical churches to explain his purpose. As a matter of fact, his three interventions in the constituent congress were exclusively aimed at promoting the evangelical cause.[3]

Fujimori's campaign represented a turning point. Most evangelicals were involved in his party Change 90 (Cambio 90); out of the fifty-two evangelical congressional candidates, fifty belonged to Fujimori's party. Fujimori's second vice-presidential candidate was a Baptist pastor, Carlos Garcia. In Change 90, apart from evangelicals, Fujimori gathered several collectives marginalized by the traditional politicians and by the white economic elite. His first vice-president was a self-made businessman from

---

[3]   Lecaros, *L'Église catholique*, 62.

Cuzco, close to the growing group of informal entrepreneurs.[4] Fujimori, himself of Japanese descent, a non-occidental minority who at the time enjoyed a favorable image, connected easily with the despised Indian and mestizo populations. Fujimori crystallized the aspirations of the many excluded and marginalized Peruvians.[5]

The unexpected success of the campaign raised many expectations among evangelicals. Some of their political mottos are quite revealing: "Change 90, Peru Evangelist country;" "Change 90, Religious change, Fuji, our hope;" and so on. Many evangelicals were actively involved in the campaign, speaking in favor of "Brother Fujimori" in a door-to-door process.[6] Upon election, their hope of a theocratic government soon evaporated. Fujimori quickly set them aside. If he needed them for his election, he soon realized that he would not be able to stabilize his government with the opposition from the Catholic hierarchy that strongly opposed the evangelical offensive.[7] After Fujimori seized absolute power in a "self-coup" in 1992, only a few evangelicals were elected anew, and by then they were presenting themselves as politicians instead of religious leaders. Following Fujimori's self-coup, evangelical candidates for Congress have been spreading in most of the political parties.

To understand the logic implied in the political field, it is noteworthy that, as Stephen Levitsky pointed out, Peru has been evolving since 1990 into a democracy without institutionalized and structured parties.[8] Following the deeply rooted *caudillo* tradition, a strong charismatic man (seldom a woman) unites several relevant leaders who in turn gather people from their respective bases.[9] Such "parties" may not survive beyond a few electoral successes in national and local politics, followed by a series of

[4]   Lecaros, *L'Église catholique*, 65.

[5]   Véronique Lecaros, *La conversión al evangelismo* (Lima: PUCP, 2016), 55.

[6]   Tomás Gutiérrez, *Protestantismo y poder: Acción política de los evangélicos en América Latina* (Lima: Prensas Editoriales Universidad Nacional Mayor de San Marcos, 2019), 27.

[7]   Lecaros, *L'Église catholique*, 72.

[8]   Stephen Levitsky, "Fujimori and Post Party Politics in Peru," *Journal of Democracy*, 10:3 (1999): 78–92; Stephen Levitsky and Mauricio Zavalata, "Why Not Party-building in Peru?" in Stephen Levitsky, James Loxton, Brandon Van Dyck, and Jorge Domínguez, eds., *Challenges of Party-building in Latin America* (Cambridge: Cambridge University Press, 2016), 412–39.

[9]   Malvina Garaglia, "Populismos y neopopulismos," in Marta Casaús and Morna Macleod, eds., *América Latina entre el autoritarismo y la democratización (1930–2012)* (Zaragoza, Spain: Prensas de la Universidad de Zaragoza, 2016), 93–118.

failures. Consequently, politicians do not feel any loyalty to their so-called party and move quite frequently from one to another, looking for the political platform that would guarantee them more exposure. The behavior of evangelical leaders-turned-politicians follows the same pattern. In this process, the ideology of the parties, shaped by the new recruits, may undergo radical changes. For the congressional election of 2020, the party of Javier Perez de Cuellar, former secretary general of the United Nations (1982–1992), presented members of the group of Antauro Humala, a jailed military coup plotter.

Two thousand ten represents another turning point in the history of evangelical involvement in politics. From 1990 onward the evangelical population was growing at a very quick pace, doubling in fourteen years and representing a significant minority. However, from an official and legal point of view, evangelicals had no recognized space in the nation. Articles 86 and 50 from the 1979 and 1993 constitutions, respectively, considered that the Peruvian state "can establish certain types of collaboration" with non-Catholic confessions. These "types of collaboration" were meant to be clarified by a law. The public debate on that law lasted for more than thirty years.

Up until 2010, although evangelicals belonged to different political parties, each congressional candidate included the project of a religious law in his campaign planning. Evangelical leaders did not agree on all of the objectives. Some, especially those who belonged to more liberal trends, were advocating for a fully fledged laical state, but most of them expected to achieve a status similar to the Catholic Church and to enjoy the same benefits.[10] Besides official public recognition, this mainly implied tax exemptions on religious premises and on donations, an evangelical version of the compulsory religious course in schools, opportunities for the creation of evangelical universities, and a status for evangelical chaplains in the army, hospitals, and jails. In the meantime the Catholic hierarchy was lobbying to prevent any legal initiative from the evangelicals.[11] For long years there was an impasse fostering tensions between Catholics and evangelicals. Finally in December 2010, the Law of Religious Freedom established a status for evangelical churches. Evangelicals reaped the desired benefits,

---

[10] Marco Huaco, "Le Pérou: de l'État catholique a l'État laïque ou pluriconfessionnel?" *Archives des Sciences Sociales des Religions* 146 (2009): 99–118.

[11] Lecaros, *L'Église catholique*, 50.

although in a minor degree compared to the advantages given to the Catholic Church by the concordat.

The law put an end to the political debate, although the topic may still come out sporadically in evangelical conversations. Consequently the agreement opened the way for the development of more peaceful relations between Catholic and evangelical leaders and facilitated the formation of political alliances. Instead of promoting and enhancing the historical trend toward a greater division between the state and religious institutions, a form of *laïcité*, the law has fostered a clientelist regime between the state and the churches. Although the discussion has become more focused and locally centered, interests remain intertwined. Recently the main evangelical churches managed to get October 31 recognized as the day of the Bible. In Congress and in the executive branch, local Catholic shrines have been pushing legal norms to be recognized as cultural national centers, which implies receiving more publicity, and thus more tourism, and above all extra financial resources for the maintenance of the shrine.[12]

From 2010 onward evangelicals have striven to develop an image as ethical leaders. Evangelical politicians have been focusing almost exclusively on the ethical perspective with an ever-growing importance given to the moral agenda. They were responding on the one hand to public preoccupation with the high level of corruption unveiled after the collapse of the Fujimori regime, as well as to growing pressure from liberal groups promoting an abortion protocol and egalitarian marriage. This process emerged with the formation of Pastor Humberto Lay's party, National Restoration (*Restauración Nacional*), in 2006, a party that mainly presented evangelicals as congressional candidates. Lay's speeches and programs stress with great emphasis their ethical "renovation" objectives.[13]

Additionally, for the first time, in 2016, a few evangelical pastors became some of the most influential leaders in the formation of the movement "Don't You Mess with My Children" (*Con Mis Hijos No Te Metas*), in which evangelicals have massively participated.[14] Among the

---

[12]   Tomas Gutiérrez, who has been working for twenty years in the Congress, is researching religion in Congress for a PhD dissertation, and he shared with us some of the data he collected.

[13]   Gutiérrez, *Protestantismo y poder*, 68.

[14]   Paulo Barrera, "'Don't you mess with my children'—Conservative Inter-religious Cooperation in Peru in the XXI Century," *International Journal of Latin American Religion* 1 (2017): 296–308; and Véronique Lecaros, "El movimiento *Con Mis Hijos No Te*

most outspoken and visible leaders, it is worth mentioning the pastor and congressman Julio Rosas and his son Cristian, who has studied at Liberty University. Although presented under a different name, this movement is active in the whole of Latin America and has represented a renewed way for evangelicals and religious people to get involved in governments' decisions by exerting pressure through massive demonstrations.[15] The official purpose of the movement is the promotion of a moral agenda: to prevent the expansion of the so-called gender ideology and to protect families (against egalitarian marriage) and life (against abortion). Beyond the impact of international networks involved in the promotion of the movement, it is worth stressing how this agenda, especially the opposition to homosexuality, resonates with deeply rooted ideals of masculinity.[16] In 2017 the movement succeeded in gathering one million people in a demonstration, putting so much pressure on the government that two education ministers had to resign, and contributing to the impeachment of President Pedro Pablo Kuczynsk.

The movement owed its success to political and religious alliances that had been going on in Congress and in other forums, hidden from the limelight.[17] Catholics, especially those who are close to conservative trends, joined evangelicals in the demonstration. The Episcopal Conference published an official statement against "gender ideology" in 2017. Moreover, Fujimori's party, led by his eldest daughter Keiko since 2005, was also involved in the movement. As Levitsky has pointed out, Fujimori's party represents an exception: it is the only party that has survived the aftermath of multiple social crises and maintained a relevant role on the political scene.[18] The party was organized enough to give Keiko the capacity to congregate supporters. Although Keiko won a congressional majority in 2016, she lost the presidential election with a very tight margin. The movement became part of her harassment strategy that finally succeeded in toppling Kuczynsk's government in March 2018.

Metas: ¿una corriente político-religiosa o un exorcismo colectivo?" in Paulo Barrera, Manoel Morães, and Donizete Rodrigues, eds., *Evangélicos e Pentecostais: alem de suas fronteiras na América Latina* (Belem: EDUEPA, 2020).

[15] Joanildo Burity, "El pueblo evangélico. Construcción hegemónica, disputas minoritarias y reacción conservadoras," *Encartes* 3:6 (2020): 1–35.

[16] Norma Fuller, "Repensando el machismo latinoamericano," *Masculinities and Social Change* 1:2 (2012): 114–33.

[17] Lecaros, "El movimiento *Con Mis Hijos No Te Metas*."

[18] Levitsky and Zavalata, "Why Not Party-building in Peru?:" 412–39.

What Is the Origin of Evangelical Political Power?

Political analysts conclude that there is no voting discipline among evangelicals, so that they have shown little consistent political alignment.[19] As a matter of fact, there is no voting discipline among Catholics either.[20] Even during the much publicized landslide of Fujimori's election in 1990, some scholars suggest that many evangelicals did not support Fujimori.[21] On the other hand, certainly, Catholics did not respond to the heavy campaign against Fujimori deployed by the clergy, among them the Peruvian primate, Cardinal Vargas Alzamora.

In later elections the lack of consistency in political alignment becomes even more obvious. Lay's party never received above 4 percent of the vote, even in local elections (2006–2011), although evangelicals had already reached more than 12 percent of the population (census 2007).[22] The congressional candidate Alda Lazo represents an emblematic case of the situation.[23] In 2006, Lazo, the wife of the head pastor of the church Agua Viva (Living Water), was elected to Congress in Pastor Lay's party. She reached the post of congressional vice-president. In the course of her mandate, she resigned from Lay's party and joined National Solidarity, the party of Jorge Castañeda, a former mayor of Lima. By so doing she acted like most politicians, in search of a party that could promote her political career. In the election of 2011, Lazo did not publicize her candidacy outside her church. Since Agua Viva is a very organized and self-contained Neo-Pentecostal church, Lazo felt secure that no matter what, the church's 100,000 members would get her into office. However, although she would have needed only 36,000 votes to reach her goal, she lost.

As a matter of fact, evangelicals as a collective are underrepresented in Congress. Even counting politicians who have turned evangelical, their share of congressional seats has always been lower than their share of the

---

[19] Pablo Semán, "Quiénes son? Por qué crecen? En qué creen? Pentecostalismo y política en América Latina," *Nueva Sociedad* 280 (2019): 26–46.

[20] Cristian Parker, "Religious Pluralism and New Political Identities in Latin America," *Latin American Perspectives* 43:3 (2016): 15–30.

[21] José Luis Pérez Guadalupe, *Entre Dios y el César, el impacto político de los evangélicos en el Perú y América Latina* (Lima: IESC, Konrad Adenauer-Stiftung, 2017), 130, 131. Gutierrez (*Protestantismo y poder*) disagrees with this perspective. He considers that evangelicals played a very significant role in the elections and that in that instance, they voted unanimously for Fujimori.

[22] Lecaros, *L'Église catholique*, 109.

[23] Lecaros, *La conversión*, 156.

Peruvian population. Only one evangelical congressman out of 130, an ex-pastor named Orestes Sanchez, was elected in the 2020 election. He plays the part of the evangelical spokesman and works to promote the evangelical ethical agenda. Peru is thus very far from the well-organized evangelical congressional group *Bancada Evangelica* in Brazil. Twenty percent of the whole 2018 Chamber of Deputies belong to the *Bancada*, a proportion more attuned to the 26 percent of the population who, according to Pew surveys, identify with the evangelical faith.[24]

If brothers do not necessarily vote for brothers, then why would politicians look for the support of evangelical pastors? One hypothesis is to consider the courting of evangelicals as a process of representation and recognition similar to that of other collectives of women, young professionals, workers, and so on. Recognition theorists, among them Axel Honneth, have stressed the importance of collective recognition through significant symbolic gestures.[25] By choosing an outstanding member of the evangelical community for their congressional list, party leaders publicize themselves as evangelical-friendly. This logic probably partially explains the way evangelical candidates are spread over the whole political spectrum. However, as we have argued in other texts, the role of evangelical pastors in politics should be understood as an element of the broader field of religion and politics.[26]

In Peru, scandals in general, and abuse scandals in particular, have not tarnished the religious institutions' reputations. In the surroundings of deliquescent and despised political institutions, religious institutions stand out as by far the most prestigious.[27] Churches still enjoy over 50 percent popularity, based on their ethical reputation and their much-valued social projects;[28] meanwhile Congress and political parties

---

[24] Brenda Carranza and Christina Vital Da Cunha, "Conservative Religious Activism in the Brazilian Congress: Sexual Agendas in Focus," *Social Compass* 5:4 (2018): 486–502.

[25] Axel Honneth, *The Struggle for Recognition: The Moral Grammar of Social Conflict* (Cambridge: Polity, 1995); Lecaros, *La conversión*.

[26] Véronique Lecaros, "Les Oxymores religieux latino-américains, Étude sur 'l'enchantement' et les processus de 'sécularisation' au Pérou," *Social Compass* 67:3 (2020): 444–60.

[27] Edward Cleary, *How Latin America Saved the Soul of the Catholic Church* (Mahwah, N.J.: Paulist, 2009); and Catalina Romero, "El Perú, país de diversidad religiosa," in Catalina Romero, ed., *Diversidad religiosa en el Perú, Miradas múltiples* (Lima: PUCP, 2016), 13–40.

[28] Véronique Lecaros, *Fe cristiana y secularización en el Perú de hoy* (Lima: Prensas de la Universidad Antonio Ruiz de Montoya, 2018).

do not reach double digits. The World Value surveys from 1996 and 2018 clearly show the evolution of the popularity of institutions. Although with a significant negative trend,[29] churches remain the most valued institutions: they received 70 percent approval in 1996 and 51 percent in 2018. On the other hand political institutions remain at the lowest level of approbation: political parties received 6 percent approval in 1996, 6 percent in 2018; Congress, 14 percent in 1996, 5 percent in 2018. The dissatisfaction with national government reveals the extent of the growing distrust toward the political field in general: it obtained 37 percent approval in 1996, corresponding to Fujimori's government that kept a relatively high level of approval during ten years, and 11 percent in 2018 in the aftermath of President Kuczynsk's impeachment.[30]

According to the World Value polls (Q113), politicians, especially in the national government, are considered by more than 90 percent of the population as the most corrupt group of people. A very high proportion of the population is aware of the omnipresence of corruption, a perception that corresponds to what Francisco Durand has called "the criminal economy."[31] The huge corruption scandal of Brazilian origin, *Lava Jato* (Car Wash), has had far-reaching consequences for the Peruvian political class. The trial has unveiled networks of a deeply ingrained scheme of bribery related to public infrastructure works. All ex-presidents in Peru since 1990 are in jail or have been in jail for corruption; many figures among local authorities, including the last few mayors of Lima, are facing a similar situation. Until recently, many people partly accepted corruption in a fatalistic way, as an ingrained feature of Peruvian culture.[32] The motto associated with the Lima ex-mayor Jorge Castañeda was "he steals but he works" (*roba pero hace obras*). However, the 2017 climatic emergency (*niño costero*) caused a number of disasters due to the poor quality of infrastructure. It put clearly in evidence that corruption results in tremendous consequences directly affecting the population's lives. Because of poor engineering planning, in Lima, a bridge collapsed and riverbeds were not capable

[29]   Parker, "Religious Pluralism."
[30]   World Value Survey, 1996; and World Value Survey, Wave 7, 2017–2020, http://www.worldvaluessurvey.org/wvs.jsp.
[31]   Francisco Durand, *El Perú fracturado, formalidad, informalidad y economía delictiva* (Lima: Fondo Editorial del Congreso del Perú, 2007); and Francisco Durand, *La captura del estado en América Latina: Reflexiones teóricas* (Lima: Oxfam/PUCP, 2019).
[32]   Alfonso Quiroz, *Historia de la corrupción en el Perú* (Lima: IEP, 2013).

of containing floods. The COVID-19 crisis has again put the effect of corruption in the medical system in the limelight.

Religious people are usually considered immune to corruption. We have argued that it stems from the image of God as an omniscient, supremely powerful, and equitable judge.[33] A true believer should be aware that "God is watching us," as Dominic Johnson put it, and that dire consequences may be looming.[34] According to a 2014 Pew survey, 66 percent of the population of Peru "believe in hell."[35] Peruvians distrust atheist people who do not "fear God."

The reputation of honesty enjoyed by religious people represents a high value of social capital in the eyes of discredited politicians. It is no wonder, then, that politicians looking for a way of cleaning up their reputation tend to appear publicly in the company of religious people and that they include (ex)pastors promoting an ethics-centered agenda in their congressional lists. Among Catholics, only clergy, sisters, and exceptionally pious people are considered honest. On the contrary, evangelicals at large enjoy this reputation. According to the Pew Research Center, one of the main reasons for converting to the evangelical faith (58 percent of those interviewed) was the desire for a "greater emphasis on morality."[36] César Hinostroza, considered one of the most corrupt Peruvian judges, converted into a pious evangelical in 2019, which makes his transformation seem credible. He is now asking for justice, citing the Bible.

In addition to the ethical dimension, in a context of instability, evangelical conservative pastors with their strong outspoken convictions produce an impression of firmness and direction that is seen as lacking in the political field.[37]

Apart from the much-publicized evangelical involvement in elections, religious leaders are, on and off, courted by politicians, especially when they are faced with a dire challenge. President Alan Garcia (2006–2011)

---

[33] Véronique Lecaros, "Dios castigador, Dios juez o Dios amado? Imágenes de Dios en medios católicos y pentecostales peruanos," *Horizonte* 15:46 (2017): 557–605.

[34] Dominic Johnson, *God Is Watching You: How the Fear of God Makes Us Human* (New York: Oxford University Press, 2016).

[35] *Religion in Latin America: Widespread Change in a Historically Catholic Region* (Washington, D.C.: Pew Research Center, 2014), https://www.pewforum.org/2014/11/13/religion-in-latin-america/.

[36] Paul Freston, "History, Current Reality and Prospects of Pentecostalism in Latin America," in Virginia Garrard-Burnett, Paul Freston, and Stephen Dove, eds., *The Cambridge History of Religions in Latin America* (Cambridge: Cambridge University Press, 2016), 430–450, at 445.

[37] Lecaros, "El movimiento *Con Mis Hijos No Te Metas*."

masterfully resorted to religious leaders to buttress his political popularity. He used to take holy communion, kneeling in front of the cameras even when scandals of diverse origin, including obvious cases of adultery, were coming out in the media.[38] He received pastors in official appointments, took part in evangelical services, and gave interviews to evangelical television channels, among them the popular Bethel channel of the World Missionary Movement (MMM), one of the most numerous churches.

Evangelicals in Politics: A Comeback of Religion in State Affairs?

José Casanova distinguishes three separate dimensions of secularization: "social differentiation," "privatization," and "decline of religion."[39] Although his perspective on religion has changed, he has maintained the relevance of those three dimensions in the course of his career. We shall not discuss the topic of levels of religiosity nor the question of privatization/deprivatization, which we have done elsewhere.[40] Rather, we shall focus on the differentiation of spheres, a feature mentioned by most scholars studying what Olivier Tschannen called the "paradigm of secularization."[41] As Casanova has noted, the "binary classification of reality, religious/secular" has become global not through a process of modernization, but through the "European colonial expansion" and its economical capitalist repercussions.[42] Applied to the political field, this binary conception implies a separation between state and religion.

The Catholic Church position expressed in *Gaudium et Spes* (§76), which became the norm after the Second Vatican Council, corresponds to and promotes this binary classification. "The Church and the political community in their own fields are autonomous and independent from each other."[43] Following the council, the Holy See has actively worked to regulate its relations with Latin American nations through concordats; such a treaty was established with Peru in 1980. It implied the elimination of government's mingling in church affairs and vice versa, as had been

---

[38] Lecaros, *La Iglesia Católica y el desafío*, 113.

[39] José Casanova, "Religions, Secularizations and Modernities," *European Journal of Sociology* 52:3 (2011): 425–45, at 433.

[40] Lecaros, "Les oxymores religieux."

[41] Olivier Tschannen, "The Secularization Paradigm: A Systematization," *Journal for the Scientific Study of Religion* 30:4 (1991): 395–415.

[42] José Casanova, "The Karel Dobbelaere Lecture: Divergent Global Roads to Secularization and Religious Pluralism," *Social Compass* 65:2 (2018): 187–98.

[43] *Gaudium et Spes*, http://www.vatican.va/archive/hist_councils/ii_vatican_council/documents/vat-ii_const_19651207_gaudium-et-spes_fr.html.

the case since the colonial period. The Church may express its opinion on social matters and does so with growing emphasis, as Michele Dillon has noted.[44] However, the Vatican II perspective entails non-involvement in political matters.[45]

By contrast, evangelicals are not bound by such rules. (Former) pastors may express their opinions publicly and come forward as congressional candidates, capitalizing on their religious positions. Although there are other alternatives for successful and discreet lobbying, the restraints imposed on religious Catholic people have opened the way for a more incisive presence of evangelicals in politics. Even though evangelicals are but a tiny minority in Congress, their involvement in politics gets over-exposed in the media. In other words, we end up with a paradoxical situation: on the one hand, evangelicals are underrepresented in state institutions and Congress in particular, and on the other hand, their public involvement in politics is over-emphasized compared to their actual share of the population.

Taking into account the renewed cautious attitude of the Catholic clergy, which has left a religious vacuum, politicians looking to clean up their reputations and gain legitimacy tend to turn to evangelical pastors. The growing presence of religion in Latin American politics is mainly driven by the flexibility of several evangelical pastors. It is no surprise, then, that in Brazil, President Bolsonaro resorts systematically to evangelical support to curb criticisms against him. The same phenomenon is at work in Peru but in a more subdued manner.

As Roberto Blancarte has rightly pointed out, "religion never left the public sphere" in Latin America.[46] Although the legal system, influenced by Western jurisprudence, shows an advanced state of secularization, the worldview of most Latin Americans never assimilated the differentiation of spheres. It remained, as many authors have underlined and borrowing the notion from Weber, "enchanted," a situation that does not preclude an

---

[44] Michele Dillon, *Postsecular Catholicism* (New York: Oxford University Press, 2018).

[45] Very few renowned clergy members have been involved in politics capitalizing on their religious aura. Among them, it is worth mentioning the former bishop, Fernando Lugo, who became president of Paraguay, and in Peru the former priest, Pedro Arana, who was elected to Congress. If at first their previous ecclesiastical career helped them, they were quickly forced to mark a distance from the Church, which is not the case with former pastors.

[46] Roberto Blancarte, "Secularism and Secularization," in Garrard-Burnett, Freston, and Dove, eds., *Cambridge History of Religions*, 331–45, at 339.

alternative modernity based on parameters different from those related to the triumph of occidental illustration. The title of an article by Gustavo Morello and others on the "Latin American religious landscape" sums up the situation in a striking formula: "Enchanted modernity."[47]

This perspective leads us to another point of entry for understanding the presence of religion in the political sphere. Pastors bring a sacral dimension into politics. In a world inhabited by supernatural entities,[48] pastors become a source of special blessing that materializes in political success. In this way evangelicals have partly assumed the role played by the Catholic hierarchy under the system of royal patronage, whose structure survived after independence until 1980.

As Daniel Levine pointed out, "politics bites back."[49] Involvement in politics implies the tremendous risk of being associated with political scandals and getting dragged down. That was true in the case of Gilberto Siura, a prominent congressman who systematically supported President Fujimori and whose career was truncated with Fujimori's fall.[50]

However, the pattern of politics in Peru, as analyzed by Levitsky, enables evangelicals to escape from the aftermath of political scandals. The (lack of) structure in political parties mirrors that of evangelical churches. The "nomadic" attitude in relation to churches characterizes the attitude of members and of pastors.[51] Moreover, unlike the Catholic Church (or other historical Protestant churches), a strong unified institution that takes responsibility for clergy members, most Peruvian evangelical churches are weaker institutions that do not request the same loyalty.

[47] Manuel Marzal, *Tierra encantada* (Lima: PUCP, 2002); Virginia Garrard-Burnett, Paul Freston and Stephen Dove, "Introduction: The Cambridge History of Religions in Latin America," in Garrard-Burnett, Freston, and Dove, eds., *The Cambridge History of Religions*, 1–21, at 17; Gustavo Morello, Catalina Romero, Hugo Rabbia, and Nestor Dacosta, "An Enchanted Modernity: Making Sense of Latin America's Religious Landscape," *Critical Research on Religion* 5:3 (2017): 308–26; and Lecaros, "Les oxymores religieux."

[48] Charles Taylor, *Encanto y desencantamiento* (Madrid: Sal Terrae, 2015); Charles Taylor, "Les anti-lumières immanentes," in Cyrille Michon, ed., *Christianisme: Héritages et destins* (Paris: Le Livre de Poche, 2002), 155–84; and Lecaros, "Les oxymores religieux."

[49] Daniel Levine, "Conclusion: Evangelicals and Democracy, the Experience of Latin America in Context," in Paul Freston, ed., *Evangelical Christianity and Democracy in Latin America* (Oxford: Oxford University Press, 2008), 217.

[50] Lecaros, *La Iglesia Católica y el desafío*, 89.

[51] Véronique Lecaros, "Estudios de recorridos religiosos: los desafiliados en context," *Estudos de Religião* 31:3 (2017): 71–90.

Peruvian pastors may easily recycle themselves across the evangelical field and eventually realize the dream of creating their own church. Consequently, denominations do not have to bear responsibility for their (former) pastors' errors.

In 2008 Levine could not foresee that political and religious evolution would enable clever evangelical politicians to become scandal-proof, at least in Peru. Notwithstanding personal convictions, Rosas' career is a good example of the evangelical ability to avoid the biting back of politics. To enter into politics, Pastor Rosas, who was then number two in his denomination, the Christian and Missionary Alliance, was invited to take a furlough from his pastoral work, as is the norm in the institution. However, he was immediately welcomed in triumph in the independent Neo-Pentecostal Church, Camino de Vida. Although technically he was not acting as a pastor, he still kept the title. Therefore, his relationship with sacred matters and his supernatural aura were preserved. He was first elected to Congress in the party of Fujimori's daughter, Keiko, in 2011. He left the party in 2015 when Keiko expressed a liberal position on same-sex union in a conference at Harvard University. He then joined César Acuña's party (APP). However, when Acuña was forced to resign from his candidacy for president due to an ethical problem not related to finance (the main problem according to public opinion),[52] Rosas did not resign, arguing that being elected to Congress would enable him, anyway, to promote a moral agenda. Rosas consistently avoided being tarred by scandal.

Who Is Involved in Politics? How? Is There a Common Perspective?

Historic Protestant churches and liberal churches represent an insignificant proportion of the Peruvian population, barely a few thousand members. Following the international religious agenda, they are mainly involved in social interreligious and ecumenical public activities. Apart from the tiny liberal minority, most churches belong to the Neo-Pentecostal movement or are greatly influenced by it.[53]

Many scholars consider that the evangelical stance on public affairs has greatly evolved in the past decades and that most evangelical pastors have changed their perspective on the so-called world, understood in the

---

[52] Acuña was convicted of plagiarism in his PhD thesis and his subsequent book. Consequently, he was forced to drop his candidacy. However, in a country such as Peru, where intellectual property does not mean much, this situation was not understood or condemned by public opinion in general.

[53] Pew Research Center, *Religion in Latin America*; and Lecaros, *La conversión*. Most of the book deals with this theme.

evangelist John's sense, no longer shunning it. When presenting his party (National Restoration) objectives, in 2005, Pastor Lay criticized the attitude about politics that had dominated the evangelical worldview: "politics is dirty [and even demoniac] and Christians should not get involved in it."[54] Through politics, Lay intended to promote laws respectful of Christian values. In other words, he was claiming that the world has to be reconquered for Christianity.

This change of attitude toward politics may be attributed to social and theological evolution. From a sociological point of view, evangelicals have grown from a small countercultural minority to a significant proportion of the population, which makes their positions more visible and worth listening to. Referring to the classical distinction of Troeltsch, Cristian Parker considers that evolving from sects to churches, from small minority communities to massive groups, evangelical denominations have relinquished their aspiration for perfection on the margin of the world to form "conservative institutions" ready to "accommodate to the world."[55]

Some specialists have also stressed the importance of a new wave of charismatic Pentecostalism which has brought about a rupture in theological convictions from a premillennial perspective to a postmillennial one.[56] Pentecostal pastors used to live with the prospect of an imminent second coming, intending to save as many souls as possible. With the second Pentecostal wave and the expansion of new conceptions related to prosperity theology and positive confession, authors state that Pentecostals have changed their attitude toward the world, getting involved in social and public matters and aspiring to improve their conditions of living.

No doubt these changes are noteworthy. However, we argue that they are not as sweeping as they may seem. We shall analyze the situation by addressing two questions: Who is involved in these changes? Have their purpose and orientation changed? That is, is it a different worldview or a different way of formulating an enduring worldview?

Churches' norms on politics differ greatly. On the one hand, for some churches, and especially Neo-Pentecostal, independent, and apostolic churches,[57] involvement in politics is considered as a logical

---

[54] Gutierrez, *Protestantismo y poder*, 76.

[55] Parker, "Religious Pluralism."

[56] Allan Anderson, "Pentecostal and Charismatic Theology," in David Ford, ed., *The Modern Theologians* (Oxford: Blackwell, 2005), 589–607, at 597; and Pérez Guadalupe, *Entre Dios y el César*, 190.

[57] Brad Christerson and Richard Flory, *The Rise of Network Christianity* (Oxford: Oxford University Press, 2017).

and dutiful prolongation of their functions. Pastor (and now Apostle, since 2012) Lazo's political career illustrates this trend. Ten or fifteen years ago, evangelical political involvement relied on scattered initiatives. Nowadays, the approach has become more structured. Through conferences at the international level, many church leaders, related to each other in networks, work to coordinate a program to promote the formation of evangelical political leaders. In March 2020 (just before the lockdown) such a conference was held in Lima in one of the city's best hotels, Los Delfines.

On the other hand, many churches that are traditional international institutions, especially those closer to the initial Pentecostal or evangelical (in this case, in the North American sense of the term) perspective, still officially maintain a distance from politics, but their position has become more ambiguous. The Assemblies of God, one of the most numerous churches, forbids its pastors from becoming candidates for Congress. However, there is a discreet, unofficial change going on. Although the denomination did not officially endorse participation in the demonstration labeled "Don't You Mess with My Children," local pastors were enticed by the central headquarters to encourage participation, and many of the panels were actually prepared on the premises of its chapels.[58]

Although the imminence of the apocalypse may not be predicted with the same eagerness as in the early days of Pentecostal formation and expansion, the eschatological horizon remains omnipresent. According to a report of the Pew Research Center, evangelicals are much more likely to believe that "Jesus will return in their lifetime." In Peru 62 percent of evangelicals believed it, compared to 43 percent of Catholics. The question is phrased in such a way that probably many more than that believe that the end of the world is near.[59] While this theme is obviously very much influenced by North American literature, it remains for researchers to investigate how much it has resonated with the local culture. Scholars have noted, for instance, the messianic tone of traditional Andean religiosity.[60]

---

[58] Lecaros, "El movimiento *Con Mis Hijos No Te Metas*."

[59] Maria das Dores Campos, "Speaking Up against Abortion and Homosexuality: Pentecostalism and Politics in Contemporary Brazil," in Martin Lindhardt, ed., *New Ways of Being Pentecostal in Latin America* (Lanham, Md.: Lexington Books, 2016), 209–24 at 214.

[60] Juan Ossio, *El Tahuantinsuyo bíblico* (Lima: Biblioteca Nacional del Perú, 2014), 38–51. Most authors analyzing the growth of the evangelical population have pondered the influence of Catholic popular piety, but there is still much research to do on

Besides occasional references in speeches, apocalypticism can be observed publicly in the way evangelical leaders deal with Israel and with ecological matters. The unconditional support evangelicals give to the State of Israel does not stem from political or ethnic reasons but from an interpretation of the Bible. Following a literal understanding of the Scriptures, as most evangelicals are prone to do—68 percent according to Pew—the end of the world will come when the Jews are back in the "promised land."[61] The creation of the State of Israel is considered a sure sign of the impending apocalypse. Besides Ezekiel (34:11–13), there are several Old Testament references to the holy land being promised to Israel by God. However, at the final stage of history, as Paul envisions in his epistle to the Romans, Jews are meant to convert to Christianity and to merge in the Christian mass. Israel is characterized as "God's prophetic clock," a familiar expression in international evangelical circles, which has also been adopted by Peruvian pastors, among them the influential Pastor Rodolfo Gonzalez from the MMM.[62] The support for Israel materializes in diverse statements from the pulpit, in money collections, and in all kinds of fancy rituals with the Israeli flag carried in triumph.[63] Pressures on the Peruvian government to develop a pro-Zionist and religiously colored stance are not comparable to what has happened in the United States, Brazil, and Guatemala, and up to now the Peruvian international position has not changed. Yet backing for Israel has become widespread among the evangelicals of Peru.

In reference to ecological disasters that are partly the consequence of global warming, evangelicals show a skeptical lack of interest, and some of the pastors consider the events clear signs of the impending end of the world. A literal interpretation of the Bible has little to say about man-made influence on the climate, since it was not obvious at the time or at

---

the relation between traditional worldviews and Pentecostalism, especially regarding eschatology.

[61] Pew Research Center, *Religion in Latin America*.

[62] The literature on the end of the world and the role played by Israel is abundant. Most of the books have been written in the United States. Some of them have been translated and are readily available on the internet. Among others, we can cite Adrian Rogers, *Apocalipsis, el fin de los tiempos* (Nashville: B&H Publishing Group, 2007), 130; and Pastor Rodolfo Gonzalez, leader of MMM in Peru, speaking about the end of the world and the role of Israel: https://www.youtube.com/watch?v=VXHWTu2KkxU.

[63] Personal observations in the Neo-Pentecostal church Agua Viva, among others, during previous research in 2013.

least was not perceived in this way. On the contrary, several pastors contest the existence of global warming. They emphasize the dominion over
nature given to human beings by God and especially the divine promise of
not destroying the world made to Noah after the flood.[64]

Catastrophes considered by scientists as partly caused by human
beings are systematically interpreted as divine signs in an eschatological
perspective. The drought in the River Euphrates has been interpreted by
Pastor Gonzalez of MMM through the book of Revelation (16:12) as an
element of the ultimate apocalyptic battle. Fires that have been raging in
Brazil and in Bolivia are also considered as omens of the final days of our
doomed world. On the other hand, the COVID-19 crisis has represented
a great financial bonus for the House of the Bible in Lima, the main evangelical cultural center renowned for its conferences and bookshop. At the
peak of the pandemic, the bookshop sold more Bibles in two months than
during the previous two years. The favorite version is that of Cyrus Sco-
field with its pre-millennial emphasis. According to the pastor in charge
of the cultural section of the institution, the impending apocalypse has
become the current talk among pastors who scrutinize the Bible in search
of a convincing interpretation of the signs of the time.

Although human beings are not to destroy the creation, they are
meant to interpret events in a biblical perspective and to foster and
guide the evolution of those events in an eschatological direction. Ultimately, worldly situations have to be thought of and acted upon to promote God's designs and those disasters are part of them.[65] From this
perspective, there is no point in worrying about ecological disasters. The
eschatological horizon haunts both Pentecostal and Neo-Pentecostal
perspectives. As Jesus Garcia Ruiz (2004) stated, "Pentecostals considered that it was necessary to isolate from this world dominated by Satan,
while waiting for the second coming of Christ who was to establish the
Kingdom of God; for Neo-Pentecostals, the kingdom of God is already
here and the Christians must work so that everything will be ready to
welcome the Savior."[66] Garcia Ruiz was researching and writing almost
twenty years ago when differences between those two trends, Pente-

---

[64] Robin Veldman, *The Gospel of Climate Skepticism* (Oakland: University of California Press, 2019), 2.

[65] Veldman, *Gospel of Climate Skepticism.*

[66] Jesus Garcia Ruiz, "Le néopentecôtisme au Guatemala: entre privatisation,
marchés et réseaux," *Critique Internationale* 22:1 (2004): 81–94.

costal and Neo-Pentecostal, were deeper. Nowadays, the eschatological horizon may be considered as a bridge that contributes to the formation of a common perspective on social and political matters among the various sections of Neo-Pentecostalism.

As Pérez Guadalupe pointed out, evangelicals do not appear to have developed a structured political program.[67] However, if we consider the importance of this eschatological horizon, then moral matters end up being essential. They represent sure guides for salvation and for preparation for the second coming of Christ. Moreover, in an enchanted world where spheres are not differentiated, incompliance with moral norms entails dire consequences. Pastor Rosas, in keeping with the logic of the "Don't You Mess with My Children" movement, published on his Facebook page that the expansion of homosexuality is responsible for the COVID-19 crisis.[68] Morality is not just about morality but about the deeply rooted perturbation of our world.[69] If we "restore" moral obedience, as Pastor Lay offered to do, then the way is paved for the "restoration" of the world to what it was before the appearance of sin, which is precisely what is destined to happen at the second coming of Christ. In this perspective, morality is the only worthwhile and efficient program.

Concluding Reflections

Since their *coup d'éclat* in Fujimori's political campaign in 1990, there is no doubt that the involvement of evangelicals in public affairs has grown in scope and visibility. Their reputation for honesty and their morally orientated agenda have made a strong appeal in the context of a liberal societal evolution and of the many scandals that have recently rocked Peruvian politics. If ethical matters have always been part of the evangelical program, after the promulgation of their legal status in 2010, their program of a moral agenda has come to the forefront. However, evangelical political power does not transit through usual channels; rather, it comes through the need for legitimacy that politicians seek to obtain from them. Moreover, the way Catholicism, after Vatican II, distanced itself from government and political affairs opened the way for a more incisive presence of evangelicals. They took advantage of the vacuum left by the secularizing

---

67 Pérez Guadalupe, *Entre Dios y el César*. It is the thesis of the entire book.

68 Cristian Rosas on Facebook (December 2020): https://www.facebook.com/xtian .rosas/.

69 Lecaros, "El movimiento *Con Mis Hijos No Te Metas*."

position of the Catholic Church that did not correspond to the enchanted worldview shared by most Peruvians.

We have argued that the eschatological horizon still dominates the evangelical worldview and that it plays an essential role in their decisions. If until the end of the twentieth century it entailed an isolation from the "devilish world" and an intent to form holy communities, nowadays it entices Christians to promote a moral renovation of the world. In other words, we are observing a different way of enacting an enduring worldview. More research is needed to understand the articulation between interpretations of the Bible, eschatological perspectives, political programs, and skepticism toward empirical scientific results. Contrary to what sociological theories expected up until the end of the twentieth century, religious beliefs are still shaping the world.

10

Brazilian Immigrants and Evangelicalism in South Florida since 1990

Matheus Reis

The first significant wave of Brazilian immigration to the United States happened in the 1980s, but it was only in the 1990s that migration flows began to move toward Florida. Today, Florida is home to one of the largest Brazilian enclaves in the United States, and the current Brazilian diasporic community in South Florida is multifaceted and complex. Brazilian immigrants often fight to break away from some of the negative stereotypes placed on Latino(a) immigrants in the United States as they work to forge their own identities as a distinct community. This journey of self-discovery is a laborious one, as concepts of identity are both fluid and are influenced by a plethora of factors, thus creating several possibilities for the conceptualization of one's identity as a Brazilian immigrant in the United States. These identity-shaping factors directly impact Brazilian evangelical churches in the diaspora, whose mission seeks to reflect and develop the ethnic identity of *evangélicos*. In Portuguese the term "*evangélico*" means "evangelical," but not with the same connotation it normally carries in the United States. For Brazilians, as is the case with other Latino(a) communities, the term *evangélico* is a catchall, and is equivalent to "Protestant" in English because it serves to represent all non-Catholic Christians. However, in the case of Brazilian *evangélicos* in South Florida, almost all would be evangelicals in the Anglophone sense—that is, the great majority of them are conservative in their theology. I will be referring to individuals as *evangélicos* because that is how they understand themselves, rather than imposing on them a Western term, such as "evangelicals," and when speaking of the movement, I will refer to it as "Brazilian evangelicalism," but it should be understood as encompassing all *evangélicos*.

The landscape of Brazilian Christianity in South Florida is very different from that of Brazil. While Roman Catholic adherence is still the leading form of Christianity in Brazil at 70 percent of the population,[1] the opposite is true in South Florida, where Catholic parishes are few and far between, and the needs of Brazilian migrants are met primarily by evangelical churches. This different dynamic between Brazilian evangelical and Catholic churches fosters new relationships that are evident between the two parties in the diaspora in South Florida. *Evangélicos* are also faced with the issue of undocumented migration, a challenge exclusive to the diaspora, and the many difficulties brought on by a lack of residency status.

This chapter will explore the relationship between Brazilian immigrants and evangelicalism in South Florida since 1990 by looking at three particular issues: 1) The identity struggles experienced by many Brazilians in the United States, who often repudiate the label of "Hispanic" placed on them by the government. 2) The fact that evangelical churches, much more than Catholic parishes (which are few and very large), fulfill the religious needs of the migrants. 3) The moral issue of how Brazilian evangelical pastors have negotiated the problem of the undocumented status of many of their congregants. This will be done by focusing first on the history of Brazilian immigration to the United States, the specific factors that influenced the earliest significant Brazilian migration wave to America, and an assessment of the size of the Brazilian community in the United States and in Florida. After this brief overview of the history of Brazilian immigration to the United States, this chapter will turn its focus to the issues of ethnic identity experienced by Brazilian immigrants in the United States. The chapter will then examine the relationship between *evangélicos* and Brazilian Catholics before addressing how pastors have negotiated the presence of many undocumented parishioners in their congregations.

---

[1]   Todd M. Johnson and Gina A. Zurlo, eds., *World Christian Database* (Leiden: Brill), accessed November 2020, https://worldchristiandatabase-org.ezproxy.is.ed.ac .uk/wcd/#/detail/country/28/98-churches.

Brazilian Immigration to the United States

During its first century and a half of existence as a nation state, Brazil was a nation of immigration rather than emigration.[2] Brazil's first emperor, Dom Pedro I, wanted to fill agricultural jobs, which caused him to loosen Brazil's immigration policies in the 1820s, and led to the arrival of the first successful Protestant settlements in Brazil. It was not until the mid- to late twentieth century that Brazilians began emigrating to countries like the United States, Japan, Portugal, and some European countries.[3] This Brazilian diaspora reached its peak as a result of the financial crisis of the 1980s, considered by many to be Brazil's "lost decade." Brazil had experienced a coup in 1964, which led to a military dictatorship that lasted until 1985. These were tumultuous years for Brazil, as the military exercised control over free speech and free expression, causing hundreds of artists, academics, and political figures to flee the country.[4] Brazil's financial crisis of the 1980s also increased the nation's levels of crime and violence,[5] and it shattered Brazil's lower and middle classes.[6] The hyperinflation was accompanied by a high level of unemployment, low wages, a high cost of living, and an economic recession, evidenced by the fact that during this period Brazil went through four different currencies, five freezes of salaries and prices, and nine government programs that attempted to stabilize the economy.[7]

Although it is not known where the first Brazilian immigrants settled in the United States, there are accounts as early as the mid- to late 1960s of Brazilian enclaves in New York City, the Catskill Mountain region of New York State, Newark (New Jersey), Boston, and California.[8] Records show

[2]   Álvaro Eduardo de Castro e Lima and Alanni de Lacerda Barbosa de Castro, *Brasileiros nos Estados Unidos: meio século (re)fazendo a América (1960-2010)* (Brasília: FUNAG, 2017), 13. According to Lima and Castro, from 1822 to 1949 Brazil received approximately 5 million immigrants, most of them being Italian, Portuguese, and Spanish, while some were German, Japanese, Polish, and Syrian-Lebanese.

[3]   Maxine Margolis, *Goodbye Brazil: Emigrés from the Land of Soccer and Samba* (Madison: University of Wisconsin Press, 2013), 17.

[4]   Margolis, *Goodbye Brazil*, 4.

[5]   Cristina Rocha and Manuel A. Vásquez, "O Brasil na nova cartografia global da religião," *Religião & Sociedade* 34:1 (2014): 13–37, at 17.

[6]   Rodrigo Serrao and James Cavendish, "The Social Functions and Dysfunctions of Brazilian Immigrant Congregations in 'Terra Incognita,'" *Review of Religious Research* 60:3 (2018): 367–88, at 369.

[7]   Lima and Castro, *Brasileiros nos Estados Unidos*, 15.

[8]   Maxine Margolis, *An Invisible Minority: Brazilians in New York City* (Gainesville: University Press of Florida, 2009), 2.

that 22,310 Brazilians were legally admitted to the country between 1966 and 1979.[9] Nevertheless, the first substantial wave of Brazilian immigration occurred only in the mid- to late 1980s,[10] when the more significant Brazilian diaspora began. The preferred destinations for Brazilian immigrants changed from the 1980s to the 1990s and beyond. In the 1980s, California and New York held more than one third of the Brazilian population in the United States, with only 12 percent of Brazilians living in Florida and Massachusetts together.[11] In 1990, immigration flows began to change toward Florida and Massachusetts, then holding 23 percent of the Brazilian diaspora, while the aggregate proportion of the Brazilian population residing in California or New York went down to 32 percent.[12] In 2000 Florida became the favorite state for Brazilians, with 21 percent of the Brazilian population, and in reports from 2014, Florida retained the largest concentration of Brazilians in the United States at 20 percent, followed by Massachusetts at 17 percent, California at 10 percent, New Jersey at 9 percent, and New York at 7 percent.[13] These five states combined hold nearly two-thirds (63 percent) of the Brazilian diaspora community in the United States,[14] and in terms of cities, Florida has five out of the ten with the largest concentrations of Brazilians.[15]

Brazilians in South Florida

The unofficial estimates of the Brazilian population in Florida vary between two hundred thousand and three hundred thousand,[16] with

[9]   Ana Cristina Braga Martes, *Brasileiros nos Estados Unidos: Um estudo sobre imigrantes em Massachusetts* (São Paulo: Paz e Terra, 1999), 47.
[10]   Donizete Rodrigues, "The Brazilianization of New York City: Brazilian Immigrants and Evangelical Churches in a Pluralized Urban Landscape," in Richard P. Cimino, Nadia A. Mian, and Weishan Huang, eds., *Ecologies of Faith in New York City: The Evolution of Religious Institutions* (Bloomington: Indiana University Press, 2013), 123.
[11]   Lima and Castro, *Brasileiros nos Estados Unidos*, 55.
[12]   Lima and Castro, *Brasileiros nos Estados Unidos*, 55.
[13]   Lima and Castro, *Brasileiros nos Estados Unidos*, 55. These estimated figures are based on the report on the Brazilian diaspora community in the U.S. sponsored by Brazil's Ministry of Foreign Affairs titled, *Brasileiros nos Estados Unidos: Meio século (re)fazendo a America (1960–2010)*, which came out in 2017.
[14]   Lima and Castro, *Brasileiros nos Estados Unidos*, 55.
[15]   Alex Guedes Brum, "A história da imigração de Brasileiros para o sul da Flórida," *Revista de História Regional* 23:2 (2018): 239–55, at 249.
[16]   Jose Claudio Souza Alves and Lucia Ribeiro, "Migração, religião e transnacionalismo: O caso dos Brasileiros no Sul da Florida," *Religião e Sociedade* 22:2 (2002): 65–90.

official American Community Survey (ACS) numbers showing a population of sixty-six thousand in 2011.[17] One of the main reasons for such a discrepancy in population sizes is the issue of undocumented migration. Margolis points out that in 2007, an estimated 63 percent of Brazilians were living without documentation in the United States, and that by 2009 Brazil became one of the top ten countries to send undocumented migrants to the United States.[18] Lucia Ribeiro's figures are even higher, estimating that 70 percent to 80 percent of Brazilians in the United States are undocumented.[19] Most of these undocumented Brazilian migrants arrived by plane on a tourist visa and overstayed their visas, thus becoming undocumented, while others attempted the treacherous and even deadly crossing of the Mexican border.[20]

The state of Florida is divided into sixty-seven counties, and Brazilians have settled primarily in its three southernmost ones, namely Palm Beach, Broward, and Miami-Dade.[21] The majority of Brazilian immigrants are found spread out across a corridor stretching southward along Interstate 95 from Boca Raton (Palm Beach County) to Broward County, with the highest concentrations to be found in the cities of Pompano Beach and Deerfield Beach in Broward County.[22]

Brazilian immigrants settled in these cities because of the lower cost of living in comparison to wealthier places such as Miami and Fort Lauderdale.[23] Unlike in other Brazilian enclaves in Boston and New York, where public transportation is both efficient and readily available, Brazilians in South Florida (with the small exception of downtown Miami) do not enjoy such access to public transport. Also, given how spread out these cities in South Florida are, Brazilians must rely on the ability to drive a car

---

[17] Margolis, *Goodbye Brazil*, 93.
[18] Margolis, *Goodbye Brazil*, 6.
[19] Lucia Ribeiro, "Religious Experiences among Brazilian Migrants," *REMHU— Revista Interdisciplinar da Mobilidade Humana* 28 (2007): 71–85, at 73.
[20] Rodrigues, "The Brazilianization of New York City," 123.
[21] Brum, "A história da imigração," 244.
[22] Manuel Vasquez, "Beyond Homo Anomicus: Interpersonal Networks, Space, and Religion among Brazilians in Broward County," in Philip J. Williams, Timothy J. Steigenga, and Manuel Vasquez, eds., *A Place to Be: Brazilian, Guatemalan, and Mexican Immigrants in Florida's New Destinations* (New Brunswick, N.J.: Rutgers University Press, 2009), 41.
[23] Brum, "A história da imigração," 251.

in order to get around, something that can be problematic for undocumented migrants who are unable to obtain a driver's license.[24]

The Brazilian diasporic community in South Florida has been the subject of a few fieldwork-based research projects. Manuel Vasquez and Luciana Ribeiro, whose fieldwork focused on the cities of Pompano Beach and Deerfield Beach in Broward County between 2001 and 2004, conducted one of these projects.[25] Vasquez and Ribeiro's survey results corroborated the Brazilian diaspora migration flow to South Florida that we have presented thus far, with 92 percent of respondents having moved to the United States after 1990, and 41 percent after 2000.[26]

I also performed fieldwork research in South Florida between 2018 and 2020 for my PhD studies, which is the basis for this chapter. My research focused on three case studies of Brazilian evangelical churches in the counties of Palm Beach and Broward: *Igreja New Wave* (INW), *Igreja Presbiteriana da Florida* (IPF), and Renovation Church Portuguese (RCP).[27] INW, a non-denominational, charismatic church, which has its roots in Baptist theology, was located in the heart of the Brazilian hub, in the city of Deerfield Beach. Although INW was charismatic, Pastor Lucas, the lead pastor, did not stress glossolalia as the primary evidence of being filled with the Holy Spirit, which differentiated him from classical Pentecostalism. INW started in 2008 as a small group of fifteen people who met together at Pastor Lucas' house. Since then, INW has met in eleven different buildings, the current one having been purchased by the church in June 2019. At that time, INW had a congregation of 563, comprising 147 males, 176 females,

---

[24]   Manuel Vasquez and Lucia Ribeiro, "A Igreja é como a casa da minha mãe: Religião e espaço vivido entre Brasileiros no Condado de Broward," *Ciencias Sociales Y Religion/Ciências Sociais e Religião* 9:9 (2007): 13–29, at 17.

[25]   Ribeiro, "Religious Experiences," 73. Vasquez and Ribeiro's findings were the source of four publications: Vasquez' aforementioned book chapter titled "Beyond Homo Anomicus: Interpersonal Networks, Space, and Religion among Brazilians in Broward County"; Ribeiro's aforementioned articles titled "Religious Experiences among Brazilian Migrants" and "Migração, religião e transnacionalismo: O caso dos Brasileiros no Sul da Florida;" and their joint effort titled "A Igreja é como a casa da minha mãe: Religião e espaço vivido entre Brasileiros no Condado De Broward."

[26]   Vasquez and Ribeiro, "A Igreja é como a casa da minha mãe," 14.

[27]   In the interest of the protection of the participants in this study, all names of churches, pastors, and interviewed participants have been replaced by pseudonyms by mutual agreement. Any and all similarities with real names of churches or people are mere coincidences.

120 youth, and 120 children. It is important to note that INW had the largest youth group of any Brazilian Protestant church in South Florida at the time of my fieldwork in 2019, with the number of young people fluctuating between 120 and 189. INW was a bilingual church, offering simultaneous translation into English, through an interpreter who stood next to the speaker at the podium,[28] for both their regular church services and youth gatherings.

Located in the city of Boca Raton, IPF was situated at the very end of Palm Beach County, but close enough to the center of the Brazilian hub, as it neighbored the city of Deerfield Beach. First established in June 2011, IPF was one of the few Reformed churches in South Florida at the time of my fieldwork. In February 2019, IPF had a total of 167 congregants, made up of 49 males, 54 females, 38 youth, and 26 children. In terms of language used, IPF's services were rendered in Portuguese, while the youth gatherings were a mix of Portuguese and English, depending on which youth leader was speaking.

Founded in 2017, RCP was the Lusophone campus of Renovation Church, a multicultural, multi-sited, noncharismatic church affiliated with the Southern Baptist Convention. Located in Palm Beach Gardens, a city in the north end of Palm Beach County, between West Palm Beach and Jupiter, RCP was quite far from the Brazilian hub in Broward County. Unlike most Brazilian Protestant churches in South Florida, RCP had an unusual setup in that they were actually a part of an American church, rather than simply renting a church building from one. In September 2019 RCP had a congregation of 103, comprising 45 adults, 19 youth, and 39 children.[29] In terms of language RCP's main services were rendered fully in Portuguese, but its children's services and youth gatherings were done in English.

Having briefly described the history of Brazilian immigration to the United States and having assessed the Brazilian community in South Florida, this chapter will now turn to current issues of identity facing Brazilian *evangélico* immigrants as it pertains to the ethnic labels employed in the United States.

---

[28]   In Portuguese the more appropriate term to refer to the whole front area of the church from which the service is led would be *púlpito* or "pulpit." The words "stage" and "platform" could be used, but the term "podium" was chosen to avoid any theatrical associations.

[29]   Unfortunately, RCP did not keep a membership record based on gender; therefore, the number of adults has been reported together.

Latino, Hispanic, or Neither? Current Issues of Ethnic Identity for Brazilian Immigrants in the United States

In her seminal work on the Brazilian diaspora in New York City titled *Little Brazil: An Ethnography of Brazilian Immigrants in New York City*, Margolis called the Brazilian immigrant community an "invisible minority" because of their lack of settled identity as a separate community. Such lack of identity begins with the ambiguous racial and ethnic categorizations employed by the census, which serves to reinforce a feeling of exclusion experienced by Brazilian immigrants, whose self-identity is deeply rooted in their perceived uniqueness as "Brazilians," rather than in their participation in pan-ethnic categories such as "Latinos" or "South Americans."

It is important to understand the terms used by the U.S. census in order to realize where the problem lies. The terms "Hispanic," "Latino," and "Spanish" can be somewhat confusing because they are often used interchangeably, even though they are not synonymous, and belonging to one group does not mean belonging to all. For example, people born in Mexico are considered Hispanic for linguistic reasons—being Hispanophone—and Latino because of their geographical placement in Latin America. On the other hand, people born in Spain are Hispanic linguistically but not Latino because their geographical placement is in Europe. When it comes to Brazilians, they are Latinos geographically, because they also come from part of Latin America, but they cannot be classified as Hispanic linguistically because they are Lusophone. One of the problems lies in the fact that in the United States., "Hispanic" and "Latino" are used interchangeably, and often synonymously, with "Hispanic" being the more common term. For instance, although the census questionnaire inquires if the person is of "Hispanic, Latino, or Spanish origin," the instructions state that the question is about "Hispanic origins," rather than Hispanic and/or Latino origins as the question implies, and both the 2000 and 2010 census questionnaires did not have a specified category for Brazilians.

Margolis rightly argues that being Brazilian in Brazil is completely different than being Brazilian in the United States, where one goes from being identified as part of a nationality to being reduced to an ethnic group, and from being the majority to becoming the minority.[30] This phenomenon thrusts members of the Brazilian diaspora into an ever-present struggle

---

[30] Maxine Margolis, "Becoming Brazucas: Brazilian Identity in the United States," in José Luis Falconi and José Antonio Mazzoti, eds., *The Other Latinos: Central and South Americans in the United States* (Cambridge: Cambridge University Press, 2007), 213.

for self-identity, a process that is performed at an individual level, where one's migrant identity is not only disputed by others, but also becomes an issue of self-doubt.[31] This struggle for self-discovery is negotiated differently by members of different generations, namely the first, the "1.5," and the second generation of Brazilian immigrants. First-generation immigrants are foreign-born, those who initially arrived in the new country in their maturity. The 1.5 generation, a term coined by Rubén G. Rumbaut in his studies of Cuban and Southeast Asian youths in the 70s and 80s,[32] serves to describe the children of first-generation immigrants who arrived in their new country during or before their early teenage years. Second-generation immigrants are the children of first-generation immigrants who were born in the new country. 1.5- and second-generation Brazilians have a more acute struggle staking their claim for self-identity. Having spent most if not all of their lives in the United States, members of these generations may struggle to be accepted as a Brazilian by their relatives in Brazil, who may view them as a *gringo(a)*, especially if they speak Portuguese with an accent. When it comes to the United States, they may also struggle to be accepted as an American because of their Brazilian heritage, regardless of whether they are U.S. citizens or not. Research shows that later-generation Latinos are more disconnected from their heritage than foreign-born ones.[33] Thus, a unique dynamic appears when these later-generation Brazilians still face the struggles of being part of a minority, even though they may not see themselves as such. This creates a phenomenon that I would call "ethnic homelessness," which is the inability to feel at home as either a Brazilian or an American.

In terms of the self-acceptance of ethnic labels, research shows that Latin Americans in general prefer to self-identify by nationality rather than by the more encompassing terms of Latino and Hispanic.[34] In the

---

[31] Rosana Resende, "Tropical Brazucas: Brazilians in South Florida and the Imaginary of National Identity" (PhD diss., University of Florida, 2009), 176.

[32] Rubén G. Rumbaut, "Ages, Life Stages, and Generational Cohorts: Decomposing the Immigrant First and Second Generations in the United States," *International Migration Review* 38:3 (2004): 1160–205, at 1166.

[33] "Hispanic Identity Fades across Generations as Immigrant Connections Fall Away," (Washington, D.C.: Pew Research Center, 2017), https://www.pewresearch.org/hispanic/2017/12/20/hispanic-identity-fades-across-generations-as-immigrant-connections-fall-away/ph_2017-12-20_hispanic-identity_11/.

[34] Helen Marrow, "To Be or Not to Be (Hispanic or Latino)," *Ethnicities* 3:4 (2003): 427–64, at 440.

1990 U.S. census, which did not have the addition of the Latino nomen-clature, 91 percent of Brazilian respondents self-identified as "not His-panic."[35] One of the reasons that Brazilians reject the label of Hispanic is because of the longstanding prejudice associated with the term in the United States.[36] Margolis points out that much of ethnicity is built upon the attempt to differentiate one's own ethnic group from another's.[37] By claiming "we are not like them," members of an ethnic group seek to dis-tinguish themselves from all things associated with other groups, and thus try to establish their own identities over and against another's. In the case of Brazilians vis-à-vis Hispanics, this self-identification operates to the detriment of Hispanics because Brazilians often contribute to the perpet-uation of negative U.S.-given stereotypes of Hispanics in general.[38] Never-theless, 1.5-generation Brazilians are more likely to embrace "Latino" and/ or "Hispanic" as a label given their higher level of acceptance of the U.S. racial and ethnic classification system, especially when there are benefits for taking on a minority label, such as in certain applications for jobs, schools, or scholarships.

The Evangelicalization of Brazilian Christianity in South Florida

> Pentecostalism is a translatable religion and not at all territorial, being based neither on a national church structure of dioceses and parishes, which is very difficult to uproot and transplant, nor on shrines and places of pilgrimage, which are also difficult to uproot. As a nonterrito-rial religion, Pentecostalism is very flexible.[39]

Paul Freston has argued that evangelicalism, especially in its Pentecostal form, is significantly more mobile than Catholicism. He points out that researchers of global Pentecostalism refer to it as "a religion made to travel, as in many ways an ideal religion for transnational migrants."[40]

---

[35] Margolis, "Becoming Brazucas," 219.

[36] Antonio Luciano De Andrade Tosta, "The Hispanic and Luso-Brazilian World: Latino, Eu? The Paradoxical Interplay of Identity in Brazuca Literature," *Hispania* 87:3 (2004): 576–85, at 579.

[37] Margolis, "Becoming Brazucas," 214.

[38] Tosta, "Hispanic and Luso-Brazilian World," 580–83.

[39] Paul Freston, "The Religious Field among Brazilians in the United States," in Clémence Jouët-Pastré and Leticia J. Braga, eds., *Becoming Brazuca: Brazilian Immi-gration to the United States* (Cambridge, Mass.: Harvard University David Rockefeller Center for Latin American Studies, 2008), 261.

[40] Freston, "Religious Field among Brazilians," 261.

This is certainly true of Brazilian Christianity in South Florida, where Vasquez and Ribeiro found thirty-four evangelical churches but only one Catholic church in the cities of Pompano Beach and Deerfield Beach, with the Catholic church building being large enough to accommodate parishioners from both cities.[41] This process of the evangelicalization of Brazilian Christianity in the diaspora in South Florida is largely the result of Catholic migrants being attracted to Protestant churches, as will be explored in this section, but it is also in part due to another factor, namely that Protestants (especially Pentecostals) in Brazil have been more likely to migrate than Catholics, as Freston pointed out, for a mixture of reasons—they may have more economic resources to enable them to relocate, or they may be more likely to be attracted to the primarily Protestant, conservative religious culture of the southern United States. This interesting phenomenon of the evangelicalization of Brazilian Christianity in South Florida could be explored in greater depth than the scope of this chapter allows. Nevertheless, a minimum understanding of it is necessary in order to explore its ramifications for Brazilian *evangélicos*, especially as to how they relate to Brazilian Catholics in South Florida.

In the current state of research, it is not possible to provide a precise estimate of the total size of the Brazilian evangelical community in South Florida, though it may be possible to arrive at a rough figure of the number of evangelical churches in all of South Florida. In 2018 I interviewed Pastor Antonio, a non-denominational Brazilian pastor who has worked in Broward County since the mid-1990s and who leads an interdenominational association of 161 Brazilian evangelical pastors in Florida.[42] Subsequently, through a third party he estimated that in the three-county area that is the focus of this study, namely Palm Beach, Broward, and Miami-Dade, there are approximately 140 Brazilian *evangélico* churches, a vastly larger number than the seven Lusophone Catholic parishes that, according to Padre Manoel, a Brazilian priest in Broward County, are in the region.[43] It is also important to note that the denominational landscape of Brazilian evangelicalism in South Florida is diverse. "[Our] association is non-denominational, and it comprises many denominations [such as] Presbyterian, traditional Baptist, charismatic Baptist, Reformed Methodist,

---

[41]   Vasquez and Ribeiro, "A Igreja é como a casa da minha mãe," 18.
[42]   Pastor Antonio, interview, August 20, 2018.
[43]   Padre Manoel, interview, May 1, 2020.

Pentecostal, and Neo-Pentecostal. We are very eclectic," claimed Pastor Antonio.[44] This diversity was also evident in my case studies, which included a Presbyterian church (IPF), a non-denominational charismatic church (INW), and a non-charismatic Baptist church (RCP). In terms of demographics, the gender breakdown in the adults of the three case-study sites did not seem to be significantly different than what it was among *evangélicos* in Brazil, where the 2010 census showed that a slightly higher percentage of women (24 percent) than men (20 percent) identified themselves as *evangélicos*, a pattern that has been on the increase in the past few decades.[45] If anything, there were perhaps more men present in Brazilian evangelical churches in South Florida than one might have guessed on the basis of similar studies elsewhere.

The main reason for the large discrepancy between the number of Catholic and evangelical churches is the lack of priests. Padre Manoel, who used to work in parts of South America prior to moving to the United States, stated that the Brazilian Catholic presence in South Florida has declined over the past ten years, a fact that he attributed to the difficulties of finding priests to pastor the community.

> The priest's profile has to be scrutinized for him to be able to come here [to the United States], it is another language. For instance, when I was in other places, in other missions in other countries, we did not have this difficulty because the language was easier, it was easier to relate to others. The church had less requirements.[46]

Brazilian evangelical pastors, on the other hand, are able to migrate more easily because of the less structured nature of evangelical churches in general. Freston's words ring true: "[A]nd why is Pentecostal supply so localized? Largely because it is a lay religion, not dependent on religious specialists who may be in scarce supply locally."[47] It is also true that while the Catholic Church has to train and approve of its priests prior to sending them, many evangelical pastors are immigrants first, becoming pastors only in the diaspora, while others have come at the invitation of local churches. Padre Manoel also mentioned that the financial autonomy that many pastors achieve in South Florida is a motivating factor for them to immigrate to the United States in larger

---

[44] Antonio, interview, August 20, 2018.
[45] "Brazil's Changing Religious Landscape" (Washington, D.C.: Pew Research Center, 2013), https://www.pewforum.org/2013/07/18/brazils-changing-religious-landscape/.
[46] Manoel, interview, May 1, 2020.
[47] Freston, "Religious Field among Brazilians," 261.

numbers. "The pastor, he can create a community and maintain himself economically with it, so it is more attractive to do this," he said.[48]

Another factor that has led to the evangelicalization of Brazilian Christianity in South Florida has been the migration of many Catholics to evangelical churches. Padre Manoel listed three reasons why he believes Brazilian Catholics in South Florida are flocking to Brazilian evangelical churches. The first reason is the availability and proximity of such churches in South Florida, an issue of which Padre Manoel is well aware.

> It is hard to travel one hour to attend mass and one hour in the week to participate in the prayer meeting. It is too far, so the distance makes it difficult. There are too few priests and it is too far to arrive at a church that speaks Portuguese.[49]

The second reason listed by Padre Manoel was the charismatic appeal of evangelical churches. He said that the Brazilian Catholic community in South Florida is very charismatic in its sympathies, making the transition to charismatic evangelical churches an attractive one. The Catholic Charismatic Renewal in Brazil is by far the largest in Latin America. The movement started off through the influence of two American Jesuits and a Brazilian priest in 1969 and it experienced exponential growth, starting with an adherence of ten thousand in 1970 and reaching as many as thirty-three million adherents by 2008.[50] The third reason given by Padre Manoel was the social work being offered by Brazilian evangelical churches, something that was very surprising to him. Padre Manoel mentioned that the evangelical pastors from the Brazilian communities he had worked with in Chile and on the Mexican side of the U.S.-Mexico border used to come to him for help, but Brazilian *evangélicos* in South Florida do not because their network of social support is stronger than that of Brazilian Catholics in the region. "Today, *evangélicos* have an excellent reputation in the area of social work for the Brazilian community," he said.[51]

---

[48] Manoel, interview, May 1, 2020.

[49] Manoel, interview, May 1, 2020.

[50] Todd Hartch, "The Heartland of Charismatic Catholicism," in *The Rebirth of Latin American Christianity* (New York: Oxford University Press, 2014), 113. For a more in-depth treatment of the Catholic Charismatic Renewal in Brazil, see Edward L. Cleary, "Brazil: The Charismatic Giant," in *The Rise of Charismatic Catholicism in Latin America* (Gainesville: University Press of Florida, 2011). See also Silvia Fernandes, "The Catholic Charismatic Renewal and the Catholicism That Remains: A Study of the CCR Movement in Rio De Janeiro," *Religions* 10:6 (2019): 397–418, at 397.

[51] Manoel, interview, May 1, 2020.

Not all Catholics migrate to evangelical churches, however, and not all those who migrate as *evangélicos* maintain their faith in the diaspora. The *evangélico* pastors I interviewed argued that a significant number of Brazilian Christians actually become non-religious upon migrating to the United States. These pastors believed that the financial security attained by some Brazilian immigrants in the United States may cause them to forgo church attendance altogether, as Pastor Samuel argued: "A Brazilian in Brazil goes to church because he needs to, while a Brazilian in the United States does not go (to church) because he does not need to."[52] It is true that many lower-class Brazilian immigrants discover Christianity out of financial need through the many community services that churches provide in the diaspora, but it is also true that for many upper-class Brazilian immigrants who are wealthier, Christianity may not hold the same appeal. There is also the fact that a significant portion of Brazilian immigrants are transient, and their lack of commitment to remain in the same place for a long period of time will usually lead them to not settle into a church.

The evangelicalization of Christianity in the diaspora in South Florida also has an impact on the relationship between Brazilian Catholics and *evangélicos*. For the most part the animosity and distrust that have been a mark of the relationship between Protestants and Catholics in Brazil is not present in the diaspora. This is primarily because Brazilian *evangélicos* are the majority in terms of the number of churches, and given their strong social support of immigrants, there is less competition for religious spaces between them and Brazilian Catholics. "The Catholic here is not a threat to our church," said Pastor Samuel. "I am not worried that the (church) members will leave because they (the local Catholic church) have a revived (charismatic) service," he added. This leads to a more amicable relationship between Brazilian *evangélicos* and Brazilian Catholics in South Florida. Although all of the *evangélico* pastors I spoke with believed that there is a need to "convert" Catholics to Protestantism, the manner in which they attempted to proselytize Brazilian Catholics was subtle rather than confrontational, as Pastor Vitor pointed out: "Our relationship with Catholics is very good because we expose (the truth), we do not impose (the truth), unlike in Brazil where there is a civil war between Catholics and *evangélicos*."[53] The Brazilian pastors I interviewed spoke of this higher level of ecumenism

---

52 Pastor Samuel, interview, July 22, 2019.
53 Pastor Vitor, interview, July 19, 2019.

that happens in the diaspora, which differs from Brazil. Pastor Antonio mentioned that in 2019, the Brazilian consulate in Miami had a council for issues pertaining to Brazilian immigrants, which included a Brazilian priest and a Brazilian Protestant pastor, working alongside each other. Many Brazilian pastors I spoke with believed that this stronger ecumenism was a result of the migrant status that Brazilian Protestants share with Brazilian Catholics. It is true that the need to help one another can make friends out of people, but Padre Manoel perceived things somewhat differently. He believed that there are two types of ecumenism, namely neighborliness and tolerance. He argued that although Brazilian *evangélicos* and Brazilian Catholics invited one another to community gatherings and celebrations, there were no real joint initiatives. For instance, our interview took place during the COVID-19 pandemic in early 2020, and Padre Manoel pointed out that there had not been any kind of joint action between the Brazilian Protestant churches and the Brazilian Catholic Church to address that current issue at the time. Padre Manoel is right to suggest that in some ways, the ecumenism between Brazilian *evangélicos* and Catholics is more about tolerance than actually working together because it is easier for Brazilian *evangélicos* to tolerate Brazilian Catholics in South Florida given the fact that they are the majority, and after all, Brazilian Catholics are not a "threat," as Pastor Samuel suggested.

Brazilian Evangelical Pastors and the Problem of the Undocumented Status of Many *Evangélicos*

As we have seen, researchers estimate that between 60–70 percent of Brazilians in the United States are undocumented, with some estimates as high as 80 percent. The lack of proper documentation to work and live in the country directly impacts the immigrant's quality of life. For the most part, undocumented migrants perform low-paying, undesirable jobs and run the risk of not being paid. This happens predominantly in the construction and house remodeling industries, where oftentimes undocumented immigrants are told that a job was not done properly and therefore they are not being paid. This is all done with the knowledge that undocumented immigrants will not be able to take legal action against the offenders without risking further problems of their own.

Leisy Abrego argues that both the media and public discourse work to dehumanize Latino immigrants, regardless of documentation status. Media coverage often depicts undocumented immigrants being treated in the same manner as potentially dangerous criminals, being carried away in handcuffs. Abrego points out that although this narrative is powerful and compelling, official records show the opposite, indicating that the majority of undocumented immigrants that have been deported do not possess a previous criminal record.[54] When it comes to deportation, things became worse in that regard after Donald J. Trump was elected president in 2016. Trump's presidential campaign was filled with anti-immigrant rhetoric geared toward all Latinos, but against Mexicans more specifically, with Trump at one point vowing to deport the estimated eleven million undocumented immigrants.[55] It is in this milieu of fear and insecurity that Brazilian undocumented immigrants are living, a state of mind that can affect many areas of one's life.

Kara Cebulko's research on the 1.5 generation of Brazilian immigrants also sheds light on the struggle that undocumented Brazilian immigrants face when trying to integrate themselves into U.S. society.[56] Gabriela, a 22-year-old informant, reported, "[Being undocumented] puts you on a lower social status than everyone else," and Tatiana, an 18-year-old undocumented informant, argued, "Here, you're like nobody."[57] The 1.5 generation of Brazilian immigrants also experiences being undocumented differently from first-generation immigrants. Abrego argues that first-generation migrants feel a higher responsibility for the undocumented migration journey, have worse working conditions, and experience a lower level of assimilation. Thus, they have a greater fear of deportation than the 1.5 generation.[58] However, Cebulko also points out that the thought of deportation can be scarier for members of the 1.5 generation because they would be returning to a country that they have little or no recollection of living in, and they would most likely lack the language skills to be success-ful in school or in the job market.[59]

---

[54] Leisy J. Abrego, "Latino Immigrants' Diverse Experiences of 'Illegality,'" in Cecilia Menjívar and Daniel Kanstroom, eds., *Constructing Immigrant 'Illegality': Critiques, Experiences, and Responses* (Cambridge: Cambridge University Press, 2013), 139–60.

[55] Tom LoBianco, "Donald Trump Promises 'Deportation Force' to Remove 11 Million," CNN, November 12, 2015, https://www.cnn.com/2015/11/11/politics/donald-trump-deportation-force-debate-immigration/index.html.

[56] Kara Cebulko, "Documented, Undocumented, and Liminally Legal: Legal Status During the Transition to Adulthood for 1.5-Generation Brazilian Immigrants," *Sociological Quarterly* 55:1 (2014): 143–67, at 152.

[57] Cebulko, "Documented, Undocumented, and Liminally Legal," 152.

[58] Abrego, "Latino Immigrants' Diverse Experiences of 'Illegality,'" 145.

[59] Cebulko, "Documented, Undocumented, and Liminally Legal," 148.

Vasquez argues that religion can provide a safe haven for immigrants in a society that seeks to vilify them by labeling them as "illegal aliens" and "lawbreakers."[60] Brazilian evangelical churches can help undocumented Brazilian *evangélicos* to feel as if they belong somewhere, and it can also give them a sense of unity with other members of society, under God, in a way that they cannot be officially, thus serving as a tool of survival for these immigrants. Ribeiro also posits the idea of undocumented migrants seeing their presence in the United States as the fulfillment of a "sacred mission" by God to lead people into salvation through an act of providential purpose. She argues that such an understanding leads undocumented migrants to no longer think of themselves in terms of illegal aliens or lawbreakers, but as those who are commissioned and protected by God.[61] Chandler H. Im and Amos Yong add that "for Christians who participate in God's redemptive purposes, the migration of people, whether forced or voluntary, should be viewed not as accidental, but part of God's sovereign plan."[62]

Brazilian evangelical pastors are tasked with the challenge of negotiating the issue of the undocumented status of many of their congregants. Paul Freston has suggested that Brazilian *evangélico* churches in the United States are in need of a what he calls "a theology of the undocumented."[63] Freston argued that such a theological response rarely ever occurs in public, or in any structured way among *evangélicos*. Out of interviews and other sources, however, Freston offered a rudimentary theology of the undocumented based on three distinct arguments: the theological, the historical, and the pragmatic.[64] The theological argument holds that since God created the world without borders, such man-made restrictions do not necessarily have to be upheld. In this argument Jesus is presented as an illegal immigrant in Egypt, the migration motif in the Bible is highlighted, and the Old Testament command to take care of the foreigner is invoked. The historical argument is based on the fact that the United States was built on multiple migration waves, and the only people who could claim an inalienable right to America as "my country" are Native Americans. Therefore, how can the descendants of

---

[60] Ribeiro, "Religious Experiences among Brazilian Migrants," 84.

[61] Ribeiro, "Religious Experiences among Brazilian Migrants," 79–80.

[62] Chandler H. Im and Amos Yong, eds., *Global Diasporas and Mission* (Oxford: Regnum Books International, 2014), 148.

[63] Freston, "Religious Field among Brazilians in the United States," 264.

[64] Freston, "Religious Field among Brazilians in the United States," 265.

other immigrants keep new immigrants from coming in? On this subject a Brazilian pastor's question is a thought-provoking one: "Which is better, to come from São Paulo on a tourist visa and overstay your visa, or to come from Britain in 1690 on a boat when nobody had to have a visa, kill a few Indians and steal their land?"[65] Lastly, the pragmatic argument focuses on the idea that Brazilian immigrants are not undocumented by choice, and that if there were a pathway to documentation they would take it. Nevertheless, Freston concludes that most pastors are willing to work with undocumented migrants in their current situations rather than shaming them for their status, albeit while encouraging members to become documented.[66]

Freston also points out that Brazilian evangelical churches are generally well-known for their moralism, and for always striving to follow the law, which can make it challenging for pastors to address from a theological standpoint the issue of undocumented *evangélicos* breaking immigration laws.[67] This quandary is evident in the response of Pastor Vitor, INW's youth pastor, to Freston's aforementioned theological argument: "Although you can look at it biblically and say that God owns the world so there are no borders, the Bible also tells us in Romans that we must follow the laws instituted by men. So, we have to obey as well, which makes this more of an excuse," he argued.[68] The theological argument also highlights the migration motif in the Bible, presenting Jesus as an illegal immigrant in Egypt. The understanding of this motif by Pastor Miguel, IPF's lead pastor, in relationship to the life of undocumented Brazilian immigrants also highlights the tension posed by Freston. Miguel argued that although the Bible has several stories of migration, such as Ruth's and Abraham's, and it also chastises those who oppress the disadvantaged, such as migrants, this does not give *evangélicos* the right to break the laws of the country they are in. He suggested that undocumented immigrants should seek to become documented if a pathway becomes open for them. He does recognize, however, that a part of the oppression faced by undocumented immigrants is the fact that the government chooses not to provide a pathway to documentation for them.[69] Pastor Miguel ultimately acknowledged that arriving at a theological

---

[65] Freston, "Religious Field among Brazilians in the United States," 264.
[66] Freston, "Religious Field among Brazilians in the United States," 265.
[67] Freston, "Religious Field among Brazilians in the United States," 264.
[68] Vitor, interview, July 19, 2019.
[69] Pastor Miguel, interview, July 19, 2019.

response to the dilemma of *evangélicos* breaking immigration laws by living in the United States undocumented is not an easy task.

> We are sensitive to the reality of undocumented *evangélicos*, and speaking sincerely, they suffer with this situation. They would like to not be in this situation, and sometimes they ask me, 'Pastor, am I in sin because I am in this [undocumented] condition?' This is a very sensitive question. It cannot be answered with a simple yes or no because a person can be undocumented and be living in sin, or a person can be undocumented and be seeking to live righteously before God. Therefore, each case is different, but there is an awareness of the leadership and of the pastors that the church is made up of people that are undocumented.[70]

Lucas, INW's lead pastor, offered the most comprehensive theological reflection on the dilemma of undocumented *evangélicos* of all the Brazilian pastors I interviewed. This is perhaps unsurprising, given his unique experience when he was placed in an immigration detention center due to an error committed by his immigration attorney, something that shaped his ministry toward undocumented *evangélicos*: "After this experience, I came back with a new ministerial vision. It changed one hundred percent."[71] Pastor Lucas shared that he received a revelation from God after much prayer and research to try to understand how to deal with the dilemma of undocumented *evangélicos* and the breaking of immigration laws.

> The issue of ministerial ethics was a difficult one for me to understand, how to deal with this situation. The person broke a law, broke a principle, and are they in sin because they overstayed [their visa]? Do I have to advise them to return to Brazil because they do not have a [documented] status? How do I deal with this? But if the person has no [documented] status, they are illegal, can I receive their tithes and offerings with no problems? How does it work? So, for me this was a very delicate question, and one that I needed to seek discernment for. Then, God showed me clearly in the word, the difference between transgression and sin. When a transgression breaks a spiritual principle, it is a sin. Thus, you can feel guilt and condemnation from a spiritual point of view because you have transgressed a spiritual principle. Now, when you transgress a human principle, a natural one, it is not a sin, but you are subject to the natural law. So, if a person overstayed [their visa], their time had come to leave but they did not leave. Is that

---

[70] Miguel, interview, July 19, 2019.
[71] Pastor Lucas, interview, September 18, 2019.

person in sin? No. They transgressed a [human] principle. What is that person subject to? To be arrested and deported. This is similar to someone driving in a highway and the speed limit is 70 [miles] per hour. If the person is driving 80 [miles] per hour, is that person in sin? No, of course not. If they die of an accident there at 80 [miles] per hour, will that person go to hell because they were driving at 80 [miles] per hour and the speed limit was 70? No. They transgressed a natural principle but not a spiritual one, it does not interfere with their spirituality. Now, if a police officer pulls them over and hands them a citation, they will have to pay that citation, there are consequences. I do not share this with everyone because not everyone will understand this, but I understood it clearly because otherwise you cannot pastor [undocumented immigrants].[72]

Pastor Lucas' distinction between transgression and sin provides a way to cope with the moral quandary expressed by Freston because it removes the sinful aspect of breaking immigration laws. These different views espoused by these Brazilian evangelical pastors demonstrate the complexity of the moral issue of how to negotiate the problem of the large presence of undocumented congregants in this Brazilian evangelical milieu. This is a constant challenge for Brazilian pastors who serve a migrant community in the United States, and a telling example of how Brazilian *evangélico* immigrants deploy evangelical theology to negotiate their distinctive situations in South Florida.

Conclusion

This chapter has surveyed the history of Brazilian immigration to the United States, and how changes in migration flows made Florida the preferred destination for Brazilian migrants, and South Florida one of the largest Brazilian enclaves in the United States. We have seen how members of this Brazilian diasporic community have struggled in their quest to forge their own identities as a distinct immigrant community, given the lack of settled identity and of a proper ethnic identifier in the United States, an issue that is only exacerbated by the lack of documentation status of most of its members. We have also examined the phenomenon of the evangelicalization of Brazilian Christianity in the diaspora in South Florida, which resulted in evangelical churches, much more than Catholic parishes, fulfilling the religious needs of Brazilian migrants, and created

---

[72] Lucas, interview, September 18, 2019. In here, Pastor Lucas is debating the difference between spiritual laws and human-made laws, though his use of the words "natural law" can be a bit confusing. When he says "natural law" he really means to say "positive law," or laws that are enacted by society or the state.

a different dynamic between *evangélicos* and Brazilian Catholics in South Florida than what is experienced in Brazil. Lastly, we explored the different ways that Brazilian *evangélico* pastors have negotiated the moral problem of the undocumented status of many of their congregants, and how their responses compared to Freston's proposed "theology of the undocumented." Overall, this chapter has demonstrated that Brazilian evangelicalism in the diaspora in South Florida is both robust and diverse.

AFTERWORD

Ronald J. Morgan

Evangelical Protestantism in Latin America is a diverse and dynamic phenomenon. As a result, the deeper scholars delve into historical, theological, and socioeconomic factors shaping it, the more we are left with the sense that we are viewing a kaleidoscopic image rather than a still life. Even so, an examination of the scholarship presented in this volume, as well as earlier scholarship surveyed in the introduction, brings out a number of themes that appear again and again.

In the first place, from their earliest permanent appearance in the nineteenth century, Protestants of all stripes have battled the stigma (and sometimes, reality) of being a foreign, culturally alien import. In his discussion of Brazilian Presbyterians of the late nineteenth and early twentieth centuries, Pedro Feitoza has challenged the conventional interpretation that has treated pre-1945 Brazilian evangelicals as "imitative, shallow, and little concerned with the pressing social situation of the country."[1] He situates the writings of key Presbyterian intellectuals in their historical contexts, noting how they reclaimed the earliest Protestant presence in Brazil as a way to rebuff contemporary allegations that their religion was culturally foreign. In a similar way, observes David Kirkpatrick, "[t]he historiography of Latin American

[1] Chapter 6, Pedro Feitoza, "Evangelical Conceptions of History, Racial Difference, and Social Change in Brazil, 1900–1940," 120.

223

evangelicalism . . . is organically connected to the lived experience of evangelical Protestants as religious minorities in the region." Commenting that the Panama Conference of 1916 not only stimulated missionary activity but also spurred interdenominational cooperation and political visibility, he illustrates the role of transnational influences on the emergence of the next generation of Protestant thinkers, who authored "some of the most significant contextualized history and theology from within Latin America." Worthy of particular note was the contextualizing work of Scottish-born John A. Mackay, whose ecumenical spirit and quest for an authentically "Latin Christ" would shape generations of Latin American theologians and church leaders across much of the twentieth century.[2] Daniel Salinas develops similar themes of the assertion of regional cultural autonomy that gave birth to the Latin American Theological Fellowship (FTL) in the 1970s. By stepping back from the shadow of North American evangelical theology, Salinas shows, a segment of Latin America's evangelicals, led by the likes of José Míguez Bonino, René Padilla, and Samuel Escobar, sought to interrupt conditions of theological and ecclesiological dependency on the Anglophone world. From the years just prior to and following the Lausanne Conference of 1974, these Latin American thinkers and pastoral practitioners refused to simply reflect back to North Americans and Europeans their own faces; now when Northern Hemisphere Christians looked south, they saw something fresh and dynamic, something that motivated and enriched their own reading of Scripture and theological imagination, enabling them to embrace a deeper understanding of the gospel and Christian mission.[3]

While historical analyses of Pentecostalism and the later charismatic renewal movements have often assumed that one-way north-to-south influences resulted in imitative religious expressions, several contributors to this collection have demonstrated alternative readings of the historical record. John Maiden's transnational approach to charismatic renewal across the Atlantic world demonstrates the flow of new spiritual currents both to and from Latin America. Spotlighting U.S. readings of events in Brazil and Juan Carlos Ortiz' charismatic ecclesiology of "one city, one church," among other examples, Maiden

[2]   Chapter 5, David C. Kirkpatrick, "The Historiography of Latin American Evangelicalism," 104, 109–10.
[3]   Chapter 2, J. Daniel Salinas, "The Theological Revolution in Latin American Evangelicalism of the 1970s."

demonstrates the role of Latin American charismatics within international renewal networks.[4] In a similar vein Joseph Florez examines
lived experiences of Pentecostal faith in early twentieth-century Chile
in order to show an indigenization process at work. Challenging the
"master narrative," which has remained largely import-focused, his
reading of personal conversion testimonies in Pentecostal journals
sheds new light on how the experience of marginality—both religious and socioeconomic—influenced the reception and personaliza-
tion of Pentecostal faith in that nation.[5] Of course, as Matt Marostica
shows, it was not easy for Argentinian heirs of Pentecostal "missionary
denominations" to escape the "myth of the missionary," that is, the
constraints that often bound them to the so-called denominational
manual. And yet, he relates, the end of the brutal military dictatorship in 1983 created conditions conducive to the emergence of a fresh,
pan-charismatic movement. Sparked by the public crusade meetings
of Carlos Annacondia and Claudio Freidzon, which featured a new
emphasis on spiritual liberation, a large segment of the evangelical
sector moved beyond denominationalism toward cooperation. Moreover, charismatic renewal began to influence the historical Protestants,
among them the Baptists and Anglicans.[6] As these cases show, there
was a persistent tension between assimilation of foreign influence and
Latin American ecclesial and theological independence.

A second set of themes emerges from several studies in this volume,
namely evangelical postures toward wider society (or to use traditional
religious language, toward "the world"). From his research on Brazilian Presbyterianism in the decades before and after 1900, Pedro Feitoza
counters the common misconception that, prior to the articulation of
theologies of liberation after World War II, evangelical Protestantism was
fundamentally conservative, "socially alienated," and unconcerned with
issues and challenges facing the nation. Similar to the work of Carlos
Mondragón González on Mexican and other Spanish American Protestant thinkers of the early twentieth century, Feitoza's chapter gives voice to
Brazilian Presbyterians Erasmo Braga and Eduardo Carlos Pereira, both of
whom emphasized the significance of evangelical faith for social morality,

[4]   Chapter 1, John Maiden, "Looking South: Latin America and Charismatic
Renewal in the United States and United Kingdom, 1945–1980," 34.
[5]   Chapter 7, Joseph Florez, "Indigenization and Believers' Accounts of Pentecostal
Faith in Chile, 1910–1920."
[6]   Chapter 8, Matt Marostica, "The Creation of the Argentine Evangelical Identity."

family and economic life, and democratic culture.[7] In the context of the Cold War, adds Daniel Salinas, the non-denominational FTL developed theological language and praxis around the concepts of a holistic gospel (*misión integral*).[8]

Although it remains the case that Latin America's evangelicals have often remained aloof from public life and social engagement—whether they have tended to be silently apolitical, acquiescent in the face of socio-economic inequality, or explicitly supportive of repressive regimes—there is almost unanimous scholarly agreement that the period since the 1980s has witnessed a major shift in the political visibility and impact of evangelicals from Guatemala in the north to Argentina in the south. In this volume Virginia Garrard and Véronique Lecaros address this shift, building on the fears and hopes raised by David Stoll in *Is Latin America Turning Protestant?* Garrard extends her scholarly production on the relationship between evangelical religiosity, politics, and violence, directing her attention to the political implications of Dominion Theology, with its origins in the United States.[9] Espoused by groups associated with the New Apostolic Reformation (NAR), she argues, Dominion Theology seems to oppose missiological principles of inculturation. With particular attention to recent cases in Brazil and Bolivia, she notes how the writings of C. Peter Wagner, with their suggestion that local religious expressions are demonic, have moved away from Donald McGavran's earlier influential call for deeper missiological understanding of local culture and epistemologies. In this regard she raises concerns about the relationship between Neo-Pentecostalism in particular, racial discrimination, and social violence, a problem acknowledged by Brazilian anthropologist Anaxsuell Fernando da Silva.[10] Véronique Lecaros provides a nuanced treatment of how, beginning with their loud public support for Alberto Fujimori's

---

[7]   Chapter 6, Feitoza, "Evangelical Conceptions of History, Racial Difference, and Social Change." See also Carlos Mondragón, *Like Leaven in the Dough: Protestant Social Thought in Latin America, 1920–1950*, trans. Daniel Miller and Ben Post (Madison, N.J.: Fairleigh Dickinson University Press, 2011).

[8]   Chapter 2, Salinas, "Theological Revolution in Latin American Evangelicalism."

[9]   Chapter 3, Virginia Garrard, "The Buried Giant: Dominion, Spiritual Warfare, and Political Power in Latin America."

[10]   Anaxsuell Fernando da Silva, "African Diaspora and Its Religious Heritage: A View from the Triple Border (Brazil/Paraguay/Argentina)," *Revista del CESLA. International Latin American Studies Review* 26 (2020): 347–76; and "'This Precarious Life': The Public Impact of Evangelical Churches in Rio de Janeiro," in Eric Miller and Ronald J. Morgan, eds., *Brazilian Evangelicalism in the Twenty-First*

presidential campaign in 1990, Neo-Pentecostals in Peru have become a more visible "part of the political landscape." She attributes this greater direct political engagement to both social and demographic factors, as well as to theological changes in the realm of eschatology.[11] The contributions of both Garrard and Lecaros point to the need for further research on the relationship between eschatological worldview and evangelical political postures, and affirm calls elsewhere for Latin American evangelicals, including Pentecostals and Neo-Pentecostals, to articulate more socially and biblically grounded public theologies.[12]

Two contributors to this volume have also published more sanguine treatments of evangelical (often Pentecostal) relations to politics and wider society. For example, as he has done in this volume, Joseph Florez has also read history from below in his study of the everyday lives of Pentecostal Chileans as they negotiated life under the repressive Pinochet regime (1973–1990), eschewing simplistic interpretations of Pentecostals, politics, and social engagement.[13] Similarly, Matt Marostica's chapter in this volume shares with his earlier published work an attention to a broader evangelical solidarity. While his attention here is to the new cooperation

Century: An Inside and Outside Look (Cham, Switzerland: Palgrave Macmillan, 2019), 159–76.

[11] Chapter 9, Véronique Lecaros, "Evangelicals in Peruvian Politics: From Impossible Theocracy to Political Influencers, 1990–2019."

[12] See Raimundo Barreto Jr., "The Church and Society Movement and the Roots of Public Theology in Brazilian Protestantism," *International Journal of Public Theology* 6 (2012): 70–98; Rudolph von Sinner, *The Churches and Democracy in Brazil: Towards a Public Theology Focused on Citizenship* (Eugene, Ore.: Wipf and Stock, 2012); "Pentecostalism and Citizenship in Brazil: Between Escapism and Dominance," *International Journal of Public Theology* 6 (2012): 99–117; and Virginia Garrard-Burnett, "Toward a Pentecostal Hermeneutics of Social Engagement in Central America?: Bridging the Church and the World in El Salvador and Guatemala," in Martin Lindhardt, ed., *New Ways of Being Pentecostal in Latin America* (Lanham, Md.: Lexington Books, 2016), 187–208. More recently, Barreto has authored a monograph and coedited two volumes on related topics: *Evangélicos e pobreza no Brazil: Encontros e respostas éticas* (São Paulo: Editora Recriar/Editora Unida, 2019); Raimundo Barreto Jr. and Roberto Sirvent, eds., *Decolonial Christianities: Latin American and Latinx Perspectives* (Cham, Switzerland: Palgrave Macmillan, 2019); and Afe Adogame, Raimundo Barreto Jr., and Wanderley Pereira da Rosa, *Migration and Public Discourse in World Christianity* (Minneapolis: Fortress, 2019).

[13] Joseph Florez, "A Prohibited History of Pentecostal Social Engagement: La Misión Iglesia Pentecostal and Authoritarian Chile," *Pneuma* 40 (2018): 287–305; and *Lived Religion, Pentecostalism, and Social Activism in Authoritarian Chile: Giving Life to the Faith* (Leiden: Brill, 2021).

that emerged around the imperatives of evangelization and the confirmation of a charismatic religious identity, he has highlighted elsewhere the rise of evangelical *political* solidarity in the face of a so-called Catholic Plot through which the post-military Argentinian state and Roman Catholic officials sought to legislate restrictions on non-Catholic religious groups.[14]

The diverse subject matters and methodologies characterizing this volume confirm the heterogeneous nature of evangelical Christianity in Latin America. The crucial importance of context—regional, national, ethnic, and historical—also shines through. One thread through several chapters is the historical development of evangelical Protestantism(s) within the context of predominantly Roman Catholic national cultures, a theme highlighted in a variety of ways by Feitoza, Marostica, and Lecaros, among others. Attention to context has led contributors in a variety of directions. Philip Jenkins innovatively applies to the Latin American context the sort of demographic analysis often used to explain the decline in religious belief and participation in Europe. In so doing he proposes that religious leaders and academics must consider the variable of declining birth rates as they assess the present and look to the future.[15] Matheus Reis' deft transnational analysis of Brazilian churches in South Florida suggests how immigrant status impacts preaching and pastoral care; moreover, he suggests, the unusual numerical predominance of evangelical over Roman Catholic believers—contrary to what prevails in the Brazilian homeland—results in a more tolerant interdenominational climate.[16]

The experience of evangelicals in Latin America has therefore been notable not only for recent growth but also for enduring distinctives. Most striking has been the difficulty of demonstrating that their form of Christianity was not an alien element, dependent on dangerous external forces and subversive of respected national characteristics. The influence from outside has been real and substantial, as several chapters in this collection show, for the Latin American movement was part of a wider international evangelical community. Yet this collection also demonstrates that a mixture of indigenization, adaptation to local

---

[14] Matt Marostica, "La nueva política evangélica: El movimiento evangélico y el complot católico en la Argentina" [The New Evangelical Politics: The Evangelical Movement and the "Catholic Plot" in Argentina], *Ciencias Sociales y Religión/Ciências Sociais e Religião*, Porto Alegre 2:2 (2000): 11–30.

[15] Chapter 4, Philip Jenkins, "Fertility and Faith: Latin America and the Limits of Evangelical Growth."

[16] Chapter 10, Matheus Reis, "Brazilian Immigrants and Evangelicalism in South Florida since 1990."

circumstances, and assertion of independent principles has been a more frequent feature of Latin American life than is often supposed. Evangelical religion is now close to the heartbeat of the region. In relating vital Christianity to the affairs of their countries, the evangelicals have shown a wide variety of attitudes. Pietistic withdrawal has been one stance, but engagement with social and political issues was not a novelty of the period of Pentecostal ascendancy since around 1990. There was close identification with liberal causes in the nineteenth century and exploration of biblical responses to social need in the twentieth. There has been major change over time in relating faith to public affairs, for the various sectors of the evangelical world, whether historic, Pentecostal, or charismatic, have been in constant flux. What has not changed, however, is their overriding imperative: the transmission of the gospel.

INDEX